# HETTY

# HETTY

The Genius and Madness of
America's First Female Tycoon

## CHARLES SLACK

An Imprint of HarperCollinsPublishers

FIRST EDITION

*Designed by Joseph Rutt*

Library of Congress Cataloging-in-Publication Data
Slack, Charles.
Hetty: the genius and madness of America's first female tycoon/Charles Slack.
p.   cm.
Includes bibliographical references and index.
ISBN 0-06-054256-X
1. Green, Hetty Howland Robinson, 1835–1916.   2. Women capitalists and financiers—United States—Biography.   3. Millionaires—United States—Biography.   I. Title: America's first female tycoon.   II. Title.

HG2463.G74S57   2004
332'.092—dc22
[B]   2004042055

05 06 07 08   BVG/RRD   10 9 8 7 6 5 4 3

*For my sisters, Jennifer Slack-Gans and Alison Slack,*
*strong women, gentle souls*

# CONTENTS

# PREFACE

At the time of her death in 1916, Hetty Green was widely regarded as the wealthiest woman in America. She left a fortune estimated conservatively at $100 million, or about $1.6 billion today. More remarkable than the sheer bulk of her fortune was the fact that she amassed the great majority of it herself, in the overwhelmingly male environs of Wall Street, at a time when women were not permitted by law to vote in an election.

She was the lone woman among a gallery of nineteenth-century rogue heroes—Andrew Carnegie, Jay Gould, J. P. Morgan, John D. Rockefeller, and the Vanderbilts. She bought and sold real estate, railroads, and entire city blocks. She owned mines, and held mortgages on churches, factories, and office buildings. Major cities, including New York on more than one occasion, came to her, hat in hand, when they ran into financial trouble. She adhered all of her life to the simplest yet hardest-to-follow financial wisdom of all: She bought low, sold high, and never panicked during a panic.

Wall Street took its name from a wall erected in the 1650s by Dutch settlers at what was then the northern edge of colonial settlement on the island of Manhattan. The wall was intended to keep the British out. It failed. But as Wall Street grew into the world's most important financial center, the wall might better have stood for the all but impenetrable barrier excluding women. In 1870, Victoria Woodhull opened the first female-owned brokerage house on Wall Street. But the brokerage, financed as a lark by Woodhull's friend Cornelius Vanderbilt, was more of a publicity stunt than a serious enterprise. Woodhull had tried her hand at newspaper publishing, running for president, and promoting the nineteenth-century religious fad of spiritualism, based on the idea that one could commune with dead relatives and friends. Wall Street was the latest venue in which Woodhull attempted to shock staid Victorian sensibilities, and the concern quickly failed. Wall Street was, in the words of historian John Steele Gordon, "universally thought to be as unsuitable to women as a battlefield."

The prevailing sentiment was captured nicely in a December 1909 *New York Times* article about women investors. "Women, it is Wall Street's conviction, are good winners but bad losers, and that's why so many brokers dislike to have women speculators among their customers," the *Times* stated. "It is difficult to reason about money and business with an angry or weeping woman. Her view of Wall Street and all its works suddenly becomes entirely emotional, and only a broker with infinite patience can calm her." The article singled Hetty out as an exception to the rule, praising her "masculine instinct for finance." "She has a broader grasp of finance than many men of prominence in the Street, and her views of the values of railroads and real estate are always worth having. She makes her investments in the logical way that a man does, and she usually makes wise ones."

As the subtitle to this book indicates, there was a certain undeniable madness to Hetty. At a time when the rich were so extravagant that their spending gave the Gilded Age its name, Hetty Green had a hard time spending a quarter. People who had millions less than she did built homes on Fifth Avenue designed after the palaces of European royals whom their ancestors had crossed an ocean to escape. Hetty took public transportation back to her small flat in unfashionable Hoboken, New Jersey, or Brooklyn.

But it is also undeniable that Hetty's madness, such as it was, served a vital purpose. By casting off the trappings and social expectations of her time, she freed herself to do as she pleased, to live life on terms that she and she alone determined.

Unlike Carnegie, Morgan, and Vanderbilt, who transformed their spotty reputations through philanthropy, Hetty Green left no monuments to herself. She therefore left it up to others to determine her legacy—and this process has not been kind to her. In her own time, she was regarded with a roughly equal mix of admiration for her financial skills and disdain for her parsimony. In the century after her death, as the immediacy of her financial prowess receded, she slipped into obscurity, remembered (when remembered at all) as a mean old woman with too much money and too little heart.

Probably the most succinct and widely disseminated version of this portrait may be found in the *Guinness Book of World Records,* where Hetty is listed, along with the largest lobster, the smallest antelope, and the champion hot dog eater, as the "greatest miser." "She was so mean that her son had to have his leg amputated because of the delays in finding a *free* medical clinic," the item states. "She herself lived off cold oatmeal because she was too mean to heat it, and died of apoplexy in an argument over the virtues of skimmed milk" (emphasis in original).

Like most legends, this description contains kernels of truth wrapped in myth, exaggeration, and caricature. She was, indeed, extraordinarily tight with her money. Some of the things she did were shocking. She never apologized for the way she lived, and it won't do to apologize for her now. But her life eludes simple classification, and "miser" is a particularly unsatisfying term, for it implies a soul that is withered, dull, and desiccated—almost devoid of life.

Hetty Green was none of these things. She was full of life, her personality if anything outsized. She was a pioneer, a trailblazer, a woman not just of wealth but of substance. She was witty and, in her younger years, beautiful. And she never backed down from an adversary, no matter how powerful. "I always try to deal justly with everyone," she once said. "But if anyone wants to fight me I'll give him all the fight he wants."

NOTE: Where does Hetty Green's fortune rank among the great American fortunes? As much art as science goes into answering such questions, given imprecise estimates of wealth, the changing value of money over time, and any number of other variables. In their 1996 book, *The Wealthy 100*, Michael Klepper and Robert Gunther ranked the net worth of one hundred fabulously wealthy Americans by the percentage of the Gross National Product their personal fortunes represented. According to the authors, Hetty's $100 million represented 1/498th of the GNP at the time of her death in 1916. Hetty, the only woman on the list, came in thirty-sixth, five places behind Microsoft founder Bill Gates, and three places *ahead* of current billionaire-investor Warren Buffett. John D. Rockefeller, whose $1.4 billion in 1937 represented 1/65th of the GNP, was ranked as the wealthiest American of all time.

# HETTY

# ONE

# NEW BEDFORD

A sleigh cut through the snowy streets of New Bedford, Massachusetts, during the early 1840s. People could not help but turn their heads as it passed. They all recognized the sleigh, the powerful black horse, and the man at the reins. Edward Mott Robinson was not a New Bedford native, but he had married into the richest whaling family in town. He had a dark, stern face with hawklike features. Black Hawk Robinson, they called him. He was known as a tough businessman, shrewd, unsentimental, thrifty, and cold. He spared little in the way of greetings to his fellow townspeople as the sleigh hurried along.

Sitting next to him, all but obscured under the folds of a thick buffalo robe, sat a girl of nine or ten. The sharp air flushed her cheeks. Her eyes were blue and lively. Lost amid the dark, arrogant ensemble of man, horse, and sleigh, the little girl was happy. She inhaled the fresh winter air and the smell of tobacco on her father's clothes. For all his wealth, he did not smoke good cigars. They were cheap four-centers. When an acquaintance offered him a ten-cent cigar, he declined. If he learned to like a ten-cent cigar, the four-cent variety would no longer satisfy him. But the smell was indescribably sweet to the little girl. Hetty Howland Robinson wished these rides, with her father sitting close to her, could last forever.

As the sleigh reached the lower portions of the city, near the waterfront, the aromas of winter air and tobacco were overwhelmed by something baser and more pungent. Whale oil, spilled and leaked a little at a time from untold thousands of casks, coated the piers that poked into the Acushnet River, the streets along the waterfront, the sidewalks, the steps of shops and factories. Under the summer sun the rotting oil gave off a funk that permeated everything. In winter the odor was more muted, perhaps, but it never went away. One backstreet leading to the wharves earned the name "Rose Alley" when some optimist planted rosebushes in a vain attempt to mask the smell left by wagons carrying casks of oil. But if the rancid smell offended delicate nostrils, the residents of New Bedford were savvy enough to recognize that whale oil smelled like money.

Within a few blocks of the waterfront, blacksmiths made whaling irons and harpoons, rivets, and nails; coopers made casks; boatwrights fashioned sturdy whaleboats from local timber. The air rang with the clank of hammers on metal and the rip of saw blades through wood. Outfitters stocked dried apples, codfish, corn, tobacco, paint, canvas, and rum in quantities needed for voyages that often lasted three or four years. An equally furious and busy industry dedicated itself to converting oil and whalebone delivered by returning ships into lamp oil, watch oil, candles, hairpins, and corsets. Language in this part of town was coarse, direct, and loud. Robinson's voice could be heard above the din, shouting at dockworkers to speed up, to load and unload faster. Hetty loved to follow her father here, when he would permit. It was her favorite part of town.

The headquarters of Isaac Howland Jr. and Company were in a three-story building at the foot of Union Street, next to the wharves. It was a serious, sturdy building of simple architecture,

made of stone and brick. On the first floor was a store for out-
fitting the company's ships with supplies. On the third floor, ar-
tisans fashioned sails and rigging. But the second floor was the
financial heart of the company—the counting room. Here,
Robinson and a small staff of managers and clerks tabulated
profits and losses, expenses, insurance costs, and wages, and kept
track of the ever-changing price per barrel of oil. Here, all of the
blood, violence, romance, lore, and adventure of whaling on high
and distant seas were reduced to a pure essence of dollars.

Perhaps the only thing about Black Hawk Robinson that
could be described as weak was his eyesight. And so from a
young age Hetty read the financial news to her father, and to her
maternal grandfather, Gideon Howland, a partner in the firm.
She read shipping statistics, tariff news, currency debates, the latest on securities and investments, and trade news from New
York. She absorbed everything. By the time she was fifteen, by
her own reckoning, she knew more about finance than many financial men. Occasionally she would detect in her father's stern
face something like approval, some faint signal, almost akin to
forgiveness, for her double sin of having been born a girl instead
of a boy, and for having been healthy and strong and full of life
when her infant brother died. Looking back on her childhood
many years later, Hetty would recall, "My father taught me never
to owe anyone anything. Not even a kindness."

Here, then, was New Bedford during the 1830s and '40s, when
Hetty was a child. The first great oil fortunes in the United
States were established not by Texans poking into the hard-
baked earth, but by New England mariners roaming the seas in
search of whales. The original whaling capital, the island of
Nantucket, faded in the early 1800s when newer, larger ships
outgrew the limitations of Nantucket's shallow harbor. The industry moved west to the mainland and New Bedford. By 1839,
212 of 498 American whaling ships called New Bedford or
neighboring Fairhaven home.

The prime quarry was the sperm whale, which had the biological misfortune to possess the best oil. Not only was the oil derived from its blubber superior to other whales', but the sperm whale had another feature that hunters found irresistible. Located at the top of its enormous head was a case containing up to 500 gallons of pure, fine oil just waiting to be scooped up. In a business where almost nothing came easy—from stalking and killing an animal the size of one's ship to "trying out" book-sized chunks of blubber over a deck fire belching black, greasy smoke—baling the case provided a sort of orgiastic release for crewmen. They clambered up the enormous head, carefully split it open so as not to spill any of the precious fluid, and dipped round-bottomed buckets, affixed to the ends of poles, into the cavern. Whalers called the oil spermaceti because, exposed to air, it thickened to the consistency of human seminal fluid (hence the sperm whale's name). As the case emptied, a crewman or two would slide in to obtain the last precious drops.

At the end of a long voyage, a fortunate ship might groan back toward home port bulging with 4,000 barrels of oil—worth more than $100,000—destined to grease the nation's machines and illuminate its nights. America ran on the by-products of slaughtered whales. Their oil lubricated watches, clocks, and guns. Wealthy young women wore corsets of whalebone and perfume containing ambergris, a waxy substance found in the whale's intestines.

Located on the western banks of the Acushnet River, about forty miles south of Boston, New Bedford was a curious amalgam of refinement and roughness. Oil revenue didn't just enrich individual whaling families; it also loaded municipal coffers—through personal estate taxes, real estate taxes, and poll taxes levied at $1.50 per voter—with enough money to turn New Bedford into a model of civic pride. In an age when one could expect to sink to one's ankles in mud, muck, and filth just to cross a busy New York City street, several of New Bedford's prominent thoroughfares were paved and their sidewalks flagged.

The central part of New Bedford was laid out in a neat grid of wide, tree-lined streets set on ground that rose rapidly away from the riverfront. In 1840, New Bedford spent more than $66,000 for highways, street lighting, and other civic improvements. The town's population increased fourfold from 1830 to 1840, from a little over three thousand to more than twelve thousand. The city boasted a membership library with more than five thousand volumes, a lyceum that offered winter lectures by out-of-town dignitaries who received honoraria to speak, two medical societies, and an athenaeum. New Bedford had an active abolitionist movement, supported by both black and white residents, and was the terminus for hundreds of slaves, including Frederick Douglass, escaping the South via the underground railroad. Although Quaker families—Hetty's included—often shipped their children off to private Quaker schools—many of the city's three thousand school-age children attended good public schools. Benjamin Evans, boys' principal at the Charles Street School, earned $600 per year. His counterpart, girls' principal Julia H. Haskell, received $300.

"There were two New Bedfords in this early day," local historian Zephaniah Pease wrote, "one a fair and dignified village on the hilltop, where were patrician mansions, with opulent gardens, the homes of the whaling merchants and captains. The other was made up of squalid sections where the sailors and those who preyed upon them [lived], the saloons, where delirium and death were sold, the boarding houses, the dance halls and houses where female harpies reigned and vice and violence were rampant." Returning sailors could relieve years of pent-up lust and thirst at brothels and saloons that flourished in red-light districts with colorful, Dickensian names such as Hard Dig and The Marsh.

Herman Melville stayed in New Bedford briefly before shipping out aboard the *Acushnet* in January 1841—the voyage that provided the raw material for his masterpiece, *Moby Dick*. In the book, he noted New Bedford's contradictions. "A queer place," he called it. "Nowhere in all America will you find more patrician-like houses; parks and gardens more opulent, than in

New Bedford." And yet a few blocks away at the bustling waterfront, "actual cannibals stand chatting at street corners; savages outright; many of whom yet carry on their bones unholy flesh." In addition to cannibals, Melville might well have seen Edward Robinson, shouting at sailors and dockworkers to pick up the pace. He might have seen Hetty, just past her sixth birthday, padding along at Robinson's heels.

Hetty Howland Robinson missed by one thin branch of the family tree the right to call herself a *Mayflower* descendant. Her direct ancestor, Henry Howland, was born in Essex County, England, and arrived in the New World with his brother, Arthur, aboard either the *Fortune,* in 1621, or the *Ann,* in 1623. Their brother, John, landed shortly before them aboard the *Mayflower.* The brothers settled in Plymouth, acquired land, and for more than twenty-five years prospered as farmers.

In 1648, a new type of Christianity, Quakerism, originated in England and spread quickly to the New World. The name was first given to the group as an insult, because followers of founder George Fox trembled when filled with the word of God. They refused to doff their hats to other men, saving this as a sign of respect for God, and dressed in conspicuously plain garments. These habits made the Quakers seem exotic and strange, but at heart theirs was a rather simple and lovely idea— that God lives within each person. They sought a closer communion with their Maker by stripping away the bureaucratic layer of priests, bishops, ministers, and other holy middlemen represented by organized religion. They met as "Friends," each individual sharing his or her experiences with God. Detractors misconstrued this as a Quaker claim that every individual *was* God, hence free to ignore Scripture if so moved. In fact, Quakers adhered closely to the established scriptures, and members could be evicted for straying too far in their personal beliefs.

The Howlands must have been extraordinarily moved by this new religion, for converting involved heavy risks. Quakers were persecuted on both sides of the Atlantic, and nowhere with more fervor than by New England Puritans. The irony of Puritan intolerance—given their own history of persecution at the hands of others—is well known. They harassed Baptists, Episcopalians, suspected witches, and anyone else whose faith deviated, or seemed to deviate, from their own. But they harbored a special distaste for Quakers. The first Quakers to arrive in the Massachusetts Bay Colony, Mary Fisher and Ann Austin, were arrested and jailed, their trunks searched, books confiscated and burned in the public market. Other Quakers were whipped, imprisoned, or even hanged, or else tied to the back of a cart and paraded from village to village for public ridicule.

The Howlands, prominent figures in Plymouth, were stripped of public positions and fined for attending and hosting Friends meetings and refusing to pay taxes for the militia. When the pressure became too intense, they pushed southward. In 1652, Henry Howland, Hetty's direct ancestor, became an original purchaser of the Dartmouth settlement, forerunner to New Bedford.

In a more congenial and accepting environment, away from the Puritans, New Bedford's Quakers excelled first at farming, then at fishing, and finally at whaling. As their fortunes rose, they lived a peculiar contradiction of their own making. They believed in humility, thriftiness, hard work, plain dwellings and furnishings, and modesty in both dress and behavior. They had no idea what to do when, applying these godly virtues to whaling, they found themselves becoming as rich as sin.

Hetty was never devoutly religious, but traditions of Quaker living filtered down to her and collected in concentrated form. It would be an oversimplification to suggest that she was solely a product of Quakerism taken to extremes. And yet those aspects of her personality that so confounded and fascinated the public during her years of great celebrity—her toughness and piousness, her accumulation of money and her seeming inability to enjoy spending it, her arch disapproval of those who *did* spend their money, her ability to claim poverty and humility while hording a fortune of epic proportions—all of these things can be traced back to that small world, at once drab and colorful, of the New Bedford Quakers.

Hetty's father, Edward Robinson, was born in Philadelphia in 1800 to a prominent old Quaker family with long roots in Rhode Island. His ancestors, as Hetty always loved to tell people, included a former deputy governor and landholder, William Robinson. Edward Robinson started his career manufacturing cotton and wool in Rhode Island with his brother, William. But he soon became involved with the more profitable oil trade and around 1833 moved to New Bedford to be closer to the center of things. By nature an ambitious, aggressive man, Robinson determined to get ahead however he could. He naturally gravitated toward the most powerful whaling firm, Isaac Howland Jr. and Company.

For several generations, Howlands had turned to the sea for their living. It was Isaac Howland Jr., born in 1755, who laid the groundwork for the whaling fortune that would accrue to Hetty and give her the starting point for her own financial empire. Isaac started modestly in business, but exhibited a thriftiness and an eye for opportunity. He noticed that sailors returning from the West Indies often wore silk stockings purchased on the islands. Isaac bought the soiled stockings off the sailors' legs, gave them a good, careful wash, and sold them at a profit to wealthy gentlemen of the town.

A tiny man, said to weigh less than 100 pounds, but with uncommon energy and drive, Isaac started Isaac Howland Jr. and Company in the late eighteenth century as a merchant shipping business. He also ran a store selling goods imported from Europe and the West Indies, as well as local produce. But as the whaling trade shifted center from Nantucket to New Bedford, Isaac recognized the potential and began investing in whaling ships about 1815. Isaac Howland Jr. and Company would grow into one of New Bedford's most active and successful whaling companies, with more than thirty ships.

In addition to the usual hazards associated with extended sea voyages during the early nineteenth century (storms, navigational error, malnutrition, potentially violent natives), hunters chasing sperm whales faced still another danger. The sperm was the only whale known to aggressively defend itself, including attacking whaleboats or even the mother ship by turning its massive head into a battering ram. Such cases, while relatively rare, were the stuff of legend. The ordeal in 1820 of the Nantucket whale ship *Essex*, rammed by an enraged whale, her surviving crew reduced in starvation to eating dead comrades, was lodged in the consciousness of every sailor. In a business fraught with dangers, both physical and financial, Isaac Howland Jr. and Company went to extraordinary lengths to protect its ships. They were outfitted with only the best rigging and supplies, often produced in their own New Bedford stores. And while the company lost its share of ships and men, most stories told about Isaac Howland Jr. and Company were of successful voyages and fantastic takes on the high seas.

Isaac's land-based pursuits also met with great success. He was a founder and director of the city's first bank, the New Bedford Commercial Bank, as well as the Bedford Commercial Insurance Company. He was a founder of the First Aqueduct Association, started in 1805 to supply the city with water. Privately, Isaac became one of the city's predominant moneylenders, foreshadowing one of the crucial methods that his granddaughter Hetty would one day use, on a much larger scale, to build her fortune.

In this tight-knit Quaker community, Isaac Howland's daughter, Mehitable, married her second cousin, Gideon Howland Jr., in 1798. In 1806, Mehitable gave birth to a daughter, Sylvia. Mehitable died in 1809, shortly after giving birth to a second daughter, Abby. By the early 1830s, when Edward Robinson arrived in town, Isaac had passed on much of the operation of Isaac Howland Jr. and Company to his son-in-law Gideon. Sylvia and Abby were by now of marrying age. With their mother dead, the girls were the sole direct heirs to Isaac Howland's fortune, worth more than $270,000, or, nearly $6 million by today's standards. Sylvia, ill her entire life with spinal ailments and numerous other health problems, was an invalid. An ambitious young man determined to marry into the wealthiest family in town had one choice: Abby.

Robinson's hard work and business instincts alone would probably have been enough to ensure his rise in business. But he left nothing to chance. He began to woo Abby right away. He had been in New Bedford less than a year when he solidified his position in the whaling company by marrying the boss's daughter. It would be difficult to envision a couple more extremely opposite than the headstrong Robinson and the delicate, retiring Abby. Abby, while physically stronger than her sister, was almost preternaturally shy and unassertive. Hetty herself rarely spoke of her mother in her later years. William Emery, the Howland family's official genealogist, provided one of the few available descriptions: "Mrs. Robinson is recalled as a lady of a most pleasant and kindly disposition." It does not require a cynical nature to divine that these were not the attributes in Abby that Edward Robinson found most appealing.

Edward and Abby were married on December 29, 1833. From a financial perspective, Robinson's timing could not have been better. Just two weeks later, Isaac Howland, the founder, suffered a massive stroke and died. With Sylvia and Abby as Isaac's only direct heirs, Robinson immediately became a major force in Isaac Howland Jr. and Company. Isaac left a total estate of $271,527.21. Edward assumed control of $90,000 (almost $2 million today) as manager of his wife's interest in the estate. Thomas Mandell, a partner in the firm, took over another $40,000 to handle in trust for Abby. The balance of the estate, some $130,000, went to Abby's sister, Sylvia.

In the summer of 1834, Abby and Edward moved into a large, leased house at 43 Seventh Street, on the corner of Seventh and Walnut. The house became available through the sudden and tragic demise of a happy family in a manner that would be astonishing in modern times but was all too familiar in the early nineteenth century. Captain Moses Gibbs, partial owner of two whaling ships, secretary of the Mechanics Insurance Company, and well on his way to becoming a pillar of the business community, had built the home for his bride, Mary. Then suddenly, within the space of two months in the spring of 1834, illness swept through the house, taking Moses, Mary, and a two-year-old son. A daughter, the lone survivor, went to live with her grandparents. On June 25, an auctioneer sold off the family's possessions. The now-empty house was put up for lease and a short time later Edward and Abby moved in.

For all of New Bedford's prosperity, 1834, the year of Hetty's birth, had been a difficult one all around. In New Bedford as around the nation, a short supply of hard currency was driving otherwise healthy businesses into bankruptcy. New Bedford sent a delegation to petition Congress to liberalize the money supply, saying "trade and confidence are in a great measure destroyed and business stopped." In August and September cholera swept through New Bedford, carrying away several dozen residents (the Gibbs family may have suffered from an earlier outbreak) and making scores more seriously ill. This swift-moving and often fatal bacterial disease, native to Asia, periodically ravaged ports such as New Bedford, where each incoming ship might bear a new round of infection. Doctors, as yet unaware of bacteria, attributed cholera in part to "suppressed perspiration" caused by drinking too much cold water on hot days. They slathered mustard poultices on the afflicted, prescribed laudanum, and restricted water intake—a treatment that only intensified suffering and hastened death since the primary danger from cholera and its related diarrhea and vomiting is dehydration.

The coup de grace of this miserable year came at five-thirty on the chilly Tuesday morning of November 18, when a fire broke out in a shoe dealer's Water Street warehouse. A light rain hardly checked the flames. The fire, refreshed by a breeze blowing from the east, spread quickly to surrounding buildings. Captain Caleb Thaxter watched in dismay as his uninsured store next door was consumed by the blaze. Captain William Blackmer lost his house, barns, and shed, but fared better than his neighbor, having had the foresight to insure his property for $5,000. The fire shifted hungrily toward First Street, consuming several houses in its path.

Among the townsfolk roused by the clatter of fire wagons and shouting voices was surely Edward Robinson, whose new home was only a few blocks north of the blaze. Robinson must have hurried down to the scene, like other residents, to do what he could to help the fire company. It would have been in his famously domineering nature not just to help but to marshal forces and begin giving orders. By 8:30 A.M., crews had the fire under control. Robinson would have noted with satisfaction that no buildings or property belonging to Isaac Howland Jr. and Company had been damaged. And as New Bedford residents, soot-streaked and exhausted, staggered home to breakfast or perhaps a brief rest before the start of another workday, Robinson would have made his way back to the house at the corner of Seventh and Walnut to calm the nerves of his bride, Abby. Frail by nature, Abby was by now confined to bed, nine months pregnant and ready to give Edward Mott Robinson the only thing as valuable to him as his fortune; an heir to perpetuate the name of Robinson: a son.

Two or three days later, on November 21, 1834, Abby gave birth to a healthy girl, Hetty Howland Robinson. Robinson spent little time doting over a daughter he had not wanted and a wife who had disappointed him. He poured his energies into the business. By the following summer, he moved his family to a home he considered more worthy of his rising status in New Bedford, a granite, Greek Revival mansion at the corner of Pleasant and Campbell streets, in the northern end of New Bedford. The house, which he leased for $920 per year, was a large square structure, with six fireplaces and three full floors, flanked on either side by large porches. It was big and institutional enough in its appearance that in later incarnations it would serve as New Bedford's first hospital, St. Joseph's, and, after that, as a convent.

Hetty would remain in this house only a short while. She was a lively child, with a pretty face and blue eyes, and much too robust for her mother. Before her second birthday, with Abby pregnant again, Hetty's parents shunted her off to the home of her grandfather, Gideon. Gideon shared the home with Sylvia, as well as Ruth Howland, the late Isaac Howland's second wife. Although Hetty would return to her natural parents from time to time, her grandfather's house would be her principal home through much of her childhood. The elderly Ruth and the invalid Sylvia shared mothering duties as best they could so that the energies of the frail Abby could be spared for childbirth. On May 20, 1836, Abby gave birth to a son, whom the couple named Isaac Howland Robinson. Here was the heir that Robinson had so desired. Young Isaac had only to survive in order to grow into a fortune that, as the sole male heir, he would one day rule uncontested. Robinson would mold the lad, shape him—teach him to be thrifty and tough, to avoid debt, to demand a hard day's work from employees, to value financial gain over sentimentality, to prosper, to trust no one. But it was not to be. The baby lacked Hetty's strength and vigor and died in infancy.

While baby Isaac's physical presence was brief and tenuous, his death would have a huge and lasting impact on the family, on Hetty, and on this story. For Abby, weakened both physically and emotionally by the birth and the loss, there was no question of having more children. Isaac's death effectively removed whatever affection there had been between Abby and Edward. For Edward, the loss reinforced his belief that the world was a hard place where only the strongest survived; he became harder. But the greatest impact would be on Hetty, still too young to mourn her brother's death. Had Isaac survived, it is difficult to imagine her evolving into the larger-than-life figure who dominated newspaper headlines for decades. His death left her as the lone direct heir to the fortune—which not only increased her wealth but intensified the sense of isolation that she carried throughout her life. She could not help but see the disappointment and bitterness in her father's eyes.

Hetty did not return immediately to that unhappy household following Isaac's death. She remained at her grandfather's home. Abby, though not absent entirely from Hetty's life, receded as the central female figure in her life. Undoubtedly the happiest times of Hetty's young life were spent not in New Bedford proper but at Round Hill, an ancestral family farm located seven miles away at the seashore at South Dartmouth, Massachusetts. The centerpiece of Round Hill was a large farmhouse, the first sections of which dated to the early eighteenth century. The house, added to by subsequent generations, sat on high land with excellent views of Buzzards Bay and the Elizabeth Islands. The house was in many ways the heart of the Howland clan. It had been the site of many Quaker meetings.

When Hetty was a girl, the extended Howland family held yearly reunions at Round Hill. These formal events drew a hundred or more relatives. The group gathered under a large tent near the farmhouse in the afternoon. After a reading from Scripture, the company enjoyed a large feast, then took a collection to pay for the meal, usually around $60. Hetty may have attended these meetings, with Sylvia or Abby. She loved the open spaces at Round Hill, the walks down to the sea, and especially, the horses. By six she was learning to drive a carriage, and all of her life she prided herself on her knowledge of horses.

She was also, in the absence of a strong, consistent mother figure, and with a father whose attentions were at best uncertain, developing into a willful and headstrong child. When Hetty was six or seven, her family instructed a servant to take her to see a dentist on the upper floor of a building on Union Street. William Crapo, a New Bedford schoolboy, was visiting the office at the same time. Crapo (pronounced CRAY-po) would grow up to become one of New Bedford's leading citizens—attorney, industrialist, banker, and three-term United States congressman. As an attorney for Hetty's father, Aunt Sylvia, and for Hetty herself, Crapo would find himself inextricably intertwined in her personal and legal affairs. Crapo, four years her senior, understood Hetty as few others did; he was able to speak to her with a directness and irreverence that few others dared—and Hetty liked and respected him for it. Even in their later years when Hetty would make Crapo the subject of one of her innumerable lawsuits, they never lost their mutual affection and their ability to tease one another.

Crapo had not yet met Hetty when he sat in the dentist's office. But he never forgot what he saw. As the dentist approached her chair, Hetty screamed and yelled, flailing her arms and legs. The dentist tried different approaches, but each time Hetty beat him back. At last, the servant produced a silver half-dollar from his pocket and told Hetty the money was a gift from her mother, so long as she behaved herself and allowed the dentist to do his work. The girl stopped screaming and looked at the silver piece. After a moment she reluctantly allowed the wary dentist to proceed. When he was finished, Hetty snatched the half-dollar from the servant's hand and, still smoldering, walked out the door.

Only later did Crapo meet Hetty and make the connection; but the scene stayed with him for the rest of his life as representing two of Hetty's defining characteristics: her fiery stubbornness and her love of money. If most children's natural inclination is to spend any booty immediately on candy or toys, Hetty showed no such urges, even as a child. Chances are that the half-dollar she earned at the dentist's office went into a box in her room for safekeeping. She received an allowance of $1.50 per week, but, unlike other children with money in their pockets, she showed no desire to spend it. When she was eight, she later claimed, she marched down to a local bank, savings in hand, and opened her first account.

Her guardians sent Hetty away to school twice. The first time, when she was about eleven, she was sent to a Quaker school at Sandwich on Cape Cod, run by a woman named Eliza Wing. It was an austere, unforgiving, humorless place, where Hetty and the other girls were given simple food, plain rooms, and copious readings in the Bible, and were generally drilled in the virtues of self-denial. She spent a year at Friends Academy, a Quaker School in New Bedford, when she was sixteen, but missed most of the spring term with illness. Not long after that, she was sent to an altogether different school, run by Mrs. James Lowell in Boston. This was a sort of finishing school for young ladies from good Boston families. It was Aunt Sylvia who pushed for Mrs. Lowell's school, in the hopes that it would rub off some of Hetty's rough edges and make her a lady.

But none of these institutions made as much of an impression on Hetty as did the education she received in the area where well-brought-up girls were not expected to spend much time at all, the center of New Bedford business, the waterfront. As an older woman, Hetty told journalist Leigh Mitchell Hodges the origins of her interest in commerce: "My grandfather's eyesight was failing and my father's, too. And as soon as I learned to read it became my daily duty to read aloud to them the financial news of the world. In this way I came to know what stocks and bonds were, how the markets fluctuated, and the meaning of 'bulls' and 'bears.'"

During these times, Hetty received the closest thing to warmth and approval that she would ever get from her father. More than a half century later, in a March 1900 article for *Harper's Bazar* about women and money, she recalled fondly: "When quite a child I was required to read the reports of the stock markets and of various business transactions to my father who would carefully explain to me those things I did not understand. I was also obliged to keep a strict account of personal and household expenses. All these things were most useful in forming the mind for business responsibilities when it became necessary to assume them."

She could not have had a better teacher than Edward Robinson. He may have married into money, but he was hardly a dandy looking for an easy life. He seized the opportunity and brought Isaac Howland Jr. and Company to its greatest heights. He was feared along the docks but always respected. His nickname, "Black Hawk," owed itself to his dark whiskers and a certain hawklike arrangement of his features; but it also gave an effective description of a man who was dark by nature and observant of everything around him. Gideon Howland, Hetty's grandfather and Edward's father-in-law, died in 1847, when Hetty was thirteen years old. With the exception of minor bequests to some relatives, Gideon passed along his estate, including his interest in the whaling company, to his daughters, Abby and Sylvia. This not only enriched Robinson, it consolidated his control. Thomas Mandell, a longtime employee, was a minor partner. As a woman and an invalid, Sylvia, despite her considerable financial interest in the company, had no role in its daily operations. Edward Robinson had virtually full control over the most powerful whaling company in the country. An anonymous New Bedford writer, quoted by Howland genealogist William Emery, called Robinson "the very Napoleon of our little business community" in 1852. "If his life and faculties are spared to him to old age, he will be one of the richest men in New Bedford, and his daughter will be an heiress of immense wealth, both from her father's and the Howland side."

# AUNT SYLVIA

For a figure who would one day garner the title "Witch of Wall Street," Hetty was a particularly lovely young woman. She was tall and full-figured, with large blue eyes, a long, straight nose, prominent chin, and generous brown hair. Her favorite place was still with her father in the counting house or on the docks, and at times she used waterfront language that shocked genteel souls. Aunt Sylvia, in particular, fretted over Hetty's lack of preoccupation with feminine things, and worried that, even by the modest standards of Quaker dress, she stood out as unfashionable.

When she was about twenty, perhaps at Sylvia's urging, Hetty spent a month in New York as the guest of Henry Grinnell, her mother's cousin. New Bedford's prosperity was well known throughout the country, and the wealthy of New Bedford found access into the upper circles of New York business and society. Born in 1799, Grinnell had left New Bedford for New York as a young man, joined a mercantile business started by his brother, and established himself as one of the city's most prominent merchants. A worldly man and an adventurer at heart, Grinnell financed several Arctic expeditions and served as the first president of the American Geographical Society.

Theirs was a lively house of six children (three more had died young). Daughters Sarah and Sylvia instructed Hetty on New York society and introduced her to their friends. Despite Aunt Sylvia's misgivings, Hetty had picked up a thing or two at Mrs. Lowell's school and could behave like a lady when she wanted. She attended balls, luncheons, parties, and concerts, and she turned the heads of young men, not just because of the money she stood to inherit, but because of her beauty. By all appearances she enjoyed herself enormously. In later years she remembered in particular one glittering affair—a dinner at Saratoga Lake, at which Martin Van Buren, the former president, and his son honored visiting English royalty, including Lord Althorp, who later became duke of Northumberland.

In 1860, Hetty wore a low-cut white ball gown with a pink sash and lace trim to a ball held at the New York Academy of Music. She wore pink slippers, long, white, kid gloves, and gold earrings. She carried an ostrich feather fan. The reason for the ball was a visit by the Prince of Wales, the future King Edward VII of England, who was in the midst of an extended tour of North America. At the ball, Hetty had herself introduced to the prince as "the Princess of Whales." The prince appreciated the joke. He laughed and told her, "I've heard that all of Neptune's daughters are beautiful. You are proof of that." They danced twice.

With her social connections, her looks, and her family wealth, Hetty, had she chosen to do so, could have shed the straitlaced provincialism of New Bedford and entered seamlessly into a life of ease in New York society, of summers at Newport and winters on Fifth Avenue. After a short stretch as a debutante she might have married a steel prince or a railroad king and spent her life raising her children with the help of French nannies. She might have organized fashionable balls to benefit the poor, held choice seats at the opera, and ridden elegant carriages around New York and, when her beauty faded, taken her place among Edith Wharton's gallery of proper New York dowagers.

But something in Hetty Robinson drew her home, back to her dour family and the seat of her family's money. Her father sent her $1,200 with instructions to properly outfit herself with dresses and gowns for the social season. Hetty spent only $200 of the money. She put the rest into the bank upon her return to New Bedford.

Between her schooling on Cape Cod and in Boston, Hetty had lived periodically with her parents in a house they had purchased on Second Street. But Hetty always maintained a bedroom in her aunt Sylvia's home, and stayed there much of the time. As Abby and Edward's marriage froze over, Abby herself spent much of her time at her sister's home, seeking refuge from her cold, ill-tempered husband. But even when Abby and Hetty shared a house, Abby was little more than an adjunct parent to her own daughter. And when Abby died, intestate, on February 21, 1860, the effect on Hetty seems to have been something akin to losing a close but not particularly vital relation—a spinster aunt, perhaps. Edward took over virtually all of her $128,000 fortune, with the exception of a house valued at $8,000 that went to Hetty. Abby's relatively modest holdings at the time of her death, given that she was one of two natural heirs to a whaling fortune, only underscored the extent to which Edward had dominated his wife. From what little is known of Abby's personality, she handed down almost nothing in the way of personality traits to Hetty; they all came from her father.

It is the actual spinster aunt, Sylvia, Abby's sister, who occupies a far greater position of importance in this story. Sylvia suffered for decades from a spinal disorder that had apparently started when she was very young. Born into wealth, she never had the health or energy to derive much enjoyment from it. Her condition precluded marriage and travel, and so she found refuge in books. She sat for hours as nurses read to her, carrying her to distant shores with the works of popular authors of the day such as Frederika Bremer and Bayard Taylor. Nurses kept her apprised of world events by reading to her from her favorite newspaper, the *Boston Journal*. She tried her hand at poetry. A poem hand-written by Sylvia survives in the collection of the New Bedford Free Public Library, in small, delicate cursive:

To Esther

*In your Album I descry a page*
*On which no pen has left its trace*
*I will endeavor to portray*
*A wish that may not be erased*

*May much happiness attend you*
*And the love of God may you implore*
*May this blessing rest upon you*
*And His name may you adore*

The poem is dated December 4, 1845, when Sylvia Ann was thirty-nine years old. The Esther of the title remains a mystery. The poem is signed "Sylvia Ann Howland"—a signature that, on different documents and a couple of decades later, would lie at the center of a raging controversy.

As she aged, and especially after the death of her sister in 1860, Sylvia lived a life of Gothic loneliness. She shuttled back and forth between her large house on Eighth Street in New Bedford and Round Hill farm, the family estate. Her world consisted of a few friends and relatives who called on her at the farm or in town, Thomas Mandell, the minor partner in Isaac Howland Jr. and Company who managed her estate, and the round-the-clock attentions of a few loyal servants and nurses. She was obsessively needy of these paid friends. When they

left her for even a few moments, she became ill at ease and im-
plored them to return They were her companions, her world.
Gradually, at her request, a small coterie of them gathered
around her, gave up their outside work, and built their own
worlds around hers. It was a clean trade of full-time attention
in exchange for steady, full-time employment. Pardon Gray, a
New Bedford livery stable owner and hack driver, was by 1855
driving exclusively for Aunt Sylvia. Pardon's most frequent
route was the seven-mile journey from New Bedford to Round
Hill, which took two hours over country roads. In the summer,
Pardon and his charge would leave New Bedford by eight-thirty
in the morning to beat the heat. In other seasons they would
leave at ten. When they arrived at Round Hill, they would eat
at the same table together, along with the nurses. There was little pretension in this household.

Fally Brownell did the cooking and housekeeping. She had
been with Sylvia Ann since 1842, and hence had known Hetty
as well almost all of the girl's life. Another vital member of
Sylvia's staff was Electa Montague, who had arrived as a nurse
for Abby in 1859, when she was staying with Sylvia. Following
Abby's death in 1860, Electa stayed on to care for Sylvia.

With Sylvia unmarried and childless, Hetty was the sole
blood heir to the Howland whaling fortune. As such, she saw
Sylvia not just as an aunt, but as the caretaker for a fortune that
would one day pass on to her. She began to fear the influence
that the coterie of nurses and servants might have on Sylvia.
Sylvia was weak and often indecisive. How could Hetty be sure
that some servant wouldn't swindle her out of a chunk of the
estate? Her gnawing fear quickly developed into an obsession,
until she could barely stand the thought of Sylvia being alone
with her staff.

In particular, she resented Fally Brownell, the cook and
housekeeper. Sylvia trusted Fally implicitly, to the point that
she gave Fally the key to a large, hair-covered trunk that Sylvia
kept in a closet in her bedroom. The trunk held some clothes,

jewels, and other belongings, but it also held money and finan
cial papers. Sylvia for years had kept the key to herself, retriev-
ing money or papers from the trunk as she needed them. But
since she had grown weaker, about 1859, she had turned the
keys over to Fally, making Fally, now in her late sixties, the de
facto keeper of the household money. Fally kept the keys
locked in a trunk of her own, under strict orders not to give
them to anyone, including Hetty, without her employer's specific instruction.

This intimate show of trust between Sylvia and Fally infuriated Hetty and deepened her paranoia. And that paranoia only
intensified in 1861, when Edward Robinson decided to move to
New York City, asking his twenty-six-year-old, unmarried
daughter to join him there. What devious plans might Fally
and the rest of them devise with Hetty more than two hundred
miles away?

Robinson's decision to leave New Bedford coincided with his
decision that same year to close up operations of the venerable
Isaac Howland Jr. and Company. As always, his business timing
was impeccable. He had entered the whaling business in the
1830s, just as it was approaching its zenith, and now he quietly
but quickly sold off the ships and other assets when he recognized unmistakable signs that the industry was headed for a
decline from which it would not recover. The recent discovery
of oil in Pennsylvania, combined with new techniques for re-
fining it, promised a new and seemingly inexhaustible supply
of oil that didn't require costly, dangerous voyages on the far
seas. But another factor greatly hastened the downfall of whaling—the Civil War.

In New Bedford, the war had started—as wars invariably do—
amid a burst of optimism and euphoria. In April 1861, just days
after the Confederate attack on Fort Sumter, former Massachusetts Governor John H. Clifford whipped the citizenry of New
Bedford into a patriotic fervor with a speech in front of City
Hall, promising "untarnished glory" and "hearty joy and honor"

to enlistees. A Ladies' Soldiers' Relief Society was quickly established, collecting flannel shirts, blankets, mittens, quilts, preserved fruits, coffee, tea, cocoa, lemons, brandy, woolen socks, undershirts, and dozens of other goods in bulk to support the troops. The state called on New Bedford, based on its population, to provide 2,100 soldiers to the cause. In the end, New Bedford sent 3,200, several hundred of whom never returned.

Whalers fortunate enough to assemble working crews during the war found themselves besieged by Confederate raiders. Confederates destroyed no fewer than twenty-five New Bedford ships, seizing or destroying a half-million dollars' worth of oil. But the coup de grace to the whaling fleet came not from the Confederate side, but from the Union. In the fall of 1861, the United States Navy commandeered thirty whalers, most of them from New Bedford, filled them with stone, and sank them in the shipping channels of Charleston and Savannah to blockade Southern shipping. The terrible truism that war is good for the winning side's economy never played out in New Bedford, which—more like a Southern city than a Northern one—had to swallow economic disaster right along with the human tragedies of battle.

Some New Bedford whaling men, attached to the city and to their way of life, would ride the industry down to its bitter end in the early 1900s, sending fewer and fewer ships out to hunt ever more elusive whales, for an oil that the world no longer wanted. But sentimentality was never one of Edward Robinson's traits. To him, whaling had been nothing more than the best way to make money, and New Bedford the best place to do it. When the time came, he cast them both off with the brisk indifference with which another man discards a worn-out pair of shoes. In New York, he joined the New York shipping firm of William T. Coleman and Company, where he found new success in merchant shipping and real estate. Hetty moved to New York with her father, but she returned frequently to New Bedford to keep an eye on things.

Each time she came, Hetty blew into and through the insular, sequestered, quiet world of Aunt Sylvia like a fresh gale. She stayed with Sylvia on Eighth Street or at Round Hill. Hetty had acquired a home of her own, the house on Second Street where Edward and Abby had lived, after her mother's death. Her father let her have it as a sort of consolation prize, after assuming control of all of Abby's money. But Hetty preferred to stay with Sylvia. Whether this preference was born of a fondness for her aunt and a desire to be the dutiful niece, or a self-centered desire to keep tabs on the cash cow, depends on who was telling the story.

Though she had as yet no legal claim on any of Sylvia's money, she felt no compunction about monitoring Sylvia's spending habits. However unattractive and at times irrational Hetty's behavior toward Sylvia was, personal greed did not seem to be among her motivations, at least, not greed in the conventional sense. She did not lust after Sylvia's money in order to one day shower herself with luxury. Indeed, the miserly habits for which she would become famous later in life point to the opposite extreme, an abject unwillingness to enjoy the indulgences that other wealthy people (or even members of the middle class) took for granted. Her concern with Sylvia's money grew instead out of her own obsession to protect the family fortune at all costs, and from her belief that the money would not be safe until it was in her hands.

What is clear, though, is that Aunt Sylvia's staff, and Sylvia herself, increasingly came to dread Hetty's visits. Physically and emotionally, Aunt Sylvia was no match for her energetic, assertive niece. Sitting in a wheelchair or in her bed, her small body curved by the disfiguring spinal condition, she felt at times helpless in Hetty's presence. And yet it is clear that Sylvia held her own in this complex relationship. Hetty hectored her aunt about expenses she felt were unnecessary. Particularly galling was Sylvia's plan to add a new section to her Eighth Street house. Hetty believed that the staff was brainwashing Sylvia into adding extra rooms solely for their own comfort.

"There's plenty of room in this house!" she cried. "You don't need to add on just to accommodate some old nurses!"

When Sylvia said she planned to go ahead with the addition regardless, Hetty threw a tantrum, sitting on the floor in front of her aunt, sobbing. When that approach failed, she marched dramatically upstairs to the room where she usually stayed, a spacious bedroom directly over the kitchen. She grabbed her belongings from the closet and bureau and took them by the armload up to the attic. If her aunt was determined to make an addition to the house—if the servants were twisting her withered arms, as she believed they were—Hetty would show by example how little space she herself required.

Heading up the attic steps, she declared, "I'll never sleep in that old chamber over the kitchen again! I would rather sleep in a cemetery."

Electa stared evenly at Hetty.

"If you want to sleep in the cemetery, go there."

"I shan't go there," Hetty replied, "until I'm carried."

With that, Hetty stormed up the steps. She took a mattress from the bedroom and laid it out across her grandfather's old sea chest and a storage trunk. Hetty's strike lasted precisely one night. When the house failed to be swayed by her display, she quietly moved her belongings and mattress back to her old room the next morning.

One day, Hetty visited the home of a cousin in New Bedford during a snowstorm. Sylvia sent a carriage to bring her home. Hetty refused the ride as wasteful—she insisted on walking. Another time, Hetty decided to have a party for some New Bedford friends and relatives. Sylvia agreed to host the party, but only on the condition that Hetty would agree not to pinch pennies on the food and decorations. But the two were soon arguing over the number of chickens and the quantity of ice cream required to adequately entertain guests. "That's too much!" Hetty shouted. Sylvia wanted expensive lace doilies, Hetty put out cheap cotton ones. Instead of hiring a waiter for the occasion, Hetty wanted to borrow a servant girl from another family. Mortified, Sylvia declared that she would never again allow Hetty to entertain in her home.

For her part, Sylvia carped at Hetty over her unbecoming clothes, and her less than astute attention to her appearance. If Hetty paid half the attention to her appearance that she did to financial matters, Sylvia reasoned, her niece would be a charming young lady. As it was, Sylvia complained to her nurses, to Hetty herself, and to Pardon Gray, the driver, who was raising daughters of his own. Once, Sylvia said wistfully to Gray, "I'd give a great deal if Hetty was like other young ladies, like your girls, or a great many others. Her dress plagues me, going down the street looking so. It's the talk of the town."

Letters from Electa to Hetty, written in rough grammar and spelling when Hetty was in New York in early 1864, reveal both Sylvia's concern over Hetty's hygiene and a genuine love sometimes overlooked in accounts of their relationship: "Dear Hetty, your not[e] cam[e] safe. Very glad to hear of your safe arrival your Aunt is so very glad that you have got such nice rooms[,] to have them *warm to[o]* we can talk about you almost see you made comfortable it gives us great joy. She thinks of that nice warm quilt you have to[o] it is [a] great pleasure to think of you and to have you dress nice and clean."

Four months later, Electa wrote another letter, expressing Sylvia's concern that Hetty had neglected to take with her a cashmere shawl that Sylvia had hoped would spruce up Hetty's wardrobe:

"Your Aunt gave you that bleak [sic] Cashmere shall [sic] that you wore last fall, expected you to take it, found you had not[;] it is such nice suitable shall for you to wear, she wants you to have it and wear it and look like a lady in your place not keep it she says she never shall wear it. She has not been as quite well since you left nearly the same. I hope to carry her out doors soon. She sends her love to you with all the rest of us and hope you are getting house cleaning setting down your things finely write soon and very often."

The letter included a postscript that constitutes one of the few hints that this insular, self-absorbed world was even aware of events raging beyond their doors: "O this awful war Oh how many are killed."

Hetty's letters, which would emerge years later as evidence in a court battle over Sylvia's estate, profess love for Sylvia, Electa, and Eliza Brown, another nurse. But they also show the conflicts and bitterness seething through the relationships. There is one letter, undated but written by Hetty presumably from New Bedford to Round Hill. From the content of the letter, it appears that Sylvia has decided to proceed with the addition to the house, and that the carpenters have shown up on Sylvia's orders, much to Hetty's consternation. The letter shows that she feels remorse, after a fashion, for her outburst, though it is couched in self-pity. "Dear Monte," she wrote, using a nickname for Electa Montague, "I am almost crazy I have my old head aches and so discourage. I had tried to be so good—and to be deceived as well as have it done was too bad. I cared more about her not telling me. . . . give my love to Aunt and tell her the carpenters are here as it will make her happy although it will take me two years at least to get over the shock. Why did you let her tell me so sudden you would scold me if I treated her so. . . . I never wanted her to give it up if it would give her pleasure but she hardly told anything about it when I had been so good. With love, Hetty."

But the warms feelings between Hetty and Sylvia's servants rarely lasted for long. One night, while visiting Sylvia, Hetty told Fally Brownell to "take your duds and clear out!"

Hetty said, "I don't want you here! My aunt doesn't want you here either. You should just go away."

"I won't," Fally said. "Not till I see Miss Howland and talk to her. Miss Howland hired me. You don't have the right to turn me away."

The antagonism between the two came to a head one chilly morning in February or March of 1862, when Aunt Sylvia, Electa, and Hetty were eating breakfast downstairs. Fally was upstairs, straightening the rooms and preparing to fill the water pitchers. Hetty excused herself from the breakfast table and went upstairs. A few moments later, Aunt Sylvia and Electa heard crashing and banging sounds.

Aunt Sylvia looked up from her plate. "What's that?"

Electa sighed. "Miss Robinson. She makes all sorts of noises."

"Go and see," Aunt Sylvia said.

In the entry, at the bottom of the stairs, Electa found Fally Brownell, disheveled, shaken, her clothing torn.

"She pushed me, and I fell down the stairs!" Fally cried. Hetty charged down the stairs, silently seething while Fally relayed the story to Electa and Aunt Sylvia.

"I can't have such goings-on in my house," Sylvia said. She sent a servant to fetch Thomas Mandell, a partner in Isaac Howland Jr. and Company and perhaps her most trusted advisor. When the servant left on his mission, Hetty's mood abruptly changed.

"Please, Aunt, don't tell Mr. Mandell about this. He doesn't have to know anything about it. Please. It will ruin my character to have this go out around town!" Sylvia reluctantly agreed and sent word to Mandell not to come, after all. But one night not long thereafter, as she lay in bed, she turned to Electa Montague and said of her niece, "How could she be so cruel and treat me so, when I have done everything in my power to make her happy?"

# THREE

# A TEST OF WILLS

Through the early 1860s the country was consumed by war, that great test of whether, in Abraham Lincoln's words, a nation conceived in liberty and dedicated to the proposition that all men are created equal could long endure. In a war notable for advanced weaponry and crude medical practices, hundreds of thousands of soldiers died particularly horrible deaths serving this lofty ideal. These years were crucial ones in another respect—they nurtured a group of people who after the war would constitute perhaps the most formidable single generation of capitalists in the history of the world.

Andrew Carnegie, John D. Rockefeller, J. P. Morgan, Jim Fisk, Jay Gould, Henry M. Flagler, Philip Armour, the list went on—all of them had been born during the 1830s, the same decade as the lone woman who belongs among their ranks in terms of the financial power she wielded—Hetty Green. They all were in their twenties or early thirties when the war broke out. Their greatest feats lay years ahead of them. In the decades to come, they would transform the landscape and the American (and the world's) way of living to such an extent that their names still are synonymous with capitalism. They would build steel mills and railroads and mass production factories. The financiers among them would lend money and arrange multimillion-dollar deals on a scale never seen or even imagined before. It is hardly an exaggeration to say that this particular generation created the modern world, or, at least, laid down its blueprints.

Yet even the most ardent capitalist must wince at their methods. The free markets they espoused were often in reality rigged markets that they freely exploited. If they were brilliant and industrious, they were not above manipulation, swindle, and fraud. The toughness and vision of the railroad builders unified a vast nation by giving it a swift means of moving from one coast to the other. Rail tycoons even gave us the concept of standardized time, unheard of until railroad schedules made it necessary for two towns located hundreds of miles apart to keep the same clocks. But the railroad builders also enriched themselves, obscenely, through enormous giveaways of public lands wherever they laid their tracks. They thanked the government for this largesse by setting up shell corporations with such names as Credit Mobilier, and Contract and Finance Company, which bilked taxpayers out of tens of millions of dollars in overcharges on construction.

The railroad builders and industrialists treated their workers abysmally, offering low wages in exchange for long hours and terrible working conditions. Andrew Carnegie was off vacationing in Scotland in 1892 when workers in his Pennsylvania mills struck for a modest increase in wages. Carnegie's lieutenants lost no time calling in Pinkerton men, the private security force, resulting in chaos and bloodshed that became known as the Battle of Homestead. Among J. P. Morgan's vast holdings were anthracite coal mines, whose fat profits added to his millions. Morgan's underpaid workforce included boys of eleven or twelve, too young to go into the mines, who earned the colorful nickname "red tips" because they sorted jagged pieces of coal with their bare hands until their fingers bled.

When the Civil War broke out, these budding world-beaters were already demonstrating the combination of intelligence, ruthlessness, opportunism, and greed that would mark their careers. For all of their professed patriotism, they found ways to avoid the fighting. As a teenager in Pittsburgh, Carnegie had written glowing letters to relatives in his native Scotland, extolling the freedom, equality, and opportunity in his adopted country. Yet when war threatened that nation's very existence, the twenty-six-year-old Carnegie paid a substitute to do his fighting for him. He spent some time in the War Department but really concentrated on amassing the fortune in oil, iron, and, finally, steel that would make him one of the richest men in America. John D. Rockefeller's younger brother, Frank, served with distinction and was twice wounded during the war. Twenty-two-year-old John, citing the needs of his growing mercantile business, bought his way out of the fighting.

Philip Armour, born in 1834, sent a substitute off to war, then concentrated on building an empire in meatpacking and grain. Armour demonstrated his patriotic fervor by selling pork futures short to a country that had endured several years of scarce provisions. Predicting that pork prices would drop as the war wound down, Armour found buyers willing to commit to paying what seemed like a bargain rate of $30 to $40 per barrel at an agreed-upon future date. When the price plummeted as he had predicted, Armour bought barrels of pork for around $18, then turned around and sold them to the committed buyers for a net profit of around $2 million.

A young J. P. Morgan, born into privilege as heir to a financial dynasty established by his grandfather and father, would seem to have had an especially large stake in fighting to ensure the survival of the United States. Yet he, too, paid someone else to dodge bullets for him. Twenty-three years old when the war started, Morgan demonstrated his patriotism by selling useless rifles to the Union. He provided the financial backing as his associate, Arthur Eastman, purchased five thousand old, defective carbine rifles for $3.50 at auction from the government. They sold the rifles back to the government for $22 apiece—a neat profit of $18.50 per rifle. When soldiers began to fire them, the rifles sometimes exploded, costing the unfortunate soldier his thumb. When the swindle became public, Morgan not only failed to show remorse or shame for his actions, he sued the government for the balance of the payment, and won. A contract, after all, was a contract.

In later years, Morgan, Carnegie, and Rockefeller would embark on a spectacular spree of philanthropy, building museums, libraries, and universities that still bear their names. In doing so they would prove remarkably successful in transforming their names from symbols of ruthlessness and greed into symbols of benefaction, artistic taste, and concern for the public good. While it is true that Hetty would never turn her millions into libraries or universities, it is also true that she never bilked the government out of tens of millions of dollars, or called out the Pinkerton boys to rough up underpaid immigrant laborers. And, during those formative years of the early 1860s, she sold neither defective carbines nor overpriced barrels of pork. During these years her ruthlessness, such as it was, played out on a more personal scale. Her efforts to get control of the family fortune, which she saw as her natural right, meant focusing on one rich aunt.

In the summer of 1860, a few months after her mother's death, Hetty approached Sylvia with a proposition. They should prepare mutual wills. Hetty would hold on to Sylvia's will and Sylvia, Hetty's. Sylvia had already written a will a decade earlier, when Hetty was sixteen, leaving two-thirds of her estate to Abby, or, if Abby was dead, to Hetty. According to that will, the money set aside for Abby or Hetty would be placed in a trust fund handled by appointed trustees. Hetty would have a steady income, but little practical control over the money. The purpose of a trust fund, of course, is to prevent an heir from frittering away an inheritance. There is irony in the name since a trust fund's fundamental message is a lack of trust in the financial abilities and wisdom of the beneficiary. In the nineteenth century, when women were presumed to have no head for money or numbers, trust funds were created for them almost as a matter of course. But a young woman weaned on the financial papers, who started her own bank account at eight, and who stashed away money given to her to buy dresses, was no ditzy heiress. Hetty wanted control of what was coming to her.

Sylvia resisted the idea. She was angry at Hetty for her behavior toward the servants, for hectoring her over the house addition. Her fortune was all she had—she wished to see a sizeable chunk go to New Bedford charities. At last, Aunt Sylvia's willpower began to crumble. She agreed to compose a new will, if only to buy some peace for herself. Hetty drew up her own will first. It bequeathed half of her estate outright to any children she might have at the time of her death, with the other half to be placed in a trust to be maintained by New Bedford businessmen Edward Mandell, Abner Davis, and Benjamin Irish. In case Hetty should die without children, all of her estate would go to the Home for Children in New Bedford. This bequest, a rare gesture of public charity on Hetty's part, was obviously included to mollify Aunt Sylvia (the Home for Children was one of her favorite charities). Hetty's will included no provision for Aunt Sylvia, who hardly needed Hetty's money.

On September 19, 1860, Hetty asked Peleg Howland, a storekeeper and relative of Sylvia's and Hetty's, along with two other townsmen, to witness the signing. They did so at Peleg Howland's home.

Hetty turned her attention to the more crucial matter of Sylvia's will, in which she "gives and bequeaths unto niece Hetty Howland Robinson all of my real and personal estate, goods and chattels of every description including Round Hill farm and everything thereon, house on the corner of Water and

School and First and everything on and belonging land and buildings to her the said Hetty H. Robinson and her children and assigns forever." In case of Hetty's death, Sylvia's money would go to the charities named in the 1850 will. Sylvia's new will was written in Hetty's handwriting. Hetty later testified in court that Sylvia told her exactly what to write. "I wrote it down on a slate, at her direction, by her direction, and then, after it was perfectly satisfactory, I copied it."

Once the will was complete, Sylvia's resolve stiffened again. To Hetty's irritation and dismay, Sylvia refused to sign the document.

"I can't, I'm not able," Sylvia protested one day, according to Electa Montague.

"Then you never will be able," Hetty shot back. "You can do it now as well as ever."

Hetty pleaded. She was alternately harsh and obsequious. But Sylvia, withered and ill and nervous, had found her gumption. She refused to sign. Later, when Sylvia was sleeping, Hetty coolly informed Electa that she, Hetty, would prevail. She said, "I never set out for anything that I don't conquer."

Hetty finally won out, by threatening not to leave New Bedford until Sylvia signed the will. On a cold, gloomy January afternoon in New Bedford, Hetty sent servant Frederick Brownell to the home of Kezia R. Price, a widow who had known Aunt Sylvia all of her life. Brownell asked Mrs. Price to come to Sylvia's home around 4 P.M. to sign a paper. Electa would serve as a second witness. The third was Peleg Howland.

Hetty instructed Peleg to arrive at four, before tea. But Howland, a man of set habits, didn't relish facing whatever Hetty had in mind on an empty stomach. He went home to tea first. Back at the house, tension built as the little assembly waited for the final witness. Sylvia, waiting in her upstairs bedroom, was wracked with nerves over the prospect of signing her fortune away. Hetty, agitated because she had waited so long for this moment, looked impatiently out the window for signs of the old man.

At 6 P.M., with no sign of Peleg, Electa helped Sylvia down the stairs to tea. She ate little, and very slowly, as Electa stood patiently by. After a time, she signaled to Electa, who helped her away from the all-but-untouched plate, and slowly back upstairs.

At his own house, Peleg Howland calmly finished his tea, either unaware of or unconcerned with the consternation that his delay was causing. It was dark when he arrived at the house on Eighth Street. The little entourage made its way up to Aunt Sylvia's bedroom, where she sat in the gloomy glow of an oil lamp.

Aunt Sylvia was visibly agitated, Mrs. Brown recalled. "Her health was very poor. I don't know if she was more agitated than common, but we said nothing to her because she was so feeble and weak."

There was a table in the room. Electa fetched a pen and ink from a drawer.

Peleg Howland cut the silence. "What is this I'm going to sign to?"

Hetty said, "A will."

Sylvia said nothing. Electa pushed Aunt Sylvia's chair, with Aunt Sylvia in it, toward the table. Hetty placed the will before her. Sylvia paused, took a breath, then, with her feeble, trembling hand, signed her name. Peleg Howland went next, then Mrs. Brown, and, finally, Electa.

The scene following the signing was as uncomfortable as that which preceded it. This odd assortment of people stayed only as long as politeness dictated, then dispersed.

With this goal accomplished, Hetty started to worry in earnest. When she was away in New York, what would prevent Sylvia from drawing up an entirely new will? She returned to New York, regretting every mile she put between herself and New Bedford, for with each mile she made it easier, she imagined, for others to exert their influence over her aunt.

Her fears, as it turned out, were well placed. About the time Hetty returned to New York, a new rival for influence over

Sylvia entered the scene in the form of a remarkably attentive physician named William A. Gordon. Born in Newburyport, Massachusetts, in 1808, Dr. Gordon had graduated from Harvard College and Harvard Medical School and, after nine years of practicing in the town of Taunton, had hung out his shingle in New Bedford. After his first few visits with Sylvia, he gradually began to focus more and more of his attention on her, until she for all intents and purposes became his sole patient, and his sole source of income.

Dr. Gordon, who had a wife and daughters in New Bedford, allayed Sylvia's neediness and fear of loneliness by spending most of his time at her side. During one stretch of thirteen weeks while Sylvia was at Round Hill, Dr. Gordon remained at the farm around the clock.

There is little doubt that Dr. Gordon provided a great comfort to Aunt Sylvia. "I have heard her say that he had done everything for her comfort, and that she could never think of having another physician," Eliza Brown, the night nurse, later recalled. The doctor designed special pillows to ease the pain in her twisted spine. He built a special sedan chair in which she could be carried around the house. He designed a bedstead with a spring lounge, so that Sylvia could be raised or lowered into bed without being lifted manually. He closely monitored her diet, and prescribed a regular regimen of swimming to ease her pain. As their relationship intensified, Sylvia began seeking his advice on other matters—including her finances. All the while, he was administering laudanum, a powerful and widely prescribed medicine of the time, whose principal ingredient was opium.

Dr. Gordon always claimed that any advice he gave to Sylvia came at her request. There is undoubtedly truth to this assertion. But it is also clear that Sylvia was susceptible to the influences of stronger people, even under the best of circumstances. In this case, the stronger individual was a physician offering relief from her pain and comfort from her fears, and also prescribing pain-deadening medicine. Whatever the underlying nature of the relationship, Hetty clearly had a new rival, and this time it was not a maid or servant. Hetty seethed from a couple of hundred miles away as Dr. Gordon became an ever-larger part of Sylvia's life.

Among Dr. Gordon's nonmedical acts on behalf of Sylvia was to write a letter to Hetty in New York advising her that she was not to visit Aunt Sylvia. No copy of the letter remains—it survives only in the memory and testimony of Electa Montague. However justified the mandate may have seemed to Electa, Fally Brownell, and others, Hetty could interpret such a letter only one way—as the act of an interloper and gold digger seeking to put distance between Aunt Sylvia and her one rightful heir.

And Sylvia's estate was growing larger and more attractive every day. Sylvia may have disliked her brother-in-law, but she had prospered mightily under Robinson's financial direction of Isaac Howland Jr. and Company, as well as his decision to get out before the whaling industry collapsed. For doing little besides signing the occasional form or financial statement, Sylvia saw her stake in the company rise from $244,000 in 1846 to $1.4 million by the time Edward began to shut the business down. Her other investments, handled by Thomas Mandell, prospered as well, from $77,000 in value in 1846 to $508,000 in 1863. On top of that, Sylvia owned real estate with a combined value of $75,000, bringing her total worth to a little over $2 million, at a time when her night nurse was happy to take home a dollar each morning.

On a September evening, a year and nine months after Sylvia had signed the will leaving everything to Hetty, Sylvia prepared to sign yet another will, undoing in one stroke of the pen all of Hetty's schemes. The location this time was Round Hill instead of New Bedford, and Hetty was nowhere to be found, but the scene carried the same Gothic drama as the earlier signing. Sylvia was now much feebler than before. At 9 P.M., as she lay in her bed, Thomas Dawes Eliot, a prominent New Bedford attorney, read to her the provisions of a new will. Eliot, a kindly-faced man with flowing gray hair and a long, white beard, read slowly and evenly so that Aunt Sylvia could understand each word. Eliot had drawn up the new will based on directions provided to him by none other than Dr. Gordon. According to the doctor, he had made up his notes based on detailed discussions with Sylvia.

The will, much longer than its predecessor, due mainly to the long list of beneficiaries now included, took some time to read. Sylvia nodded her head as Eliot read. When he was finished, the will was placed on a board and set across Sylvia's lap. Although at times she had been too weak even to pick up a pen, Sylvia now was able to sign her name without assistance. She signed each page of the will separately, to avoid any charges later of pages being added in without her knowledge. Then, all the witnesses in the room signed. They included Eliot, Simpson Hart, and Dr. Jacob Bigelow, a prominent Boston physician whom Dr. Gordon had consulted regarding Sylvia's condition.

The new will was certainly far more catholic in its dispersal of Aunt Sylvia's estate. She took the opportunity to thank with money those who had cared for her and been her friends. She left money for indigent widows—including some who were strangers to her.

Sylvia left $10,000 each to New Bedford widows Hannah Mc-Cofftry, Hepsa Sherman, Sylvia H. Almy, and Phebe Allen and several other women who were relations or friends. One widow, Elizabeth A. Wood, received $20,000 in the will.

Fally Brownell, the beleaguered housekeeper, was to receive $3,000, on top of the generous gifts Sylvia had already given her to compensate for putting up with Hetty's tirades. Electa Montague, the loyal nurse and confidante, was to receive $5,000 outright. Eliza Brown, the night nurse, was remembered with $3,000.

For those employees who didn't get outright payments,

Sylvia set up trusts of $10,000 each. The trusts would ensure an income, and ensure that the recipient didn't waste all of the money foolishly. Aunt Sylvia apparently made the decisions based on her judgment of the personal responsibility of each recipient. Those receiving trusts included Frederick Brownell, her handyman (and husband of Fally), and Pardon Gray, her driver and livery keeper. "I supposed Miss Howland thought she did it all for the best, as I generally spent all the money I made," Pardon Gray recalled years later. "And I finally concluded myself it was for the best."

She left money to New Bedford for a variety of works. To an outside observer, this was a particularly enlightened document, compared with the earlier will that left everything to Hetty. Among her general bequests, Sylvia left $20,000 to the New Bedford Orphans' Home and $50,000 in trust "to be divided among the poor, aged and infirm women of New Bedford."

The will also called for a total of $200,000 in bequests to the city of New Bedford. These included $100,000 for the city treasury, to be used toward bringing water into the city, for manufacturing purposes. This bequest was particularly prescient, as it anticipated the importance of steam power. "I give this legacy to my city, because I believe that its prosperity depends much upon the establishment and encouragement of manufactures within the city." The other $100,000 would be given to the city council, half "to promote liberal education" and the other half for enlargement of the New Bedford Free Public Library.

She also set aside large sums for certain individuals. Among these was Thomas Mandell, the partner in the whaling firm, manager of her money, and the designated executor of her will, who would receive $200,000. She provided $100,000 to Edward Robinson, whom she detested—a bequest most likely included to discourage Hetty's father from trying to break the will. Sylvia, like any other objective observer in September 1863, would have assumed that the hearty, aggressive Robinson would outlive her. And Sylvia had always felt cowed by her brother in law. She also provided a $50,000 outright gift to each of the three trustees to the will, one of whom was Dr. William A. Gordon. The gifts were intended "as a token of my esteem and regard." In addition, the trustees would receive "a reasonable amount"—thousands of additional dollars each year for as long as they handled the estate.

The remaining million dollars—about half of what Hetty had expected to receive—would go into a trust, of which Hetty (after taxes, commissions, trustee's fees, and other payments) would receive the income. It was enough money to make her a wealthy woman, with around $65,000 a year in income. But if she had any inkling of what was being done in that farmhouse bedroom on that September night, it would have confirmed all of her worst fears. Hetty herself would have no control over the bulk of the money. It's direction would be in the hands of others—and one of the guiding hands, reaping rewards for himself all the while, would be the detested interloper, Dr. Gordon. Even if the arrangements were entirely Sylvia's idea, the doctor emerges as a dubious character, if not an outright cad. He was, after all, prescribing mind-altering medication to a dying woman whose last-minute financial decisions stood to make him rich.

And there was another feature of the will guaranteed to infuriate Hetty. Upon Hetty's death, the remainder of the trust was to be divided among the multitudinous heirs of Gideon Howland Sr., Sylvia's paternal grandfather.

The breadth of Sylvia's new will, promising to scatter manna into so many hands, did more than just increase the number of beneficiaries of her goodwill. It also severely isolated Hetty and even, in a way, put a price on her head. Dozens of people stood to inherit money when Hetty died. Even if Hetty was not aware of Aunt Sylvia's plans, she was extremely suspicious. Banned from Round Hill, she seethed in New York. Hetty would later claim that she knew nothing of the new will until after Sylvia's death. According to their agreement, Sylvia had to inform Hetty of the new will, a point that would become a central argument in Hetty's case to have the will overturned. There is, however, compelling evidence that Hetty soon learned about the existence, if not the details, of the new will.

On August 1, 1864, Edward Robinson wrote to Thomas Mandell a letter that, introduced as evidence in the trial, would severely weaken Hetty's claims to have been in the dark about Sylvia's new will:

> Hetty has heard from some person confidentially that her Aunt S.A.H. has made another Will. I am indifferent about it myself—strange as it may seem to you. Hetty is much troubled about it—made sick, etc.— If you could without a breach of confidence let me know if you know anything I shall be obliged. I have not hinted to her that I should or had written to you or anyone. One of Hetty's connections told her, (so Hetty said to me) she had better get or take all her aunt would give her, as no one knew what might happen.

If Edward was indifferent to the existence of Sylvia's new will, it is safe to say he would have been less so about Sylvia's next step, which she took four months after he wrote that letter. On November 28, 1864, she signed a codicil to her will. Some of the provisions were unremarkable: trusts of $2,500 to $10,000 were made to a few relatives, and $20,000 toward the establishment of a National Sailors' Home, to care for indigent seamen. But then the codicil (like the will, dictated to Dr. Gordon) gets interesting. First, it revoked the $100,000 bequest to Robinson, "for reasons which I think sufficient." Sylvia had never cared for Robinson, but she had been intimidated by him. But she felt increasingly confident in the strength of her will. "I have made it good and strong," she told a servant one day. "I have made it so strong that Edward M. Robinson cannot break it."

The primary beneficiary of Sylvia's codicil was Dr. Gordon.

In addition to the $50,000 and perpetual trustee fees awarded in the will, he would now receive an additional $50,000, "in grateful acknowledgment of his professional and other services and kindnesses rendered to me by him." In addition, Maria Gordon, Dr. Gordon's wife, would receive $10,000. His daughters would split another $5,000. In all, Dr. Gordon and his family stood to earn $115,000 outright, none of it tied up in the sort of trusteeships that Dr. Gordon and the other trustees would be managing for *other* heirs. And he would be earning a healthy income besides, simply for acting as a trustee. The man who drafted the codicil was Judge John M. Williams, of Taunton, former chief justice of the Court of Common Pleas—and father-in-law of Dr. William A. Gordon.

In the spring of 1865, Edward Robinson, the hale, blustering fellow whom it seemed might live forever out of simply being too stubborn to die, suddenly fell ill. He held on for a few short months, and died on June 14, 1865.

Hetty had spent so much time worrying about her aunt's will, in part because she assumed it would be years until she saw much from her father. An inventory made after his death showed an estate of nearly $5.7 million. Of that, only $163,350 remained invested in whaling ships, showing the extent to which he had succeeded in extricating himself from the business that had made him rich. The rest was in stocks, bonds, cash, interest in merchant ships, and outstanding claims considered good. Robinson left virtually his entire estate to his only heir, his daughter. Five months shy of her thirty-first birthday, Hetty Robinson found herself a rich woman.

But there was a catch. Robinson had arranged to leave Hetty a little over $900,000 outright, along with some property in California that he owned. The rest, almost $5 million, would be bound up in a trust, with Hetty as beneficiary, but with two associates of her father's, Henry A. Barling and Abner Davis, as managers.

On one level, Hetty had little to complain about. The bequest was beyond the imaginings of most Americans of her time, ensuring a life of ease and comfort, should she want that. And, certainly, Robinson was free to distribute the estate as he saw fit. And yet Robinson had been wholly aware of Hetty's consuming interest in money and finances. She had been his eager student, reading to him, following him around the docks, soaking up any and all of his financial wisdom. Had she been a young man, she would without question have been groomed to take over his money and his business concerns. But she was a woman, and Robinson followed the conventions of the day and kept some 80 percent of his fortune in trust for her, so that she would not fritter it away. Hetty could interpret the will as nothing other than a deep and burning insult. She would carry anger over her father's will throughout her life, transferring her rage from her father to the men he had selected to administer the trust.

Just two weeks after Robinson was laid to rest next to Abby in New Bedford's Oak Grove Cemetery, Sylvia took a turn for the worse. She lay in her bed in the house on Eighth Street. Her last days underscored the poignant irony of her life. She was rich—probably the richest woman in town—and her fortunes were steadily increasing as her health declined. In just the last year of her life, she earned some $200,000 from her investments. Yet her physical ailments had confined her travels, outside of the well-worn seven-mile path between New Bedford and Round Hill, to the pages of romance novels. Her closest companions in these final days, however sincere they may have been in their affection for her, were largely her paid staff. Even discounting their financial interest in Sylvia Ann, their affection for her seems to have been quite genuine. Electa Montague, the nurse, recalled after Sylvia's death: "I regarded her as my sincere friend, and felt to love her, and respect her, and do for her, and would do for her anything in my power to comfort her, and re-

lieve her sufferings and her long confinement." And yet the sad
reality of this arrangement seems to have haunted Sylvia right
to her deathbed. Nobody knew better than she that her companions were bought and paid for. A few months before her
death, she called Fally Brownell to her bedside and confided, "I
have remembered you in my will. I want you to make yourself
comfortable with the money I have left you. You will miss me
when I am gone, for Hetty will never treat you as I have
treated you." It was not a point that Fally, with memories of
being shoved down the stairs, was likely to dispute.

In the days just before her death, she lay in bed in a
laudanum-induced haze, courtesy of Dr. Gordon. In the still-
ness of one evening, Eliza Brown, the night nurse, was at her
bedside. Filled suddenly with a fear of being alone, a fear that
dogged her all of her life but intensified in her final days, she
said to Eliza, "You know that I have given you so much money,
and I want you to stay with me as long as I live."

Eliza could think of nothing to say besides, "Yes, Miss Howland, I will." Sylvia held on for a few days longer, with Electa
or Eliza Brown always by her side. It must have taken some
fortitude to serve this mistress, particularly toward the end. If
one of them so much as left the room, she would ask nervously where they were going and when they would be back.
Dr. Gordon stayed in the next room. Sylvia frequently called
for him; other times she simply asked Electa or Eliza to reas-
sure her that he was still nearby, in case she should need him.
But for all of her fears, and her desperate need for companionship, nothing could forestall the journey that she would soon
have to take all alone. On July 2, Sylvia Ann Howland died.
She was so worn down by her inactive life, so frail, so thin, so
withered, so unfulfilled—it seems difficult to imagine that she
was only fifty-nine years old.

# FOUR

# ALONE IN A CROWD

etty was just getting herself settled in New York when she received news of Sylvia's death, news that beckoned her back to New Bedford for the second time in three weeks to bury a close relative. Her grief over Sylvia's death was tempered on her northbound journey by the knowledge that she was steeling for a fight. At last, Sylvia's death promised to force the secretive drama of her will to a very public conclusion.

New Bedford was, suddenly, a different place for Hetty, home only to ghosts. Every member of that extended cast of relatives who had taken a hand in raising her was dead. Among the living residents of New Bedford she had hardly a friend whom she felt she could trust. Rumors regarding Sylvia's will swirled around the town, visions of dollars dancing in one parlor, parsonage, and counting house after another, from Hard Dig to the top of the hill. Anticipation rippled through not just those expecting direct bequests, but a much larger stratum of distant Howland relatives who learned that, upon Hetty's death, the remainder of the trust would be distributed among them.

Decades later, when Hetty was an elderly woman, a friend of hers named C. W. deLyon Nicholls, described her experience at Sylvia's funeral, in a 1913 article for *Business America* magazine:

> Her aunt's establishment she found to be in the custody and under the ironclad rule of a band of avaricious doctors and nurses. One of the former [presumably a reference to Dr. Gordon] transfixing her with a hypnotic stare, exclaimed, "Really, Miss Robinson, I am very sorry to see you looking so miserable. At best, you cannot hold out longer than a year." . . . The day of the funeral arrived. Every remote ramification of the family tree able to walk, with or without crutches, put in an appearance. Miss Robinson slipped in so deeply swathed in crepe that she was not recognized. With her head bowed against the piano and almost prostrated with grief, she overheard a couple of these distant relations chuckling to themselves, 'When Hetty dies we will have a whole greenhouse built onto our house."

Since the only possible source for this account was Hetty herself, it is impossible to verify this scene. It is difficult to imagine Hetty being able to appear incognito at Sylvia's funeral. Sylvia's maids and nurses would later recall not a niece "prostrated with grief" but a hard-eyed, calculating woman eager to get down to business. But the real value of Nicholls's description is not the relative veracity of the details but the vivid window into Hetty's mind as she stepped off the train in New Bedford and saw greed in every face—just as they, surely, saw greed in hers.

At the reading of the will following the funeral, Hetty sat stewing in a silent rage as she listened to each provision. The news that she would receive lifetime income on a $1 million trust did not move her. All she could hear was a litany of insults large and small. She was to receive no cash. In essence, she was to be less trusted to handle money than the assortment of widows who received direct cash payments of $10,000 or $20,000. The huge cash payments to Dr. Gordon and his family outlined in the will and the codicil stung Hetty, but the greatest outrage was that the hated Dr. Gordon would serve as one of the trustees for her inheritance. He would be the one making financial decisions for her and reaping thousands of dollars each year in commissions.

A final insult came freighted with irony. The $100,000 that Sylvia had initially left to Hetty's father would have been hers because of his untimely death. But the codicil had removed the gift to Edward. To whatever degree Hetty knew the specifics of Sylvia's last will beforehand, this reading confirmed all of her worst fears. In a fever of righteous anger she set about planning ways to stop it dead.

Hetty's New Bedford lawyer, William Crapo, recognized the strength and care with which Sylvia's new will was drawn. He was also in the rather delicate position of having served not just Hetty and her father, but Sylvia, for a number of years. Although he would ultimately testify on Hetty's behalf in the upcoming court case, and serve as one of a battery of seven attorneys, he had little stomach for the battle and was never more than lukewarm in the support of her cause. About the only stalwart ally she had as she entered the fray was a new figure, a wealthy man who had recently moved to New York, Edward Henry Green.

Green, a native of Bellows Falls, Vermont, had met Hetty in February, at her father's home. Edward Mott Robinson was already ailing when he introduced his thirty-year-old daughter to the forty-four-year-old bachelor, a sometime business associate of his. The son of a prominent merchant in Bellows Falls, Green had left his hometown in 1838, at seventeen, to seek his fortune in Boston. Nine years later, having established himself as a merchant, Green left for the Philippines, where he remained for some twenty years, earning a fortune trading tea, silk, and other goods for the firm of Russell, Sturgis and Company. By the mid-1860s, he returned to the United States, and the New York office of Russell, Sturgis. His decision may have been influenced by a large earthquake that struck Manila in 1863, killing many residents and burying others under the rubble of their homes and businesses. Green had been on a business trip in Hong Kong at the time, but the close call sobered him. "A narrow escape, to be sure," he relayed in a letter to a friend in Pennsylvania.

There are several stories about how Hetty and Edward first came to be introduced. One suggests that Green had heard about Hetty during a gathering of American businessmen in Japan when someone offered a toast to the "richest American heiress"—Hetty Howland Robinson. Hearing this, Green is supposed to have banged his fist decisively on the table and announced, "I'm going to marry her." The story is colorful, but probably not true. Hetty was not yet rich, let alone America's richest heiress, nor was she yet famous enough to have her name bandied about by strangers on the other side of the world. Another story has Green hearing of Hetty at a banquet in New York. The likeliest scenario is that they were formally introduced at Edward Mott Robinson's home in February of 1865 and within a few weeks were inseparable. By June first, two weeks before the death of Edward Mott Robinson, Edward and Hetty were engaged.

With the exception of their mutual affection for money, Edward and Hetty had little in common. They were an odd pairing, and their differences would intensify in the years to come and make them both frequently miserable. For one thing, Edward was not a Quaker, but an Episcopalian. This did not pose much of a theological barrier—neither was particularly devout. But the Quaker traditions that drove Hetty to save, scrimp, and deny herself luxuries were utterly lost on Edward Green. He was a physically large man, over six feet tall and stout, with a gentle nature and an easy laugh. Throughout his stay in the Far East, he had regularly sent money home to his widowed mother, and bought her a comfortable home in Bellows Falls. He loved fine food and wine, dressed well, and enjoyed the easy camaraderie of clubs. He was a generous tipper and a soft touch. He enjoyed the luxuries, comforts, and prestige that his money could buy. New York, he wrote to a friend, "is rather a pleasant place for a stranger. Lots of Balls, Dinners, Parties going on all the time." The letter was written in July 1865, and Hetty, although not mentioned, undoubtedly accompanied him to many of those balls, dinners, and parties.

The fact that Hetty and Edward thought they could find happiness together represents a considerable gap in judgment by both. They could hardly have been more different in what they wanted out of life and in the ways they defined happiness. What did they see in each other? Edward undoubtedly admired Hetty's knowledge of business—rare in a woman. She was pretty, and possessed a sharp wit—another quality Edward admired. And, of course, there was the fortune she stood to inherit—although he had to know that getting his hands on any of her money might be more trouble than it was worth. Edward did not need her money, as he had amassed a fortune of close to a million dollars on his own. More likely, Hetty's money simply lent her a certain glitter that in Edward's eyes compensated for her rougher qualities.

For her part, Hetty knew that Edward liked to spend. But his self-made fortune attested to his business abilities, and her father, whose business judgment she valued above all others, liked Green. If he spent his money, what of it, so long as he didn't try to spend hers. If Hetty had any doubts about Edward, he proved himself to her by accompanying her to New Bedford and serving as her loyal friend at a time when she needed one.

The will Hetty heard following Sylvia's funeral was airtight. It had been witnessed by respected men and was thorough and exact. If she had any hope of reversing the inevitable, she would have to somehow establish the preeminence of the mutual wills that she and Sylvia had signed in 1860 and 1862. She would have to present some document specifically invalidating any subsequent wills. And she would have to move quickly.

Her campaign began at Sylvia's house on Eighth Street the

evening of the funeral. Hetty summoned Fally Brownell, the aged housekeeper who guarded the keys to Sylvia's trunk. In the dim light of an oil lamp, Fally, Electa Montague, and Hetty climbed the stairs to Sylvia's room. Edward waited downstairs. According to Hetty, she asked Fally to open the trunk and retrieve some papers, which Fally did. One, a lemon-colored envelope, contained Hetty's will. The other, a white envelope, contained a copy of Aunt Sylvia's 1862 will. Attached to it, Hetty insisted, was a second page that had been added at Sylvia's request shortly after she signed the will. This second page contained Sylvia's explicit request that any subsequent will be automatically invalidated by the probate judge.

Edward corroborated Hetty's version, although he erred in his testimony by saying the search for the papers happened in the morning, a couple of days after the funeral. Fally and Electa insisted Green wasn't even in the house, and that it was Hetty, not Fally, who rummaged through the trunk. "Miss Montague and I stood at the door of the closet. She [Hetty] went in and went to the trunk. I did not see what she did. I went downstairs in a very few minutes," Fally recalled. Electa said she saw Hetty retrieve some papers but had no idea what they were. The distinction was crucial. Hetty needed to establish that someone besides herself had seen this second page actually attached to the will, to counter suspicions that Hetty had fabricated the second page after Sylvia's death and forged her aunt's signature.

As she launched her "second page" scheme, Hetty attacked on another front: She set about trying to win support among Sylvia's beneficiaries. She tried to convince Electa that Sylvia had slighted both of them. "We are not capable of taking care of our money," she said. "Yours is in trust, and so is mine." In fact, Electa had received $5,000 in cash outright.

The next day, Hetty tried another approach. "We were at Sylvia Ann's homestead, and Miss Robinson asked me into the parlor," Electa recalled. "She talked about the will, said her aunt had not given me as much as she ought to, and said if I would

come over on her side she would give me as much as or more."
Electa turned down the offer.

Hetty traveled frequently between New York and New Bedford that summer, with Edward by her side much of the time.
One day in July, Pardon Gray, Sylvia's former driver, saw a
horse and buggy roll up to his door, bearing Hetty and the
large stranger from New York. "Isn't it strange that Dr. Gordon
hasn't come to see you since your aunt's death?" Edward asked
Hetty, in a voice loud enough for Pardon to hear.

Hetty said, "Maybe it is conscience keeps him away."

Then the pair turned their attention directly to Pardon Gray,
pointing out that his $10,000 bequest was all in trust.

"Wouldn't you rather have the money outright?" Hetty asked.

Green added, "You will have to go to Dr. Gordon, hat in
hand, and ask him for your dividend. If it is not agreeable to
him, he will tell you to call again some other time."

Hetty later testified that she had, indeed, visited Pardon
Gray, but only for advice in buying a horse.

Frustrated with her lack of progress in swaying townspeople
to her side, Hetty one month later boarded a train for the short
ride from New Bedford to Taunton to see Edmund H. Bennett,
judge of the Probate Court for Bristol County and the man who
would decide whether to admit the will. Hetty had already written Bennett a letter earlier in the summer, complaining about
"improper influences" brought to bear upon Aunt Sylvia, and
asking him to investigate the levels of laudanum prescribed to
her around the times she signed the will and the codicil. The
letter invited the judge to visit her the next time he was in New
Bedford. She included her name and address. Bennett ignored
the letter, so Hetty decided to pay the judge a surprise visit.

She launched an attack on the cabal of men behind Aunt
Sylvia's new will, focusing particular wrath on Dr. Gordon.
Then she said, "I can get somebody to serve as trustee who
won't charge any commissions. You can have the commissions
for yourself."

The judge stared at her for a long moment.

"Do I understand correctly what you just said?"

Hetty repeated the offer.

Bennett looked at her coldly. "Young lady, I must decide the case upon the law and the evidence. I do not want to hear any more from you."

Fortunate that the even-tempered judge hadn't tossed her in jail for attempted bribery, Hetty left the office to catch the noonday train back to New Bedford. Unbowed, she had one more errand to take care of before boarding the train. When Judge Bennett arrived home for lunch, he found an envelope containing money as a gift for his child. The judge returned the money to Hetty by the next mail. A month later he approved Sylvia's last will.

Hetty appealed to the Supreme Judicial Court, then withdrew the appeal, deciding instead to sue the trustees, filing in the United States Circuit Court in December of 1865. Hetty's suit charged that she, as the only direct heir to the Howland fortune, was by law and nature entitled to the estate. She claimed that Dr. Gordon and others manipulated a drugged, enfeebled, and vulnerable woman into crafting a fraudulent will. When in her right mind, Sylvia had always wanted Hetty to have the full inheritance.

In their response, lawyers for the trustees painted Hetty as a bitter, coldhearted schemer. Witnesses called forth by the defense, among them Fally and Electa, described in excruciating detail Hetty's tantrums and her single-minded persistence. It was an extremely unflattering portrait, delving even into Hetty's wanting habits of personal hygiene. "She told me many times that she did not want to be left with Miss Robinson," Electa said of Sylvia. The trustees, by extension, represented the interests of every widow, charity, servant, or relation Sylvia Howland had known, dozens of people waiting in the wings for their share of Sylvia's largesse. It was Hetty against the world, or, in any case, that corner of the world that for most of her life she had called home.

The case as it played out in court essentially became two separate trials. On the one hand was the intrigue of the rich spinster aunt and the ambitious, covetous niece, the lonely nights in the gloomy lamplight at Round Hill farm, the servants' gossip, nurses being shoved down stairs, temper tantrums and frayed nerves, all of it reading like the precursor to some modern-day soap opera. On the other hand was a painstaking scientific case involving the signatures and allegations of forgery. This side of the case was in its own way as fascinating as the former, not the least because of the collection of famous minds assembled to offer opinions.

The piece of physical evidence upon which Hetty pinned her highest hopes was the now-notorious "second page"—the addendum to Sylvia's 1862 will. Introduced into evidence, the page read:

Be it remembered that I, Sylvia Ann Howland, of New Bedford, in County of Bristol, do hereby make, publish and declare this the second page of this will and testament made on the eleventh of January in manner following, to wit: Hereby revoking all wills made by me before or after this one—I give this will to my niece to shew if there appears a will made without notifying her, and without returning her will to her through Thomas Mandell as I have promised to do. I implore the Judge to decide in favor of this will, as nothing would induce me to make a will unfavorable to my niece, but being ill and afraid if any of my care-takers insisted on my making a will to refuse, as they might leave or be angry, and knowing my niece had this will to show—my niece fearing also after she went away—I hearing but one side, might feel hurt at what they might say of her, as they tried to make trouble by not telling the truth to me, when she was here even herself. I give this will to my niece to show if absolutely necessary, to have it, to appear against another will found after my death. I wish her to shew this will, made when I am in good health for me, and my old torn will made on the fourth of March, in the year of our Lord one thousand eight hundred and fifty, to show also as proof that it has been my lifetime wish for her to have my property. I therefore give my property to my niece as freely as my father gave it to me. I have promised him once, and my sister a number of times, to give it all to her, all excepting about one hundred thousand dollars in presents to my friends and relations.

In witness whereof I have set hereto my hand and seal this eleventh of January, in the year of our Lord one thousand eight hundred and sixty-two.

Sylvia Ann Howland.

Whenever (and by whomever) this document was conceived, it was painfully obvious that the author sought to allay not Sylvia's fears, but Hetty's. The wording is almost comically inept. A skilled con artist would have made the document more general, more ambiguous and sweeping. As written, it is difficult to read the second page and see it as anything other than a rather pathetic last-minute response to Aunt Sylvia's final will. The ham-handed appeal to the judge anticipated too closely the court case. The reference to $100,000 for friends and relations seemed an obvious component of Hetty's campaign to sway Electa and others to her side. Beyond the wording, Hetty's explanation of how the will was written and signed stretched credulity, to say the least. Why had the contents of the second page not simply been written into the will? As presented into evidence, the papers had pinholes around the edges. Hetty suggested that she and Sylvia sewed the sheets together so as to keep prying eyes away from the contents. They had written the second page as a separate document in order to spare embarrassment if, upon Sylvia's death, her caretakers had not succeeded in forcing her to write a new will. "If they did not get the advantage of her, then I could detach it, only showing it to Mr. Mandell, and perhaps the Judge," Hetty explained.

It took the defense no time at all to label the document a fake. But what occupied a lion's share of the case was not the document itself, but Aunt Sylvia's signature at the bottom. Nobody questioned the authenticity of Sylvia's signature on the 1862 will—which, after all, had been made in the presence of three witnesses. But Hetty was the only witness as Sylvia supposedly signed two copies of the second page, one for each of them to keep. The signatures on all three items looked almost exactly alike, indicating that someone had copied or traced the two "second page" signatures from the signature on the will. Was Hetty Robinson a forger?

Rarely had such a collection of scientific celebrities been assembled for one case. In their zeal to top one another, both sides sought the greatest names they could find for their professional opinions—among them Louis Agassiz, Oliver Wendell Holmes, Benjamin Peirce, and John Quincy Adams, grandson and namesake of the sixth president of the United States. Their depositions were taken separately over several months, mostly in the Boston office of Special Examiner Francis W. Palfrey. But the collective star power, combined with the lure of the wealth involved, made the case one of the most watched civil cases of the century.

Of all the expert witnesses called, Louis Agassiz, the eminent Harvard naturalist, seemed to take the greatest pleasure in the assignment. The Swiss-born Agassiz had published groundbreaking works on zoology and geology in Europe, including a study of glaciers that first shed light on the existence of the Ice Age. His work had made him famous on both sides of the Atlantic, and in 1846 he had come to America to lecture and study. By 1848 he was in place as chairman of the Department of Natural History at Harvard, where he founded the Museum of Comparative Zoology. He was at the height of his fame, and just a month shy of his sixtieth birthday, when Sidney Bartlett, lead council for Hetty's side, delivered Sylvia's signatures to Agassiz at his office at the museum on a spring day in 1867.

Agassiz set about examining them under a microscope. He was delighted with the opportunity to demonstrate his skills.

Agassiz basked in his reputation as a scientific genius. Testifying for Hetty's side, Agassiz said, "I have been devoting my whole life to the study of natural history. I began as a child, and have pursued it to this day; I am studying now; I am a student; that pursuit involves the use of the microscope very extensively." Asked if he would consider himself an expert with a microscope, Agassiz replied, dryly, in his heavily accented English, "He that has had long training is a master, if he brings the proper application, proper care, to his work."

In this case, Agassiz had been asked specifically to check for signs of pencil marks underneath the ink in the two signatures in question. Pencil, of course, would be a dead giveaway that the signatures were traced first.

Agassiz testified:

I have examined these papers very carefully, in the way in which I generally examine objects submitted to various magnifying powers. First, with my naked eye, and with spectacles, and with simple lenses of various powers from one half to two diameters. Such a preliminary examination I always make, in order to become acquainted with the object in its totality, when the low power permits to see the whole object at one time, and ascertain its general appearance. I next examined it with the compound microscope, with three-inch power, when entire letters or even words might be seen simultaneously. I then applied higher powers, half-inch, and four-tenths. Handwriting does not admit of higher than these powers, because then only small parts of the letters can be brought under the focus.

Then, with the excitement of a child seeing for the first time a tiny world enlarged to the gigantic, Agassiz described the structure of the paper like some foreign landscape of dips and hills, transversed by rivers of ink frozen in time:

The highest powers used disclosed clearly the texture of the paper, and the manner in which the materials used for writing— the material—is distributed in its structure. With such a power, it appears that the paper consists of fibers felted together, inter-crossing each other in every direction, not unlike a pile of chips, pressed together. It is easy to trace with the microscope the fibers that lie at the surface, and distinguish these with those at succes-sive greater depths. Into this felt the ink has penetrated, and pen-etrated unevenly, the thicker parts of the ink being accumulated along the more superficial fibers of the felt, the more fluid part penetrating deeper, and here and there both merging together.

The ink, Agassiz said, lay in varying thickness on the paper; "under the microscope, the thicker clots of ink resembled mud, caught up under brush on a riverbank, after a spring freshet." All of this indicated to Agassiz that the signatures had been composed in a natural hand. With regard to pencil marks, he said, his examination "did not disclose the slightest indication of materials foreign to the ink as seen in any part of the signa-ture. Pencil not being a fluid substance, if used in this case, would have left its mark on the superficial fibers of the paper, and remained there, while, in every part of the letters which look lighter than the others, the lighter color is deeper in the substance of the paper, and the accuracy with which the focus of the microscope may be made to bear in succession from the surface deeper, leaves no doubt upon this point." He added, "I have carefully compared the three signatures, besides examining them singly, and in not one of them can I detect indications of the use of two kinds of materials tracing the letters."

Three weeks after Agassiz's testimony, Bartlett delivered the signatures for examination to Dr. Oliver Wendell Holmes, the famous author and Parkman Professor of Anatomy and Physiol-ogy at the Harvard Medical School. Trained in both law and medicine, Holmes was at fifty-seven one of the most revered figures in Boston, indeed, in the country, a true Renaissance figure. He was equally at home writing light verse, psychological novels, or disquisitions on "The Contagiousness of Puerperal Fever." He was a founder of and one of the most prolific contributors to the *Atlantic Monthly*. As a twenty-one-year-old law student at Harvard, he had written the poem "Old Ironsides"— which was credited with saving the historic ship *Constitution* and remains a staple in anthologies of nineteenth-century poetry. But it was his expertise with a microscope that attracted the attention of Hetty's lawyers.

"With the mechanical arrangements of the microscope, not the optical, I have made certain improvements, I think," Holmes modestly told a questioner the morning after his examination of the signatures. Holmes had examined the paper using simple and compound microscopes, by both daylight and gaslight. His analysis essentially corroborated that of Agassiz. "I found nothing to show that either was traced," Holmes declared.

But it would not be sufficient simply to establish the absence of pencil marks. Hetty's lawyers had to overcome the improbability of Sylvia's signature appearing almost identical on three separate documents, when even the most consistent penmanship is likely to produce slight variations from signature to signature. With or without the aid of pencils, this stretched credulity to the breaking point. So the lawyers rounded up examples of individuals whose signatures repeated often, demonstrating a capacity for repeating words as well as signature traits. Among these people was one Samuel W. Swett, president of Suffolk National Bank in Boston, who said, "The remarkable uniformity of my signatures has been remarked upon. I should think that if a man was signing his name a good many times a day, his signature would become very uniform. . . . I suppose this uniformity in my signature arises from my signing my name so frequently."

Of course, this argument might be seen as just as valuable for Hetty's opponents, for it threw into stark contrast the image of a hale and hearty bank president signing dozens of docu-

ments per day, and a lonely, disabled shut-in, who had quite literally to be placed in front of a document, at times with a pen
inserted between her fingers, in order to sign anything at all.
No matter, the complainants charged on.

Lawyers for the estate located a variety of other individuals
with consistent penmanship, the most prominent among these
being John Quincy Adams. The sixth president had been dead
for nearly twenty years, but he became an unwitting participant
after his thirty-three-year-old grandson discovered in the president's old study a chest containing dozens of canceled personal
checks. The grandson's testimony served primarily to establish
that the checks were, in fact, in the handwriting of the president, and that the president never used a stamp of his signature
on checks, always preferring to sign them individually.

A series of engravers, tracers, and penmanship experts were
then enlisted to examine the various multiple copies of signatures
of these individuals, to see whether their handwriting might du-
plicate, or "cover," as well as or better than the signatures of
Sylvia. What followed was a detailed, exhaustive digression into
the arts of penmanship, mapmaking, photography, and assorted
other fields with ever more tenuous relation to the issues at hand.
John A. Lowell, a twenty-nine-year-old Boston engraver, found,
upon examining hundreds of sets of signatures, "quite a number . . . covered quite as well, or better, in my opinion" than the
purported Sylvia signatures. No doubt Lowell was an expert in
his field but it is difficult to imagine a judge following or paying
attention for long to his testimony, a small segment of which
serves to represent the overall tone: "I found of the J. Q. Adams
lot, No. 24 matched with No. 49, covered as well as the best one,
and that No. 51 with 58, did not cover as well as does No. 10 does
with No. 1, but better than 15 does with one."

George Mathiot, head of the electrotype and photographic di-
vision of the United States Coast Survey Office in Washington,
submitted to no fewer than five days of mind-spinning,
posterior-numbing testimony on ever more arcane subjects. An

expert on tracing, Mathiot had devised a method for reducing table-sized maps to standard paper size, for publishing purposes. Hetty's lawyers had enlisted him to examine signature pairs and testify with authority, as had Lowell, that lots of signatures covered better than Sylvia's. Mathiot did so, but his testimony, especially under cross-examination, drifted onto subjects ranging from the attributes of various lens types, the manufacturing process of paper, and the type and configuration of clamps used to hold paper to drafting tables at the Coast Survey Office. One excruciating session, covering much of an afternoon and extending into the following morning, concerned the relative merits of the Voigtlander lens. When, nearing the end of his testimony, Mathiot was asked by one of the respondents' lawyers whether his examination of the signatures had been a long or short one, he replied, "A long and tedious one." It is safe to say that everyone present could feel his pain.

The respondents' lawyers, for their part, produced an equal number of witnesses claiming precisely the opposite, that signatures so uniform and precise could be nothing but forgeries. George A. Sawyer, a forty-four-year-old teacher of penmanship and bookkeeping, said of the copies of the second page: "They are not natural; they are studied. They exhibit great effort to make them look exactly like No. 1 [the signature on the will]." Sawyer described his suspicion of fakery as immediate and visceral. "It is my conviction—it was my conviction when I saw it at first. Detectors of counterfeit money and those in the habit of studying manuscript often form an opinion without being able to express the reason in words. It would be impossible for me to express in words all the reasons for not thinking those signatures 10 and 15 [the copies of the second page] were genuine."

George N. Comer, president of Commercial College, a Boston trade school specializing in penmanship, bookkeeping, and similar arts, was called in to provide two important points. One was to show that the signatures could easily have been traced without the use of a pencil, thus deflating the impact of the august Agassiz and Holmes. The second-page signature appeared to be "written over No. 1 without the intervention of pencil or other tracing, and is consequently more flowing," Comer said. But he added, "The whole signature bears the evidence to me of having been written over or copied from another, and does not have the character which the genuine signatures have."

But the defense wasn't all just obscure penmanship experts. The lawyers for the estate showed that they would bring out the celebrity firepower by producing as witnesses famed Harvard mathematician Benjamin Peirce and his celebrated son, Charles. An astronomer and mathematician born and raised in Salem, Peirce had spent the first part of his career teaching and writing dry and somewhat unremarkable textbooks, before his landmark *A System of Analytic Mechanics* in 1855 made him a celebrity. He had taken a leading role in establishing the Harvard Observatory, making many notable astronomical discoveries and observations. He had served on the committee drawing a plan for the Smithsonian Institution. For fifteen years he had served as director of longitude determinations for the United States Coast Survey, and in 1867 had just been appointed the Survey's superintendent. This must have made for interesting office politics for the beleaguered George Mathiot, who had testified at such length for Hetty's side.

Peirce's twenty-seven-year-old son, Charles, had followed closely in his father's footsteps. The elder Peirce had provided much of Charles's early mathematics education, and, after graduating from Harvard, where his father taught, Charles went to work in 1861 for the Coast Survey, where he would spend the next thirty years. At his father's direction, Charles Peirce closely examined the three Hetty signatures for improbable similarities that would have been unlikely to occur in the natural course of signing separate documents. The Peirces paid special attention to the downstrokes of the pen, which would have the greatest tendency to vary from signature to signature if written naturally. "The proposed signature must be analyzed into its characteristic lines," Peirce said. "The safest and surest mode of performing this analysis is to adopt for the characteristic lines all those which consist wholly or in part of a downward stroke."

In poring over the signatures, Charles Peirce had found no fewer than thirty identical downstrokes—downstrokes being, as the term implies, the two times in the forming of, say, a "w," when the pen makes a downward slash. In addition to being a mathematical genius, Benjamin Peirce possessed an eye for the marketable quote, the sound bite in a pre–sound bite age. Sensing that thirty identical pairings of downstrokes might not possess sufficient force to impress the judges and the press, Peirce converted this finding into a mathematical probability that would be repeated in virtually every newspaper account of the trial. "In the case of Sylvia Ann Howland," he said, "this phenomenon could occur only once in the number of times expressed by the thirtieth power of five, or, more exactly it is once in (2,666) two thousand six hundred and sixty-six millions of millions of millions of times, or 2,666,000,000,000,000,000,000,000."

With his flair for drama and language, Peirce added, "This number far transcends human experience. So vast an improbability is practically an impossibility. Such evanescent shadows of probability cannot belong to actual life. They are unimaginably less than those least things the law cares not for."

It was almost anticlimactic when Peirce introduced another variable making the odds against the signatures being genuine even more remote. This was that the signatures, despite having been written on unlined paper, were all written with each letter on the same level. This would add an additional improbability on the relatively minor and anticlimactic order of one in 200 million.

As if it needed being stated, Benjamin Peirce offered his personal assurance that the signatures were not genuine and that, by implication (though he didn't say this), Hetty was guilty of forgery. In this matter, he intoned, "I have the utmost degree of confidence."

# FIVE

# SELF-IMPOSED EXILE

The horde of would-be trustees, heirs, and beneficiaries would have to wait more than a year for Justice Nathan Clifford to hand down his decision. Not surprisingly, the only parties assured of getting substantial chunks of Sylvia's fortune were the teams of lawyers representing both sides—seven for Hetty; three for the trustees. Hetty's side had included a former governor, John H. Clifford (no relation to the judge); the trustees' roster included a former Massachusetts Supreme Court justice, B. F. Thomas. The reams of testimony (covering more than one thousand large pages) gathered from all those scientific experts and celebrities had not simply made for entertaining legal theater. It was also a world-class case of churning on the part of attorneys who, by the time they were finished, had racked up more than $150,000 in fees.

Hetty retreated into the company of the one man who had showed her unstinting loyalty—Edward Henry Green. In the two years since they met, Edward had barely experienced a time of peace, first supporting Hetty through the deaths of her father and aunt, then being plunged into Hetty's bizarre world of intrigue, recrimination, scheming, and anger. While he was eager to help Hetty, Edward had put his own reputation on the line by making himself a party to her schemes; and, to the extent that he corroborated portions of Hetty's fabulous tale of the "second page," Edward Green quite probably lied under oath.

Hetty and Edward were married on July 11, 1867, more than two years after becoming engaged. The scene of their wedding was, significantly, not New Bedford. The ceremony took place in New York, at the Bond Street home of Henry Grinnell, the relative who had hosted her on her earlier visits to the city. Edward was forty-six; Hetty was thirty-three, well into her spinster years according to the customs of the times, but still a lovely young woman with a fair, clear complexion, blue eyes, and attractive figure.

Among the small wedding party was her maid of honor Annie Leary, a young society woman whom Hetty had met during her earlier stays with the Grinnells. Annie and Hetty were opposites in many respects and this, perhaps, helped explain their attraction. Leary, a Catholic, was one of six children of James Leary, a Manhattan hatter whose business was located at the corner of Broadway and Vesey Streets downtown. Leary made his fortune serving some of the most prominent New Yorkers, among them, John Jacob Astor. Annie reveled in her fortune, and in the power her money gave her, both to enjoy the finer things and to support charitable and civic causes. For her efforts on behalf of Catholic charities, in particular to help the children of poor Catholic immigrants, she would be named a papal countess. She spent much of her adult life in a large limestone house at 1032 Fifth Avenue. Although she never married, Annie was an extrovert, a social creature who loved to throw elegant parties with her home lit up and smart people coming and going throughout the night. She had a fondness for fine objects, with a special appreciation for large, ornate, gilt-edged mirrors. According to one count she had sixty-eight. Their enduring, lifelong friendship was a remarkable feature of Hetty's life, given that Hetty has frequently been portrayed as a dour woman to whom friendship meant nothing.

Shortly after their wedding, Mr. and Mrs. Edward Green sailed for England. This was more than just a honeymoon—they planned to live there, temporarily at least. While in Asia, Edward had developed a strong network of business contacts in England. But undoubtedly there were other reasons for the change of scenery. Hetty wanted to put as many miles as she could between herself and her recent past. Much of the testimony at the trial had been humiliating; every unattractive act or personal shortcoming was publicly exploited. New York, it seems, wasn't far enough from New Bedford—an ocean would provide a more secure distance.

And then there was the looming issue of the trial, still waiting to be decided. This was a civil, not a criminal, trial, and Hetty had been the plaintiff, not the defendant. And yet the tables had turned during the course of the trial; as everyone knew, if the now-infamous "second page" was not genuine, then Hetty was by definition guilty of forgery. If Hetty was a forger, could criminal charges be far behind? Some of Hetty's opponents had made rumblings about that possibility. Hetty may well have feared that she had finally gone too far. Some people suggested the relocation to England was a means of removing her from the arm of American justice. Hetty rejected any such insinuations as ridiculous. But still, she left.

One of the most persistent stories regarding the marriage is that Edward signed a prenuptial agreement laying no claim on Hetty's fortune should she die first. It's impossible today to verify whether such a document ever existed. But during this early phase of the Greens' married life, Edward was making the choices about where and how they lived and he paid all the bills.

The Greens settled in London in the Langham Hotel, where they indulged Edward's taste for the good life. The Langham, among the city's first grand hotels, was just four years old when the Greens arrived in 1867, but already it was regarded as among London's best and most fashionable addresses. It was located in Marylebone, in the northwestern portion of the city, along Portland Place. The Langham commanded fine views of Regent's Park. It had been built for £300,000, with the latest plumbing and fire-resistant technology available. Four large pipes ran the height of the building, delivering water to each floor from tanks containing 50,000 gallons. The hotel boasted of its pure water sucked up from an artesian well sunk 365 feet into the ground. Shortly after the opening, the Langham became the place for visiting celebrities to stay. Guests included everyone from Napoleon III to Mark Twain. Twain wrote to a friend from the hotel in 1873, describing the rooms as "luxuriously ample" with fine views from broad windows out onto one of London's best neighborhoods.

Marylebone was "the richest and most populous metropolitan parish," according to *The National Gazetteer of Great Britain and Ireland* of 1868. The immediate neighborhood had a rich history. Boswell had lived in the area when he wrote his great biography, *Life of Johnson,* and Edward Gibbon had lived there for a time while completing his masterpiece, *The Decline and Fall of the Roman Empire.* Marylebone, according to the *Gazetteer,* "contained some of the finest squares, crescents, and mansions in the metropolis, including Cavendish and Portment-squares, Park-crescent and square, Manchester-square, Portland-place, the finest street in London, 100 feet wide, &c., and is inhabited by many of the first families in the empire, and likewise the Langham Hotel. . . . The inhabitants are chiefly gentry and trades-people, there being scarcely any manufactures." It was, in short, just the sort of place Green adored, and just the sort of place for which Hetty liked to profess unbridled contempt.

The Greens lost no time in starting a family. Swathed in fine sheets and with all of the attentive care that the Langham staff could provide, Hetty became a mother on August 22, 1868, a lit-

tle over a year after she had become a wife. It was a boy. The
Greens gave him a long name befitting his lineage and honoring
both sides of the family: Edward Howland Robinson Green. To
distinguish him from his father, the boy would be called Ned.
The boy was less than three months old when word came from
New England that Judge Clifford had reached a decision in the
Aunt Sylvia case. The news couldn't have surprised Hetty. The
trustees had a much stronger case all along. But the decisiveness
with which Clifford, on November 14, 1868, rebuked Hetty's
claims left little room for comfort.

The most damaging element of Clifford's ruling was to ex-
clude all portions of Hetty's testimony related to the mutual
wills she and Sylvia signed. Clifford's basis for this decision was
a Massachusetts law forbidding one member of a mutual will
from testifying in his or her own favor, unless the other party
was also alive and able to testify. Although the case was heard in
a federal court, Clifford cited recent precedent that federal will
cases should respect the laws of the state in which they are tried.
Because of this ruling, it has been suggested that Clifford, in
essence, tossed out the great will case on a mere technicality. In
fact, Clifford's detailed, exhaustive decision went on for some
nineteen pages and left little wiggle room for Hetty's side on any
element of the case.

Even if Clifford had admitted (and believed) every word of
Hetty's testimony regarding the mutual wills, it is clear that his
decision wouldn't have changed, because he was deeply unimpressed by the wills themselves. "The two wills under consideration [Sylvia's January 1862 will and Hetty's from 1860] are
not mutual wills in any proper sense, as recognized in the law
of evidence or the decisions of the courts," Clifford wrote, because they were signed at different times and because Hetty's
will left no money to Aunt Sylvia.

Ironically, the portions of the case that had made it such a
crowd-pleaser—the mysterious contents of Aunt Sylvia's hair-
covered trunk, with its yellow and white envelopes being

passed in the dim light after Sylvia's funeral; and the star-studded testimony revolving around the forgery issues—had little bearing on the decision.

Clifford did not care whether the documents were genuine or forged, he said, or who passed them to whom and under what conditions, because, "viewed in any light, and assuming all the papers to be genuine, the evidence fails altogether, in the opinion of the court." But the forgery portion of the trial was not a total waste of time—as Clifford himself predicted in his decision, the voluminous expert testimony would prove "highly important" in establishing rules of evidence in future forgery cases.

Hetty responded to the decision through her lawyers a month later with a notice of appeal to the United States Supreme Court. But before the appeal process began, Hetty and the trustees reached a compromise. Hetty agreed that each beneficiary would receive his or her bequest, plus 6 percent annually from the date of Sylvia's death. But just when the matter seemed to have been settled, Hetty held up the process over the matter of taxes. She wanted the taxes on each gift deducted from the gift itself, or from the capital of the trust, rather than from the income. In other words, Hetty did not want to be paying the taxes on the gifts from her own income. It was a fairly nit-picking point, and yet the debate kept beneficiaries from getting paid for another year; the court decided that the taxes would be paid from the capital.

With the great battle at last over, the munificence from Aunt Sylvia, stalemated for seven years, began to flow in 1872 and spread around New Bedford like whale oil from a leaking barrel. Electa Montague, the loyal nurse now sixty-eight years old, received her $5,000 in cash, plus accrued interest. Pardon Gray, the old livery driver who had driven poor withered Sylvia on that shaded seven-mile ride from New Bedford to Round Hill, began to receive his modest stipend from the $10,000 placed in trust for him. Widows around town, those who lived to see the will enacted, saw their lives grow a measure more secure in their old age. In recognition of her $100,000 gift for the New Bedford Free Public Library and other educational purposes, the city erected a marble tablet praising Sylvia's "enlightened liberality" in "extending to the children and youth of the city the means of wider and more generous culture." The library placed a bust of Sylvia on its second floor.

Two decades later the city built a red brick schoolhouse and named it Sylvia Ann Howland School. The $50,000 she had left "to be divided among the poor, aged and infirm women of New Bedford, to the most neediest cases," was used by the trustees to found a private charity. The New Bedford Orphans' Home found itself with $20,000, and the City of New Bedford received $100,000 to pipe water into the city. Twenty thousand dollars went to establish a sailors' home, to care for the men whose toil and risk had helped make the fortune possible. Sylvia, who spent so much of her life shut away from others, taking refuge from her tortured body in the pages of romance novels set worlds away from New Bedford, became a benefactress and public figure in death that she had never been in life.

Dr. Gordon, already receiving thousands of dollars each year in commissions as trustee, received a lump sum of $100,000 plus $15,000 for his wife and children, along with 6 percent accrued annual interest. Thomas Mandell, the head trustee, took home $200,000 plus interest. For all those lump payments, there remained a $1.3 million chunk of principal—enough to supply Hetty with an income of $65,000 a year for life. She also received a large up-front payment. Mandell had invested much of the estate in U.S. government 6-percent gold bonds, and reinvested both the interest and dividend. When the estate battle was settled, Mandell handed Hetty's lawyer, William Crapo, a stack of bonds worth $600,000 face value. Their value on the market was worth considerably more than that. Crapo, who transferred the bonds to Hetty, noted dryly in his introduction to William Emery's *The Howland Heirs*, "Mrs. Green apparently had not suffered by the long delay and expensive litigation."

On January 7, 1871, thirty-five-year-old Hetty gave birth to the Greens' second child, a girl, named Hetty Sylvia Ann Howland Green. The girl would always be known as Sylvia, rather than Hetty, and Hetty would point to her daughter's name as proof of the love that had existed between Hetty and her aunt.

When the children were old enough, she took them for walks around London. Hetty prided herself on the Quaker traditions of home healing, and on her own abilities as a nurse. Years after returning to the United States, she recalled an incident that occurred one day as she walked with Ned and Sylvia on Prince of Wales Terrace, a small street on the south side of Kensington Road, near Kensington Gardens. The driver of a passing cart suddenly fell from his vehicle, Hetty told reporter Leigh Mitchell Hodges of *The Ladies' Home Journal*. As Hetty told it, the man went into seizures and the small crowd that gathered had no idea what to do. Hetty told Ned to watch Sylvia carefully and stand next to a tree. "Mrs. Green sent one man for water and another for a doctor. Then with her handkerchief she washed out the cuts received in the fall, and bandaged them, and ordered the man carried into the shop nearby."

" 'It wasn't any more than I would have done for anyone,' " Hetty told Hodges. " 'But those simple folk would have let him bleed to death while they wondered what to do. You can imagine my surprise when, as I started back to the children, a footman in gorgeous livery bowed to me and said "The Marchioness of Something" wished to present her compliments and desired to see me. Curious to know what she wanted I followed him to a great house on the Terrace. The Marchioness came out and greeted me warmly. She said she had watched the whole proceeding from her window and wanted me to know how she admired what I had done. I was just the woman she was looking for. A charity hospital in which she was interested needed a superintendent. If I would accept the place she would have me appointed, and there was a cottage near the hospital in which my family might live.' "

Hetty continued: " 'I didn't like to hurt her feelings by telling her I didn't have to work for my living, so I thanked her and said I could not then accept the offer. She insisted, but I declined. As we walked home I noticed her footman following quite a way behind.' " The footman followed her and was stunned to see Hetty enter the Langham. He asked her identity at the front desk. " 'An hour or so afterward a note came from the Marchioness. She begged to apologize; she hadn't the least idea who I was when she sent for me, and all that. A whole lot of tickets to bazaars and entertainments, of which she was a patroness, were enclosed. I sent these back with thanks, and a day or two after that called on her and told her she needn't have offered any apology, as I indeed felt highly honored that anyone could consider me at all fitted for such a position as the one she offered me.' "

Edward spent his London years as a gentleman banker, serving on the boards of several London banks, making the rounds of clubs, and enjoying the life of a gentleman. Hetty was already busy tending to her fortune. The extent to which Hetty and Edward worked together on financial matters is unclear, and Edward may well have advised her on investments in the early stages. But she was already establishing the patterns of investment that would define her career, sticking with conservative instruments such as United States bonds, and having the cool head to stay on her course when others panicked. From the time she inherited her first lump from her father in 1865, Hetty had been buying up United States "greenback" notes.

The government had printed large quantities of these notes immediately after the Civil War, to cover its huge expenditures. The Union had won military victory, but people were still quite apprehensive about the prospects, particularly the economic prospects, of the ragged and still-fragile reunified country. Unease caused a rush to gold, and the greenbacks dropped to as low as forty or fifty cents on the dollar of gold. While others lost their nerve and sold greenbacks, Hetty bought. John T. Flynn, who wrote about Hetty's career a few years after her death, summed it up nicely in his book, *Men of Wealth*:

> Here was an excellent chance for any far-seeing person to pick up government securities at half their value. All it required was a little faith in the nation that had just demonstrated in a most extraordinary way its ability to come through a terrific civil war. Looking back at it now, the recovery of the country ought to have seemed a sure thing to any observer. The war had given an immense impetus to the resources of the continent—coal, iron, oil, copper, gold, and silver were just being discovered and developed. But for all that, the nation's credit was at a low ebb and through 1865, 1866, and 1867 Hetty Robinson bought all the government bonds she could lay hold of.

She continued this strategy in England, claiming in a single year to have made $1.25 million from her bond investments alone. Her income from the two trusts was now very substantial. Her father's estate of some $5 million, even under management she openly detested, was yielding her several thousand dollars per week in interest and dividends. She was able to put all of this money to work in U.S. bonds, and she began branching out in railroad bonds issued to finance the rapidly expanding rail network. With Edward handling the living expenses, Hetty had nothing to do with all of her money but to keep investing and reinvesting principal and income. Within a few years her fortune doubled, tripled, quadrupled.

"Two hundred thousand dollars is the largest sum I ever made in a single day," she told Leigh Mitchell Hodges of her days in London, "though I've cleared more than that on single deals." As her cash piled up and she sought new investments, she became a de facto bank. Her holdings, indeed, were growing larger than those of many banks of the day, in England or America. Banks in need of cash would sell Hetty loans they had made to parties using property as collateral. When inevitably some of the borrowers defaulted on their loans, Hetty began to accrue property. This was the beginning of what would become a real estate empire.

Hetty (and Edward) had also begun to invest in U.S. railroads, expanding rapidly in the wake of the Civil War. It was this interest, probably, that led to their family's decision to return to the United States after six years in the winter of 1873–74. It was one thing to invest in relatively static U.S. notes from abroad, quite another to keep tabs on the volatile world of railroads, which were as full of potential disaster as of promise. In 1873, the markets were particularly uneasy. Banks had extended loans to hundreds of railroads, in various states of completion— some amounting to little more than grand words in a prospectus. Bonds for these railroads flooded the market. In the fall of 1872, within less than three months, three major U.S. banks—the New York Warehouse and Security Company, Jay Cook and Company, and the Union Trust Company—failed. Other banks soon suspended operations. To stem the panic, the New York Stock Exchange closed for ten days. The distress that lingered through the entire next year became known as the panic of 1873. Before it was over, some eleven thousand companies had failed, and combined losses reached $380 million. Under the circumstances, Edward and Hetty decided they needed to be closer to the seat of their respective fortunes. After a brief stay in New York, they headed north to Edward's hometown of Bellows Falls, Vermont.

# SIX

# PRIDE AND PAIN

Bellows Falls buzzed with the impending arrival of Edward Green and his family in the spring of 1874. Despite its somewhat remote location, thirty miles north of Brattleboro and tucked away on a bend in the Connecticut River, this was no hayseed town. The name came from an early settler named Benjamin Bellows, but the rather industrial image it conjures is appropriate. The village was founded principally on paper mills and the transportation industry. A man-made canal cut through the heart of town, and by the mid-nineteenth century Bellows Falls was an important railroad junction, connecting Burlington and Montpelier upstate with Hartford, Boston, New York, and New Hampshire. There was a prosperous downtown with good hotels and fine old homes lining a promontory overlooking the river. Visitors were not uncommon. But this was no ordinary arrival.

Edward Green, the scion of a prominent Bellows Falls family, was returning to his hometown as a wealthy man of the world. The Tuckers, on his mother's side, owned the toll bridge leading from Bellows Falls across the river to Walpole, New

Hampshire. His father, Henry Atkinson Green, had come to
Bellows Falls from Massachusetts and established Hall and
Green, a large store on the river side of the main town square.
Older residents remembered Edward Green as a tall, lanky, affable youth who loved to play along the river with other boys,
watching and imitating the river men who guided their craft
through the canal that bisected the town. One day, as Edward
stood on a wooden bridge watching his hero, Jack Adams, navigate the canal, he leaned so far over the barricade that he fell
twenty feet into the water and nearly drowned. Jack Adams
added to his local legend by fishing the boy safely out of the
water; Edward added to his reputation as a bit of a dreamer.

But in the years since he had left town, no one could deny
that Edward Green had made his dreams come true in the most
spectacular fashion. His mother, Anna, had kept the town well
informed of Edward's progress, his business successes and his
adventures in Asia. As a bachelor, Edward had returned from
time to time, bringing along a bulldog and a manservant. He
spent money freely, wore fancy clothes, and impressed old
friends with snippets of Chinese and other languages he'd
picked up overseas. He invariably bore expensive gifts for his
beloved mother, including an ornate Chinese lacquer workstand,
embossed with gold figures and set on thin legs supported by
golden dragons. When he learned that his mother planned to
visit New York, he directed her to buy furs and charge them to
his New York agent. When she returned with a nice but not ex-
ceptional mink coat, Green gave it to his sister and replaced his
mother's coat with Russian sable. He sent her money regularly
from the Philippines, particularly after his father's death in 1863,
and bought her a neat cottage on Henry Street, one of the most
prominent residential streets in town. And now, to top off his
legend, Edward was returning home with two children, ages six
and three, and a fabulous millionaire wife.

Anticipation over Edward's arrival was overshadowed by the
gossip, excitement, and expectations surrounding his wife. Ed-

ward was rich, but his wife had money on a scale that people in Bellows Falls could not comprehend. What would this woman be like? Would she be dour or sweet? Would she put on airs or mix with the common folk? Was there a house in town grand enough to suit a woman of her wealth, or would she direct Edward to build for her some Xanadu on a hillside? Would she hold grand balls and elegant teas? Would they be invited? What gowns and jewels would she wear? What should *they* wear? Just how did one behave in the presence of *so much money*?

It is safe to say that when the Greens stepped off the train in their new home, the reaction was not so much disappointment as quiet wonder. At forty-one Hetty still had a pretty face and a fine complexion, but her dress was downright homely. Her hair looked as though she hadn't given it a thought. She spoke not in the low, regal manner they might have expected, but in harsher, earthier tones, and, when angered, she could cuss like a dockworker. Within a few weeks of her arrival, if any of the townsfolk even remembered their predictions of aristocracy in their midst, it was only with an ironic laugh.

The Greens moved in with Edward's mother, into the house on Henry Street that Edward had bought as a gift. Nobody was more shocked by Hetty than Anna Green's Irish cook and maid, Mary. On the day of the Greens' arrival, Mary spent all day in the kitchen, preparing a homecoming feast. She curled her black hair and put on a crisp white muslin uniform with a starched overskirt and ruffles. She did not greet the family at the door, but waited in the kitchen in order to make a proper appearance. When the family was ready to eat, Mary adjusted her uniform, took a deep breath, and entered the dining room. The heiress staring back at her wore old, soiled-looking garments. Later, Mary swore that Hetty's hands were not clean.

Hetty and Mary disliked each other from the start. Hetty thought Mary wasted money shopping for family meals. In fact, she considered Mary herself a wasteful expense and would have fired her had she not been Anna's maid. Hetty insisted on doing most of the shopping herself, and would return to the house bearing the cheapest flour she could find, and bags of broken cookies that grocers sold cheap. Grocer Patrick J. Keane said she always redeemed her berry boxes for a nickel refund, and asked for—and received—free bones for the family dog.

A half century later, Mary, interviewed by a Bellows Falls historian named Lyman Simpson Hayes, was still scathing in her assessment of Hetty Green. One day, Mary recalled, Hetty brought from the butcher "a bit of meat no bigger than half my hand. And one would eat the meat and the other gnaw the bone."

People began to view Edward in a different light. He had not changed so much in personality—he still loved the companionship of friends, loved a hearty laugh over lunch downtown, was still generous on an individual basis with friends in need. And yet to the extent that any marriage is a battle of wills, Hetty clearly held the upper hand. Her parsimony ruled the home and Edward, instead of insisting on the luxuries he adored, quietly acceded. When the Greens first arrived in town, they took pleasure rides in Edward's barouche, a fancy, four-wheeled carriage with a collapsible top, double seats facing each other inside the carriage, and an outside front seat for the driver, along with a pair of fine horses. Hetty decided the rig was too fancy. She sold the carriage and horses, and paid $10 for an old horse and a modest jump seat wagon, barely large enough to fit the family. In the subtle way that reputations shift, Edward was no longer the conquering hero to the admiring throngs of Bellows Falls, but a man making the best of a difficult situation.

Edward's mother was no match for Hetty's forceful nature. Anna had no doubt expected to live out her remaining days in genteel comfort and contentment, surrounded by Edward, his bride, and the two grandchildren. Instead, she found herself sharing her suddenly too small home with a loud, opinionated woman who questioned every incidental expense, harangued her beloved maid, and didn't even bother to make herself presentable. Neighbors on Henry Street were shocked one day to see Hetty on the roof, seated, wearing hoop skirts, hammering away. Why pay workmen for a simple repair job?

It was all too much for Mary. She threatened to quit. Anna, terrified at the prospect of days alone with her daughter-in-law, begged her to stay. Mary agreed, and remained until the next summer, when on June 28, 1875, at seventy-three, Anna died. Regarding Anna's death we have only Mary's wholly biased and nonmedical diagnosis that distress over Hetty's overbearing ways sped her decline. At any rate, Anna's funeral led to one of the few times that Mary (or anyone else) saw Edward react violently to Hetty. As the family gathered for a postfuneral dinner, Edward raised a drinking glass to his lips and noticed it was old and cracked. This was not his mother's prized crystal, but cheap kitchen ware.

"Where is the crystal?" he asked evenly.

Hetty told him she'd packed it away. No point risking valuable heirlooms when everyday glasses hold liquid just as well. Edward stared at the glass, his face slowly flushing with anger. He stood, hurled the glass against a wall, shattering it, and walked out of the room.

At other times, Edward's protest was more reserved. One day, as he headed to the station to catch a train for New York, Hetty discovered that he had forgotten to take along an extra pair of pants. She followed him to the train and handed him the pants, which he took without comment. When the train rolled out of the station, Edward discreetly tossed them into the canal below.

Soon after that, Hetty and Mary had the mutual pleasure of parting company. Mary dragged her bags to the door and insisted that Hetty open and examine them so she could never accuse Mary of stealing. They argued over her final paycheck. Hetty refused to pay. Mary found Edward having lunch with some friends at a hotel. She approached his table and said, "Don't you think it's about time I had my pay?" Green, cha-

grined, sent to the hotel's office for pen and ink, and promptly
wrote Mary a check for the full amount.

In 1879, five years after the family arrived in Bellows Falls, Edward Green made what would prove to be the last major material purchase of his life, his final grand gesture in the face of
Hetty's irresistible penury. He bought a large, square, yellow
brick home on a bluff overlooking the Connecticut River,
around the corner from Henry Street. Built in 1806, the house
had been owned by his grandfather, owner of the toll bridge.
Known as the Tucker House, it was an imposing structure with
immense chimneys and a widow's walk crowning the roof. The
house occupied a choice piece of ground just south of the town
square, at the corner of Church and Westminster Streets. From
a rocking chair on the broad front porch, you could look down
to the river or across to the sheer face of Mount Kilburn in
New Hampshire.

Inside, the house was dominated by a wide central hallway
and a beautiful winding staircase. On the left side were two
large rooms connected by a wide passageway; on the right, a
parlor and a dining room. Among the furnishings was a portrait
of Hetty, painted years earlier, which hung over the mantelpiece.
There were also a few valuable pieces that Edward had picked
up in the Far East, including the Chinese lacquered stand Edward had bought for his mother. Hetty may well have disap-
proved of the purchase of the Tucker House. It was too big; it
cost too much to heat. It was said that in later years when she
stayed there she added makeshift partitions to cut the size of the
rooms, and the expense of fuel. But she grew undeniably fond of
the house. For a woman who had shuttled from house to house
from infancy, the Tucker House became the closest thing she
would ever have to her own home. Even when she moved away
from Bellows Falls, she returned often to the refuge of its walls.

When the children were old enough, they were enrolled in
local schools. Sylvia attended the rectory school at Immanuel

Episcopal Church. She was a shy girl by nature, overshadowed throughout her life by a strong and domineering mother. She seems to have had few close friends at any period of her life, but one of her first became one of her best, Mary Nims. Mary lived outside the village center, so she carried a lunch to eat at school while the village children went home. Sylvia ate a hurried lunch at home, then rushed back to school to keep Mary company. Mary recalled Sylvia as a shy but sweet girl who always shared her candy. "Her school dresses were clean and inexpensive. She wore glasses and a stiff little sailor hat that was too small for her was perched on her head. When we all dressed for last day exercises she appeared in a very elaborate dress made with many ruffles of white embroidery that looked like a Godey print. She said it came from England."

Once the town folk got used to the fact that Hetty Green would not reign as the queen of Bellows Falls, they began to see her, with a mixture of consternation and affection, as a celebrated oddball. Hetty stories developed into a local currency; everyone had at least two or three, and they were handed down by word of mouth, some even to this day, until it is not always clear which are apocryphal and which based on fact. She was, as one local historian put it, "at once the pride and pain of the town."

Stable hands traded stories about Hetty's penny-pinching over the family's carriages and horses. Boarding a horse for the winter, she drove a hard bargain with one stable owner, refusing to pay more than two dollars per week. When the owner informed her that such a small payment could buy only hay for feed, no grain, Hetty is supposed to have replied, "Just hay, then." The next spring, Hetty discovered the horse looking thin and haggard. The hostler is said to have fed the horse grain from his own pocket. But a winter epidemic had besieged the horses. When the hostler explained the situation to Hetty, she was unimpressed. She refused to pay the bill, saying, "If the horse had had decent feed he would not be so thin."

Local merchants and others with whom Hetty traded heard

her talk at length about her Aunt Sylvia's estate—in particular about the large number of people awaiting their share of the fortune. "They're only waiting for me to die so they can have my money," she would say. "But I'll fool them. I'll take such good care of myself that I'll never be ill. They'll see who laughs last."

Among the most celebrated stories in town concerned her obsessive search for a postage stamp. The story began when Hetty took a daylong drive with her horse and carriage, returning the rig to the stable in the evening. "Some time later, after bedtime, there came a knock at the hostler's door," Lyman Simpson Hayes wrote. "Mrs. Green presented herself to say that while absent that day she had bought a two-cent stamp which she was now unable to find. The man must get up and help her look for it. With a groan he arose, lighted a kerosene lantern, and the two searched the wagon and stable, but without success. The next move was to The Island House, a Bellows Falls hotel where she had spent some time in the afternoon. Together on hands and knees by the smoky gleam of the lantern they searched the grassy lawn inch by inch, to no avail. Long after his visitor had departed, when silence had descended upon the stable, the hostler was again aroused to be informed that the valuable piece of property had at last been located—inside her clothing, where it had been placed for safe keeping."

Merchants reportedly tried to lie low when they saw Hetty Green approaching. She was known to demand the cheapest possible goods and, still, to haggle endlessly over a bill. One shopkeeper remembered that Hetty had come into his shop and, as was her custom, began handling the merchandise. The storekeeper watched in dismay—her hands were black. She explained that she had been pulling some reusable nails out of some boards that had been damaged in a fire in her barn. When she brought her skirt to Wheeler's Laundry, she is said to have asked that only the bottom portions be washed—the parts that swished through the alternately muddy and dusty street.

In later years, when the family traveled and rented out the

Tucker House for periods while they were away, Hetty rented a
room over a Bellows Falls bank to store some furniture. A cat
apparently entered the room and, unable to find a way out, began
to wail. Hetty had taken the key with her to New York, so someone raised a ladder at the rear of the building, broke a window,
and retrieved the cat. Months later, Hetty is supposed to have returned to Bellows Falls and found the broken pane upstairs. Fearing she might be charged for the breakage, and as yet unaware of
the cat incident, Hetty supposedly picked up a loose cobblestone
and presented it to a bank employee, saying, "There's a lot of
glass broken upstairs. Don't expect me to pay for it. Someone
threw this stone through the window. I found it on the floor up
there." As Hetty marched out, the cashier turned the stone over
and discovered that it was still damp on one side—a sure indication that Hetty had just picked it up from the street.

Whether consciously or not, Hetty courted the reputation that
followed her throughout her life. The more outrageous tales
were merely extensions of her habits and behavior and the way
of life she followed. More than most people, she had the resources to create for herself any life and any reputation she
chose. For her children it was another matter entirely. Ned and
Sylvia spent their early years living an odd double life as rich
kids whose mother behaved as if they were poor. They wore
ill-fitting clothes and got used to being pointed to and whis-
pered about, not out of jealousy, but out of pity.

Ned's awkwardness was accentuated by a pronounced limp,
the result of a childhood sledding accident. The accident is generally believed to have occurred in Bellows Falls during one of
the family's first winters there. But Mary Nims remembered
Hetty saying the accident took place earlier, in New York,
shortly after they returned from England. "She told my mother
that during their first winter in New York there was a snow
storm and they bought Edward a sled so that he might slide
with the other boys in the park. He had never before seen

snow so his enthusiasm over the sport was so great that he injured his knee jumping onto his sled." As for the nature of the
injury, it does not seem to have been a fracture, because Edward continued to walk on the leg after it happened. According
to some reports, he dislocated his kneecap. At any rate, the
problem was chronic and worsened over time.

Of all of the myths and legends about Hetty's miserliness
handed down from generation to generation, the most persistent and unflattering is that she allowed her son's leg to worsen
over the years because she was too cheap to seek the care of
doctors. As with most myths, the actual story is more complex.
It is true that Hetty's contempt for doctors and their bills, ex-
ceeded only by her contempt for lawyers, led her to take advantage of doctors in ways that were unseemly. Fearful of being
charged a millionaire markup should she and Ned use their real
names and visit doctors in their offices, Hetty was not above
hauling her son to a free clinic, dressed in tattered clothes,
where those same doctors volunteered their time. For her to
take advantage of doctors' goodwill in this manner was of
course reprehensible. For her to even think of money when her
son's well-being was at stake was inexcusable, except to say that
Hetty Green never thought of anything without evaluating its
cost, and never received a bill that she did not question.

And yet the suggestion that Hetty stood by cavalierly while
Ned's leg withered away is both inaccurate and unfair. In fact,
Hetty did seek medical care, repeatedly. Her son was the principal love of her life. Looking across the broad canvas of their
odd but loving relationship, their devotion to one another until
the day Hetty died, it is inconceivable that Hetty would have
endured Ned's suffering in order to save money. It is equally inconceivable that Edward, for all of his acquiescence to Hetty in
other matters, would have allowed Hetty to neglect Ned's condition. Without knowing the exact nature of the injury it is impossible to say whether this treatment or that might have saved
the leg. But the Greens did try. When not seeking formal med-

ical opinions, Hetty, who always fancied herself a nurse, tried innumerable home remedies in her futile effort to make her son whole again. The first time Mary Nims met the Greens, Hetty was on just such a mission.

"We heard much gossip about the fabulous Mrs. Green and her peculiar way of living, so when the Greens in their ancient carriage drove into our yard, there was considerable excitement," she recalled in memoirs written decades later. "It was a warm day and the blinds on the south side of the living room were closed. From behind this screen a little girl friend and I, with our maid, had a good view of the visitors and made appreciative comments. Mr. Green, who was driving, did not get out of the carriage. His wife did, and attended to the errand on which they came, while two children, a girl my age and a very lame boy, played about the yard.

"My father raised tobacco and Mrs. Green had heard that tobacco leaves bound on Edward's leg would loosen the contracted ligaments," Mary recalled. "He furnished Mrs. Green liberally with the dry tobacco leaves and had an interesting talk with Mr. Green about Manila and his experiences with earthquakes."

Hetty's homegrown tobacco remedy failed to correct Ned's condition, as did all of the other cures suggested by laypeople and physicians alike. Ned was tall, like his father, and as he grew his weight put added strain on the weakened leg.

For all of the oddities that others saw in Hetty and her family, these years in Vermont were the most outwardly conventional of her life. Edward traveled frequently to New York on business by train, leaving Hetty behind with the children. Hetty was still a relatively obscure figure on Wall Street in comparison with her husband. He was an active trader in railroad stocks and bonds, and for a time served on the board of directors of the Louisville and Nashville Railroad, in which he was a heavy holder. He conducted his transactions through John J. Cisco and Son, a prominent Wall Street financial house. When

Edward traded, he did so with his own money. Hetty had laid down the law in no uncertain terms that he was not to use her principal in his transactions. Hetty did her banking with Cisco as well. She had a little over a half-million dollars in cash deposits with the bank, a fraction of her overall wealth but enough to make her Cisco's largest depositor. The rest of her fortune, now totaling more than $26 million in mortgages, bonds, and other securities, and growing all the time, was stashed safely in Cisco vaults, away from the hands of Edward, Cisco partners, or anyone else. She visited New York only on occasion, and concentrated on keeping her house and raising her two children. All of that was about to change.

# HETTY STORMS WALL STREET

In late January 1885, what had been an unusually mild winter in New York suddenly took a turn for the worse. The temperature dropped seventeen degrees in a single day to well below freezing, and gale force winds battered the coast. Ships, unable to approach the harbor, rode out the storm just offshore. The brig *W.N.H. Clements* finally limped into the Atlantic Dock under tow after a terrifying night at sea with her sails shredded, her anchor cables snapped, her crew nursing frostbitten hands and feet, and her entire length encased in ice. On shore, winds whipped angrily around the banks and brokerage houses of lower Manhattan, kicking up clouds of sand and dust from the street that temporarily blinded carriage drivers and pedestrians and lodged into every fold of clothing. Brokers and traders could be seen dashing down streets chasing high hats blown from their heads. But Hetty, who had arrived in New York a few days earlier, alone, was far more concerned about the financial storm raging in the offices of John J. Cisco and Son at 59 Wall Street.

---

Some celebrities burst onto the scene so suddenly and with such force that the Before and After of their fame is as obvious as two cities separated by a fissure in the earth. For Hetty Green, the precipitous time was that January, when Cisco and Son, where Edward invested and where Hetty kept her securities, collapsed. She was two months past her fiftieth birthday, a time of life when most people have already settled into the routines that will define the rest of their lives. But Hetty's life would never be the same. After the Cisco failure, she would declare independence from her husband, and war on the world.

Both Hetty and Edward had a long history with the bank. John J. Cisco was an erstwhile dry goods merchant who had served as assistant United States treasurer before starting the bank in 1867. Edward had done his banking with Cisco for quite some time. Hetty trusted the bank's conservative, staid reputation enough to place her securities there for safekeeping. Cisco was amused by Hetty's eccentricities when she came to New York from Bellows Falls to check on her holdings or add something to them. He loved to tell of the day he was looking out the window of the company's building at 59 Wall Street and saw Hetty stepping off of a public coach on Broadway, carrying a bulky parcel. He went to the front door to greet her, and learned that the parcel contained $200,000 in negotiable bonds.

"Don't you think it was risky for you to have brought these bonds downtown in a public stage? You should have taken a carriage," Cisco said.

Hetty arched her eyebrow. "Perhaps you can afford to ride in a carriage. I cannot."

Since Cisco's death in March 1884, the firm's business had been handled by his son, John A. Cisco, and his partner Frederick W. Foote. As managers, the junior Cisco and Foote were less cautious and conservative than the elder Cisco. The bank had been financial agents for the Houston and Texas Central Railroad. Cisco and Foote didn't just handle the financial arrangements; they bought heavily in the railroad's bonds, both personally and on behalf of the bank. In 1884, a conglomerate bought the railroad as a possible link in a new transcontinental railroad, one that would mirror and augment the northern route. The man behind the conglomerate was Collis P. Huntington, the forceful, fiery, and headstrong leader of the Big Four, the cadre of tycoons that had carved the Central Pacific Railroad, the western portion of the first transcontinental line, through mountains and forests. But no sooner had the sale gone through than Huntington and his associates shocked investors by defaulting on a bond payment due January 1. The Houston and Texas Central, Huntington announced, was in far worse shape than originally thought. The railroad's bonds plunged. The bank's Houston and Texas Central holdings dropped in value from $304,000 to $182,400. Foote and Cisco had also invested heavily in another railroad, the Louisville and Nashville, which had run into trouble as well. In a short time, Cisco's personal assets dropped in value from $77,000 to $32,000. Foote's decline was even more dramatic, from $153,500 to $21,500.

Word that Cisco and Son was in trouble spread around Wall Street and made its way up to Hetty in Bellows Falls. She wasted no time in writing a letter to the principals. The bulk of her fortune—her securities—was not exposed, but her cash deposit of more than $550,000 might be in jeopardy if the bank failed. She demanded that the entire deposit be transferred at once to the Chemical National Bank. Cisco and Foote gulped when they read Hetty's letter. She was not the only one to ask for a withdrawal as the rumors spread. But the desperate partners could not afford to lose their largest single depositor.

Hetty had every right to expect Cisco and Foote to do as she had asked. But there was a complication, which the partners cited in refusing to honor her demand. It seemed that while Hetty was the largest depositor at John J. Cisco and Son, Edward Green was its largest debtor. The pride of Bellows Falls, Far East trader extraordinaire, owner of thirty-one suits, generous tipper,

and man-about-town, owed the bank no less than $702,000.
Green had been a close associate of Foote and Cisco's, and had
been involved with them in a variety of investments. Like them,
he had been a major investor in the Louisville and Nashville Railroad, serving on its board of directors and even for a short time
as its president. Doubtless the collapse of the L&N had hurt him
badly, but the overall economy of the early 1880s offered any
number of opportunities for a speculator to lose money. Whatever Edward's specific investments, his performance during this
time tells an all too familiar tale of a man chasing one doomed investment after another in a desperate bid to recapture a lost fortune. As Edward sank further and further into debt, John J. Cisco
and Son was only too willing to continue extending credit to
him. Edward never explicitly offered Hetty's fortune as collateral—at least, the bank presented no evidence of this. Nevertheless, creditors did not hesitate lending money to a man whose
wife sat on a pile of $25 million. Now, Cisco and Foote asked
Hetty to make good on the debt.

It's not clear just when Edward's serious troubles began, but
a quitclaim deed, buried in an old record book in the town
clerk's office in Bellows Falls, provides a clue. It is dated June
19, 1884, three months after the death of John J. Cisco. The
deed, signed by Cisco's son, relinquished the elder Cisco's claim
to the Tucker House, for the sum of one dollar. The new
owner specified in the deed is Hetty Green. There seems only
one reasonable (and utterly poignant) inference to draw from
this document: Edward had put up his house, either as collateral or as direct repayment of a loan, and lost it. The New York
bankers, with little practical need for a house in Vermont, in
turn agreed to hand the house over to their largest depositor, as
a gesture of goodwill. As of June 1884, Edward was living in his
ancestral family home as a guest of his wife.

Hetty was sitting in that very house, seething, when she
wrote a second, and much sterner, letter to Cisco and Foote.
Her husband's finances were his own affair. She had no inten-

tion of covering loans she had not taken out. Should the bank refuse to release her money at once, she would sue. When Foote and Cisco received this missive, they took what they saw as their only remaining recourse.

The New York Stock Exchange had already closed for the day on January 15, 1885. Moneymen from the city's banks and trusts were already bundling on their coats against the winter chill in wind-whipped lower Manhattan. Cisco and Son issued a terse announcement that it was suspending operations. Then as now, bad news was usually relayed after the close of the business day, to allow traders to mull and sift and sleep on news before reacting to it.

Despite the rumors about Cisco that had circulated for days, the announcement took Wall Street by surprise. Cisco and Son was still known as a conservative house, not given to rash speculation. The *New York World* wrote the following day: "The fact that the firm did not do a speculative business to any great extent, that it received very large deposits from innumerable persons and corporations, that it had acted as fiscal agent for several railroads and as correspondent for many out-of-town bankers; that it did a large business in issuing letters of credit to travelers in Europe, made the failure a more than ordinary disaster."

Bankers, investors, and financial reporters around lower Manhattan immediately began looking for the villain responsible for bringing the house of Cisco to its knees. As it turned out, there were several possibilities. They turned their anger and resentment first on Collis P. Huntington, the leader of the Houston and Texas Central. To anyone with more than a passing interest in the affair, the railroad's failure to make the bond payment looked less like financial distress than a calculated and insidious plan by Huntington and his associates to marginalize outside bondholders and consolidate control of the company. No sooner had the bonds plummeted in value than the Huntington group started buying them up at bargain prices from distressed bondholders. It was the sort of act that today might earn Huntington and his cronies at the very least a hot seat before the Securities and Exchange Commission, various Senate and House committees, and an intimate examination by the Justice Department, if not jail time.

In the wilder and woollier nineteenth century, the average investor could do little but gnash his teeth in anger as Huntington himself pleaded ignorance and mild surprise at the whole controversy. In a self-serving letter to the *New York Daily Tribune* two days after the Cisco failure, Huntington wrote that his Southern Development Company had acquired the Houston and Texas Central indirectly, as part of a much larger acquisition of industrialist Charles Morgan's Louisiana and Texas Railroad and Steamship Company. Huntington claimed that since he had neither built the railroad nor issued the bonds, he was not responsible for paying interest on them. "I have been and am wholly unable to bring myself to the conclusion that any legal or moral obligation existed for my payment from my own resources the maturing coupons upon bonds of a railway company with which I have become connected only in the indirect way which I have mentioned." As for his subsequent eagerness to buy the depressed securities, Huntington explained that he did so only as a favor to investors who felt themselves "inconvenienced" by holding nonpaying bonds.

Two other obvious culprits in the episode were John A. Cisco and Frederick W. Foote. Their crime was one not of malice but of gross naivete. As one anonymous investor wrote the day after Huntington's letter appeared: "The Messrs. Cisco were the financial agents of the Texas Railroad Company for a long series of years, and ought to have known precisely what was its financial condition." What the letter writer didn't say is that Cisco and Foot should also have been more wary in dealing with Huntington, whose reputation for devious tactics was already well established.

Within a few days of the collapse, the press and the financial community had identified a new villain. The headline in the *New York World* of January 18 stated it succinctly:

HETTIE GREEN'S MILLIONS
HOW SHE CAUSED THE RECENT FAILURE OF
JOHN J. CISCO & SON

"John J. Cisco & Son have nearly eight hundred creditors," the article began. "The report in yesterday's WORLD that Mrs. Edward H. Green was the heaviest of these received further confirmation in Wall street yesterday. The amount of her deposit in the bank is about $475,000 [*sic*]. Curiously enough while she is a creditor of the firm her husband is its principal debtor." The *World*'s story explained the crux of the argument against Hetty:

> The friends of the house say that if Mrs. Green had taken up the loan made to her husband it would not have been forced to suspend. It makes her largely responsible for the failure and subjects her to much criticism for the selfishness which actuated her conduct towards a firm which for twenty years has acted as her financial agent, collecting her interest and looking after her interests, besides guarding with honor the securities held by it in trust for her, amounting to the enormous total of $25,000,000. The friends say that if, under a strong pressure, the firm had but used for a day or two a million or two of her securities in its possession, it might have bridged over the gulf and saved itself from financial wreck.

As the *World* thus praised Cisco and Foote for their gallantry in resisting the temptation to pilfer a million or two from Hetty's securities (which, given their recent record, they might well have lost), the *Tribune* concurred that Hetty's "peremptory demand for the transfer of a large sum of money precipitated the failure of the firm."

The *Times* described the events like this:

> Soon after rumors affecting the credit of the banking firm were started, Mrs. Green wrote from Bellows Falls, Vt., where she is re-

siding, requesting the firm to close her account, stating that she desired to place her cash in other banks. The letter reached John J.
Cisco & Son while a heavy run was being made upon them by
their depositors. Friends of the firm say that to have paid the large
amount called for by Mrs. Green at that time would have crippled
the concern and caused a sacrifice of the interests of other creditors. The firm replied to Mrs. Green's letter informing her that her
husband, Mr. E. H. Green, formerly Vice-President of the
Louisville and Nashville Railroad, owed them more than $700,000
and requesting her to allow her deposit to remain for the time
being as an offset to that loan. This she promptly declined to do,
as it has always been her invariable rule to keep her own financial
matters entirely separate from those of her husband.

The Cisco affair marked the beginning of the public fascina-
tion with Hetty Green that would follow her for the rest of her
long life. At that point she was still referred to as "Mrs. E. H.
Green." Within a short time, as her fame eclipsed that of her
husband, the papers would rarely refer to her as anything but
"Hetty Green." "Mrs. E. H. Green is well known, by reputation
at least, in Wall-street," the *Times* reported. "She is believed to
be the richest woman in America, a title earned by her own
business sagacity, energy, and watchfulness." The article added
later: "She has lived a frugal life, exercised extraordinary keen-
ness in her investments, and by embracing every good opportunity that the stock market afforded she has more than
quintupled her inheritance. Old Wall-street operators give Mrs.
Green credit for having as intimate a knowledge of railroad securities as any person they know." Her idiosyncrasies also were
attracting attention: "The 'richest woman in America' has some
strongly marked characteristics," the *Times* said. "She does business on the strictest business principles, regardless of sentiment
or relationship, and she is economical in the most elaborate
sense of the word. She seems to have made it a rule of her life
to indulge in no personal luxuries. She has been known to

walk from her hotel in this city to a social reception through a heavy snowstorm rather than pay for the use of a coach."

An enterprising reporter from the *World* journeyed to Bellows Falls. "Mrs. Green looks to be about forty-five years old [she was fifty], is of robust form, usually wears her iron-gray hair in a French twist and her sharp eyes continually dart from one object to another. She is a woman of tremendous will power, her determination being quite as remarkable as her parsimony. Overdress, according to the townspeople, is not one of her weaknesses. . . . Frequently she rides or promenades wearing on her head a hat with iridescent trimmings and in cold weather she invariably uses old hosiery for overshoes. She seems to have an innate desire for bartering, and notwithstanding the Yankee shrewdness of these Vermonters, Mrs. Green seldom loses a dollar by any of her small trades."

The *World* was also among the first to suggest publicly what would become a stock characterization of Hetty—that she must be unhappy. "Health and wealth she may have, but there is scarcely a villager here who has less happiness or less of the things to be enjoyed in life than Mrs. Edward H. Green."

Hetty cared far less what people were saying of her than she did about the fate of her money locked away at a now-bankrupt firm. Since his financial difficulties started, Edward had been spending more and more time away from the family, at the Union Club in New York. One hopes for his sake that he was in New York rather than Bellows Falls when these events transpired. Hetty always had a temper, especially when she felt her money compromised, and her reaction to the Cisco fiasco must have bordered on pyrotechnic, the walls shaking with every colorful epithet she had soaked up on the New Bedford docks. She packed a bag and marched down to the Bellows Falls station to await the next train to New York.

By the time she arrived, control of John J. Cisco and Son had passed from Cisco and Foote to Lewis May, an appointed assignee. May issued the following announcement upon taking charge: "The rumors started some ten days since about the old established banking house of John J. Cisco & Son, and which were telegraphed all over this country and Europe, have caused a very severe run upon them on the part of their depositors. In addition to this, they were largely interested in the bonds of the Houston and Texas Central Railroad, which have been greatly depreciated by the severe blow against the credit of that company caused by the action of C.P. Huntington in purchasing the coupons of the first mortgage bonds. These matters with the general great depression of all securities have compelled them for the benefit of all their creditors to make an assignment without preferences for the purpose of a gradual liquidation of all their affairs. All the depositors will undoubtedly be paid in full as soon as the securities can be realized upon. The firm has no outstanding contracts at the Stock Exchange."

The assurance that all depositors would be paid hardly mollified Hetty. As soon as she arrived in New York, she marched into the Cisco offices at 59 Wall Street, looked May in the eye, and said, "I've come to get what's mine."

Hetty might have been able to browbeat the dispirited Cisco and Foote into complying, had they still controlled the bank. But May did not flinch. A familiar and respected figure on Wall Street, he had been a partner in May and King, an investment house, and, more recently, had presided as assignee over the failure of a large dry goods company. He had, in the words of the *Tribune,* "won a reputation for prompt business methods."

An extraordinary scene developed over the next several days. Hetty threatened, screamed, and pleaded, stomping her foot and at times sobbing. May matched her fire with a cool (and, to Hetty, infuriating) calm. Bystanders gathered at the windows of the Cisco headquarters to watch. Many more followed the saga in the newspapers. Hetty's $25 million in securities were not technically among Cisco's assets, and were therefore not part of May's jurisdiction in settling Cisco's affairs. Hetty's cash deposit of $558,851 accounted for more than a quarter of the firm's total. The next largest depositor, the estate of founder John J. Cisco, had a mere $218,593 on the books. In a rather pathetic footnote, at the bottom of the list of depositors was Edward Green, holding in trust for his son $1,106. But the physical presence of Hetty's securities at the locked-up bank gave May a powerful negotiating tool. However much Hetty valued her cash deposit, May knew that the securities represented virtually her entire net worth.

May said he would be pleased to release Hetty's massed securities—as soon as she made good on her husband's $702,000 debt. At first, Hetty haughtily repeated what she had told Cisco and Foote—that her husband's finances were no concern of hers. She demanded to examine the securities. May agreed. Hetty sat for several hours, meticulously counting, and found to her relief that nothing had been taken.

As Hetty twisted and writhed, May let it be known (both in person and through the papers) that he had all the time in the world. Quoting "a friend of the assignee," the *Tribune* reported: "Mr. May could wind up the affairs of the depositors in four weeks, but he prefers, for the sake of all, to nurse matters, and is willing to devote a year to bringing things out straight. Not a man of the depositors has asked for his money; on the contrary, most of them are willing that the assignee should take his time about payment." The line about "not a man" may or may not have been a sly reference to Hetty's gender, but the article closed with this: "No information as to Mrs. Green's attitude was furnished by the assignee."

The prospect of having no control over her fortune for weeks or even months at last wore Hetty's resistance down. In early February, she curled her fingers around a pen and forced herself to scrawl out a check for $422,142.42. She also agreed to relinquish half of her deposit, or, $280,015.62. This brought her total payment to $702,159.04. With that, she packed up her securities and took them in a hired cab—an unaccustomed luxury, but a necessary one, considering the size of the bundle—to the offices of the Chemical National Bank.

Hetty would never forget the many indignities done to her through the Cisco fiasco. She held a grudge against Lewis May and, in particular, against Collis P. Huntington, the railroad magnate. She patiently planned her revenge on May, waiting almost two years to the day from the time of the Cisco failure, when May had at last sorted out the finances and was preparing to pay off the long-waiting creditors. Hetty filed objections with the New York State Supreme Court, claiming that May had defrauded the creditors by paying himself inflated commissions as assignee. According to the *New York Times,* Judge William S. Keiley had agreed to hear Hetty's objections, but only on the condition that she pay all court expenses should she lose. The fact that the costs would easily reach $10,000 shows the depth of her anger.

Keiley, who had been appointed by the court to approve May's handling of the Cisco failure, had already found his work exemplary. But Hetty claimed his commissions of $139,500 to be exorbitant. She claimed that the law firms handling the case had earned too much—$27,000—and that May had erred hiring Frederick Foote, one of the Cisco partners, for $10,000 per year, to assist him in handling the case. As with the earlier Aunt Sylvia trial, the action against May had the practical effect of holding up payments to a large number of potential recipients, in this case depositors who now had to wait another year to get their money. Her goal, no doubt, was to embarrass May. Hetty hired a New York lawyer named Nelson Smith to handle the proceedings, but she took practical control herself, attending every hearing and often personally questioning witnesses. Her conduct exasperated the judge and left even her own lawyer groping for words.

May added fuel to Hetty's anger by boasting on the witness stand that he may not, in retrospect, have been able legally to force Hetty to cover her husband's debts. His acknowledgment that Hetty might have been able to walk away with all of her cash, in addition to her securities, was a double slap, both in the loss of money and in the gleeful implication that Hetty had been bested in a deal. May called his and his lawyer's handling of Hetty, "One of the greatest things ever accomplished in the city of New York, and I was daily complimented for it."

Hetty was still steaming when she assumed the duties of questioning John A. Cisco on the witness stand. According to the *Times* account, "she went for him like a tigress and nothing could hold her."

"May I ask you a few questions?" she began, brushing past her attorney, Nelson Smith. She launched an attack accusing the witness and his late father of deliberately hiding the fact that Edward had used Hetty's money to staunch the flow of his own losses. "When your father was writing to me did he ever say to you that he was writing me? Here are these letters where he says none of my money will be used in anything. Yet Mr. Green was using it all the time." She even suggested that the Ciscos had "sent a man" to Bellows Falls to intimidate her. "Then did you think when you had a sham failure and a sham assignment and sham lawsuits—"

"Mrs. Green!" The objection came not from May's attorney nor the judge, but from Hetty's own counsel, trying to prevent her from self-destructing.

May's lawyer, delighted by Hetty's outburst, objected to her lawyer's interruption and urged her to continue. She did so, now accusing both Cisco and Foote of participating directly in the attempts to intimidate her, or worse.

"Did you think I had a tendency to heart disease, and you would put me out of the way and get all the money?" At the audible gasps from various corners of the room, Hetty explained, "I am only asking him if this was a nice little game, because the people in the country said my life wasn't worth it. I only want to give him an idea of that."

Finally, a bewildered Cisco was able to respond: "All I can say is that I have no knowledge of any of the circumstances Mrs. Green speaks of."

Hetty offered this blanket explanation of her own conduct, repeated several times during the proceedings: "I come of good old Quaker blood. All I care for is to do right. Then I am sure to go to heaven."

Judge Keiley, unmoved by the protestations of righteousness, sided with May, finding his conduct in handling the Cisco failure exemplary. Hetty was required to pay the court costs—estimated at $10,000–$15,000. For all her frugality, she always seemed to consider such expenses money well spent, if she was able to turn the screws a bit on her enemies.

If the financial community had settled on Hetty as scapegoat for the Cisco failure, Hetty herself blamed Collis P. Huntington. His actions had caused the collapse of the firm, putting her deposits, and perhaps even her $25 million, in jeopardy. Hetty's seething, burning, spitfire hatred of Huntington was inevitable. She set about slowly to take her revenge on the well-known bully, who frightened her not in the least. In time, Huntington's dislike for Hetty would grow to match hers for him.

But the Cisco failure caused another turning point in Hetty's life, a more personal one; it marked the effective end of her marriage to Green. Actually, that is not quite so. Hetty and Edward never officially were divorced. In fact, over the years they effected a sort of reconciliation; things would be cordial between them, and for stretches, at least, they would stay under one roof. But it was the effective end of anything resembling a conventional marriage. Hetty had had enough of convention; she had had enough of the masquerade of herself as the dutiful wife and Edward as the financial brains behind the family. He had violated a trust through his mismanagement of money. He had not simply squandered his own fortune; he had sliced into hers. Even at his most confident and robust, Edward was hardly a match for Hetty's steel-minded determination. When she packed up her two children and walked out, Edward was left, for all intents and purposes, a broken man, without money of his own, reduced to a sort of genteel subsistence. Following the Cisco failure, Hetty was a free agent, in her personal and financial life.

---

# EIGHT

# THE VIEW FROM BROOKLYN

For an ambitious capitalist in the United States, the period between the end of the Civil War and the beginning of the twentieth century was the most golden of golden ages. The Civil War had settled once and for all the nettlesome question that had haunted the country for generations: would the Union survive? It would. In Europe, the end of every war dumped another horde of unemployed soldiers into crowded and already mature cities. But the American landscape was ample and open enough to absorb hundreds of thousands of ex-soldiers looking for work and opportunity, in addition to hundreds of thousands of immigrants who came each year to work in factories or to till fields that stretched beyond the horizon. Alexander Noyes, in his classic volume *Forty Years of American Finance*, wrote: "Almost at the moment when a million citizens were turned from organized destruction to pursuit of peaceful industry, the avenues of American employment and production were widened in a degree unprecedented in the history of trade."

The pace of growth and production was staggering. Every

industry, from manufacturing to agriculture, boomed. American farmers, who in 1867 planted just over 64 million acres of wheat, corn, oats, rye, and barley planted 100 million by 1878. The combined yield increased to 2.3 billion bushels. Moving those vast supplies of grain, as well as a restless people, required a new and extensive transportation network. The transcontinental railroad was rightly hailed as a monumental construction feat when the two sides were linked in Utah in the spring of 1869. But those 1,800 miles were a drop in the bucket of overall railroad development. In the eight years after the end of the Civil War, crews laid some 30,000 miles of track across the United States. Russia, also aggressively building its rail infrastructure, put down just 11,000 miles during the same period.

And every new mile of railroad required steel for rails, timber for ties, and capitalists for cash. If the potential rewards of investing in railroads were great, so were the risks. For every strong, healthy railroad with sound management there were many more that failed for mismanagement, natural obstructions, or outright fraud. Corrupt politics, frequent panics, and a shaky money supply unsettled on the issue of whether gold, silver, or paper ought to be the standard, left a financial landscape strewn with the corpses of would-be tycoons. One of them was Edward Green.

Hetty Green holds the considerable distinction of being the only woman to make her mark in the financial markets during the Gilded Age. But if repressive and constricting attitudes toward women presented serious obstacles for Hetty, the Gilded Age in almost every other regard was tailor-made for a financial genius looking to get rich. A roster of financiers and industrialists of Hetty's generation, whose fortunes flowered along with hers during this remarkable period, reads like a who's who of American capitalism. Jim Fisk, whose notorious financial schemes made him the embodiment for the term "robber baron," was born in 1834, seven months before Hetty. Fisk's partner, Jay Gould, was born in 1836. Steel magnate Andrew

Carnegie was born in Scotland in 1835. J. P. Morgan, the financier and banker who would buy Carnegie's company (over a golf game) to form the colossus U.S. Steel, was born in 1837. John D. Rockefeller, the muscle and brains behind Standard Oil, was born in 1839. Henry M. Flagler, Rockefeller's onetime partner who later became a real estate developer who invented Palm Beach, had been born in 1830. For the shrewd and lucky, this Darwinian environment, before regulation, labor unions, and income tax, presented opportunities almost without limit.

Most of these men and their wives and families lived on a scale unprecedented in the history of the world. New York's Fifth Avenue, laid out in 1811 and completed in 1824, drew Wall Street swells away from their downtown mansions in the postwar years and became the wealthiest and most fashionable address in the United States, if not the world. The stretch of Fifth Avenue in the vicinity of Central Park became known as Millionaire's Row. Testimonies to wealth and privilege rose in block after block of French manor houses and royal palaces and opulent châteaux, each built by and for some industrial captain whose family a generation or two earlier had been trapping furs, butchering meat, tilling soil, or keeping shop. There were Rockefellers on Fifth Avenue, and Flaglers and Guggenheims, and Russell Sage, a grocer-turned-financier, and Hetty's archenemy, Collis P. Huntington, who got his start peddling hardware to miners during the California gold rush. The Vanderbilts erected a section of fabulous homes on a ten-block section of Fifth Avenue below Central Park that became known as Vanderbilt Row. In 1879, Henry Vanderbilt commissioned not one but two houses. A few months later, William Kissam Vanderbilt settled on plans for a grand home on Fifth Avenue at Fifty-second Street, to be designed by noted architect to the rich Richard Morris Hunt. Fawning critics pronounced the home a triumphant combination of the Palais de Justice, the Hôtel du Bourgtheroulde at Rouen, the Hôtel Cluny at Paris, and the Château de Blois. When it was completed, Alva Vanderbilt,

William's wife, christened the house with a costume ball at which each guest dressed as a member of European royalty.

This great fat feast was the New York that Hetty found when she arrived after the Cisco failure. But when she left Bellows Falls with her two children in tow, she did not erect a mansion next to the Vanderbilts, although she could have afforded a home as fine as the finest on Millionaire's Row. She chose instead the teeming, dense borough of Brooklyn, populated by immigrants and, laborers, where nobody dressed up as royalty, European or otherwise. With the exception of short stretches in low-rent quarters in lower Manhattan, Hetty would call Brooklyn home for the next decade. She rented apartments in hotels and rooming houses, usually paying by the month. A large house, beyond the price to buy or build it, would mean an endless stream of payments for upkeep, not to mention a staff of servants to keep the place running. And there was another reason. In order to collect personal property taxes, collectors first had to establish proof of residency. By paying monthly rent and moving frequently, Hetty preserved the ability to deny that she lived in any given city or state whose tax collectors became too persistent. During the course of her life she would be a resident of Bellows Falls, New Bedford, New York, and New Jersey, all of them and none of them at the same time.

Hetty, Sylvia, and Ned moved first into a modest apartment house on Pierrepont Street in Brooklyn Heights. No childhood with Hetty Green as the mother could ever be called normal, but with their move to Brooklyn Ned and Sylvia entered a new, surreal phase of their lives. While they were among America's richest children, Ned and Sylvia's lifestyle was more akin to those constantly struggling for the next meal. Hetty never failed to tell them how rich they would be one day, and she meant it, for her goal was to leave them as the richest people in America.

Ned, despite the severe limp that made walking awkward, and despite the rigors of life with his mother, was developing into a tall, gregarious young man with an easy laugh. At seventeen, he was already six feet tall, built like his father. Sylvia, on the other hand, seemed to retreat inside of herself. Tall and not pretty, she was a painfully, shy, self-conscious girl. People who spent time with her were often unable to detect any trace of a personality. To acquaintances, she seemed to go through the motions of life without ever taking a part. She was Hetty's constant companion, and did chores around the apartment.

This odd little family naturally aroused the curiosity of fellow Brooklynites. As Hetty's financial prowess became more celebrated, her reputation as an oddball preceded her. A reporter for the *Brooklyn Eagle* noted: "Nobody ever saw her with a dress which was not severely plain, and seldom has she been noticed when she did not carry an old style and well worn black satchel. Her appearance would never cause the uninitiated to think that she was anything more extraordinary than an old fashioned woman of moderate means and simple tastes, who was on her way to the corner grocery or the bakery on the block below. Yet, if money is power, this same staid looking person is one of the most powerful human beings in the country."

People found her modest living conditions in Brooklyn and, later, in Hoboken, New Jersey, endlessly fascinating and amusing. Hetty rarely lost sleep worrying what others thought of her, and yet there was a certain irony in the public's reaction to her. For all of her faults, she was no snob. She sneered at all forms of pretense, and was unimpressed with titles.* She didn't just mix with the common folk; she lived among them, ate at their restaurants, rode their streetcars and ferries. Clerks and storekeepers, delivery boys and washerwomen who would not

---

*One of the most delightful Hetty stories, perhaps apocryphal, concerns an Englishman passing through Bellows Falls who was supposedly chased by a cow on her property. The man knocked on Hetty's door to complain and, not getting the apologetic reaction he wanted, reeled off his impressive-sounding title. Hetty said, "Tell it to the cow."

be allowed through the front door of Alva Vanderbilt's Fifth Avenue mansion lived side by side with Hetty and her children. And yet it was her very reluctance to live like a queen that evoked derision and ridicule.

The public never seemed to begrudge Andrew Carnegie his sixty-four-room house on Fifth Avenue, a structure so large it required a special railroad spur running into the basement to deliver the two tons of coal needed for a single day's heating in the winter. Carnegie himself justified personal extravagance in his 1889 essay, "Wealth": "It is well, nay essential, for the progress of the race that the houses of some should be homes for all that is highest and best in literature and the arts, and for all the refinements of civilization, rather than that none should be so." Untold thousands living in the same city but struggling to maintain their tenement flats seemed to agree with him, according to Carnegie's biographer, Joseph Frazier Wall. Wall astutely assessed this public sentiment on wealth, using Hetty Green by way of example. The public, he wrote, "expected its millionaires to live in style in big houses; it looked with contempt upon Hetty Green, living penuriously in a small apartment in Hoboken."

Nor did her lifestyle inure her to criticism from populists that she was just another self-important member of an overmonied class. A reporter once asked her why she lived the way she did. "I am a Quaker; my early training disciplined me towards pomp and show," she replied. "My family has been wealthy for five generations. We need make no display to insure recognition of our position." An editorial in the *New York World* went after her with a vengeance: "The insolence of this utterance would be astonishing if we had not been accustomed to it by the words and ways of our Plutocracy for years past."

In 1883, after buying the *World* from robber baron Jay Gould, Joseph Pulitzer had made a point of beating the populist drums against all wealthy financiers, Gould included. The editorial continued:

The assumption needs only to be examined in order to make its absurdity appear. What 'position' do five generations of wealth give which the public must perforce 'recognize'? Does Mistress Green mean to say that people who are wealthy are better or more honorable or entitled to greater consideration than people who are not wealthy? Or is her claim merely that people who have been wealthy for five generations are superior to people who have not been wealthy for so long a period?

The public recognizes the fact that Mrs. Hetty Green is rich, if that is any comfort to her; but it declines to recognize any sort of virtue or superiority on her because she happens to own more money and property than other people do. It has no greater respect for her than her personal character may entitle her to claim, and not one whit more than it gives to an equally worthy woman who lives in a tenement and takes in plain sewing for a living.

It was a strong reaction to what had been, especially for Hetty, a fairly innocuous comment. And the irony, of course, was that, unlike Pulitzer and his editorial writers, Hetty Green actually did live in a tenement.

For all of her aversion or indifference to matters of society, Hetty's one connection to the world of wealth and privilege was her lifelong friendship with Annie Leary, who lived in a large limestone house at 1032 Fifth Avenue. Leary, who had been a member of Hetty's wedding party so many years earlier, was one of New York's, and hence, the nation's, leading philanthropists. She didn't just throw money at good causes, or organize high-toned balls to support some home for the poor. She rolled up her sleeves and became active in a dizzying array of causes. Annie donated the Christopher Columbus monument at Columbus Circle in New York; she served as vice president of Stonywold, a home in the Adirondacks for sufferers of tuberculosis, and as president of the Flower Guild. She built churches and mission houses, and built a chapel at Bellevue Hospital named for her late brother, Arthur. For her efforts with the Catholic Church, the pope conferred upon her the honorary title of papal countess.

Annie saw in Hetty a side that others did not—a side that ran contrary to her public image. Annie appreciated Hetty's humor and loyalty as a friend. Annie was also secure enough in her social position not to care how her friendship with Hetty would reflect upon her. In some ways, Annie, the do-gooder, took on Hetty and her family as a social project. When Hetty appeared at parties or balls, or events at Newport, Annie Leary was the one who orchestrated it. Hetty's daughter, Sylvia, was of particular interest to Annie, who was determined to bring her out of her shell. If Hetty believed she was bringing Sylvia up to respect money and to be wary of gold diggers who might be after her (and Hetty's fortune), it was Annie Leary who saw clearly the devastating effect this was having on the girl.

The friendship with Annie notwithstanding, Hetty lived her life convinced that, as a businesswoman, if not as a woman, she was fundamentally and completely alone. Nobody else would watch out for her interests. She mistrusted all forms of alliances and cabals. Where other investors sought the safety of numbers, the soothing ring of consensus, Hetty felt most comfortable on her own, trusting her own judgment and instincts. She was a free agent in the truest sense of the term, and anyone going into a deal assuming he had Hetty Green in his corner, or that she could be pushed, harassed, or cowed into going along with a crowd, learned difficult and expensive lessons to the contrary. Her shrewd conduct during a takeover attempt of the Georgia Central Railroad a year after the Cisco failure offers an excellent glimpse at the tactics and style she would use over and over for the rest of her career.

Based in Savannah, the Georgia Central had been pieced together from a number of smaller southern roads. It was a large railroad, with some two thousand miles of track around the Southeast, but it was unwieldly, inefficient, and complacent. The stock languished at $69 per share, and the company had been paying stockholders a meager 2 percent semiannual dividend. In a story that sounds more out of the corporate raider days of the 1980s than the 1880s, a group of wealthy investors, mainly from New York, spotted a ripe takeover opportunity. They were particularly interested in a steamship line, owned by the railroad, which ran regular service between Savannah and New York. The steamship line, they figured, had been badly undervalued among the railroad's jumble of assets. The investors began buying up the stock during the summer of 1886 with the idea of installing their own managers and directors.

Over the next few months, an increasingly bitter and nasty battle ensued, as the New York group tried to round up a majority of the voting stock in time for the directors' election in January. The New Yorkers charged the railroad with sloppy management and failing to properly reward stockholders. The Georgians dismissed the New Yorkers as greedy manipulators and outsiders who would simply break the company apart for a quick profit. Hovering in the near background, informing and inflaming sentiments on both sides, was the Civil War, barely twenty years past and still fresh in everyone's mind. The Yankees, it seemed, were marching across Georgia once again.

Hetty got wind of the plan early on and began quietly buying up Georgia Central stock at around $70 per share. By early summer she held 6,700 shares. She waited patiently as passions reached their peak. She took no sides. True, she was a New Yorker, and a Yankee, but people who mixed sentimentality with business were fools. If these breast-beating old soldiers wished to relive Bull Run and Gettysburg in the boardroom, so much the better.

By November, the stock had shot up to $100 per share. She could easily have sold at this point for a quick $200,000 profit. She chose to sit tight, figuring that, as the clock ticked, the New Yorkers would grow ever more nervous. In a close election, her chunk of stock might just mean the difference. E. P. Alexander, the New Yorkers' handpicked candidate for president following the planned takeover, approached Hetty with an offer of $115 for each of her shares, a $15 premium over the already inflated going rate. He was offering her more than $300,000 above what she had paid.

Hetty told Alexander he could have the shares—for $125. It was a bold gamble. After all, the New Yorkers might simply decide they could win without her and leave her with wads of shares and no buyer. But part of Hetty's genius was to recognize when the other side was sweating. Alexander did the frightening math—$837,500—in his head, declined the offer, and left. Hetty waited. A short time later, Alexander returned with a new offer. She could have her $125, but not until after the election. Instead of selling her shares now, she would promise to vote their way. When the election was over, she would get her money, in full, regardless of the results of the election and the going rate of the stock. Alexander could hardly believe he was making such a generous offer to this stubborn woman.

Hetty replied, "If I have to wait for my money, the price is $130."

Alexander had come too far, the election was too near, for him to go away empty-handed again. He countered with $127.50. Hetty agreed. First, as was her custom, she demanded that Alexander's group post collateral for the entire amount in advance of the vote. On January 3, shareholders elected E. P. Alexander president of the Georgia Central Railroad, and installed a new board of directors. Hetty's shares provided nearly half of Alexander's 15,000-share victory. The new managers went about trying to salve wounds of the previous months' battles, assuring Georgians that southerners, not northerners, would continue to operate the railroad and that the new owners wished only to improve, not dismantle, the company. Hetty Green washed her hands of the entire affair, having sold her shares for $854,250—at a profit of $385,200.

# NINE

# GROOMING A PROTÉGÉ

Hetty disproved the prevailing idea that women were incapable of handling finances. Her skill, tenacity, and fearlessness made her a feminist long before that term became a rallying cry for generations. Her money gave her power over men and companies and financial markets, and yet she never proclaimed herself an example, or even an advocate, of women's rights. And when it came to deciding which of her children would succeed her in handling the family fortune, her choice couldn't have been more conventional; from the start, it was going to be Ned.

Hetty explained her position on women in business years later in a *Harper's Bazar* article that ran under her byline in 1900. "Mentally, I do not believe woman to be inferior to man, save as she has become so by a mistaken course of training," Hetty wrote. "A certain amount of business training would be an excellent thing for women, but it should be begun in their infancy." She frequently cited her own training from reading the financial papers to her father and grandfather. "A mother will say to her boy, 'Go out and play,' while to the daughter of the house she observes, 'Do this piece of sewing and I will give you a pretty ribbon,' thus incidentally sewing the seeds of vanity, and imparting a restricted and wrong view of the value of things in relation to life and labor. The boy becomes broadened mentally and physically by his robust out-door life, while the girl's natural inclinations are cramped to a narrow groove, which, after a time, becomes second nature to her."

Judging by the plain, unfashionable clothes Sylvia wore as a child, Hetty spared her daughter the developmental problems associated with pretty ribbons. But neither did she encourage her daughter to "go out and play" in the sense of discovering the world and making her own decisions and mistakes. Sylvia did get a financial education—nobody spent more time with Hetty over the years; nobody had a better view of Hetty's methods; nobody endured as many of Hetty's homilies and maxims on the value of thrift and avoiding waste. But Sylvia remained a half-formed person, painfully shy, socially stunted, and lacking any great curiosity about the world and its inhabitants. When in Hetty's presence, as she was most of the time, Sylvia was as unremarkable as a shadow.

Ned was different. Though Hetty intended for her children to share equally in the money she left behind, she expected Ned to act as shepherd of the fortune. And so as Ned entered adulthood Hetty prepared for him a trial by experience, thrusting him into positions where he could make business decisions, without jeopardizing too much real money, at least at the beginning. But before Ned could enter the adult world, he would have to face one particularly difficult and punishing trial, the matter involving his bad left leg.

The limp, the legacy of that childhood sledding accident, was now a defining feature of Ned's life. Well over six feet tall, and stout, he moved about awkwardly—his one good leg bearing most of the pressure of carrying his large frame. Periodically, he reinjured the leg in falls, only adding to his troubles. In addition to experimenting with any number of poultices and other home remedies, Hetty took him to see a number of specialists. One, Dr. Lewis A. Sayre, recalled that a woman arrived at his office in New York with her son in tow, wearing old clothes and presenting themselves as charity cases. Dr. Sayre was a respected orthopedic surgeon who would leave his mark—quite literally—on untold millions of males in succeeding generations by being the first American physician to promote the idea of routine circumcisions of infant boys. Dr. Sayre said he took the boy to Bellevue Hospital and exhibited his mangled leg to medical students. But when someone recognized the boy's mother and pointed out to Dr. Sayre that his charity case was in fact the son of a woman worth tens of millions of dollars, he refused to see either of them again unless she paid in advance. Hetty and the boy left and never returned.

She clearly loved her son with greater intensity than she hated doctors. Nevertheless, she preferred to pose as a pauper, a tactic she would use not just for Ned, but for her own care as well. On January 19, 1898, a prominent physician used Hetty as his primary example in a speech titled "The Abuses in Medical Charity," given before the Medico-Legal Society at New York's Hotel Marlborough. The physician, J. H. Brudenshaw, said Hetty, this time seeking treatments for herself rather than her son, arrived one day at the offices of an unnamed physician. The next day the *New York Times*, under a provocative headline reading, in part, "The Case of Hetty Green," quoted at length from Brudenshaw's speech. "That woman put on an old gown and worked upon the sympathies of the attending physician to such an extent that out of sheer pity he advised her to come to his private office, where he could give her better treatment and save her the trouble of the long waits. She gladly accepted, and for a considerable time came to the physician's house, where he gave her the best of treatment absolutely free of charge."

A friend of the physician visiting the office one day recognized her as "Hetty Green, the richest woman in all this land."

"The physician could hardly believe his own ears," Brudenshaw continued according to the *Times*. "He went out and questioned Mrs. Green. At first she totally denied her identity, but when confronted with the man who knew her, she was compelled to admit it. The young physician promptly rescinded his charity and sent a bill to her for $600, which she was compelled, though much against her will, to pay."

At any rate, Ned's bad left leg progressively deteriorated. In July of 1888, Dr. Charles McBurney, an eminent surgeon, removed it above the knee in an operation performed at Roosevelt Hospital in New York. After recovering from the operation, Ned was fitted with a cork leg. The operation, of course, gave a grim permanence to Ned's affliction. But the procedure at least stabilized his condition, allowing him to move ahead with his life and take his place as his mother's budding protégé.

In the days when he followed his mother along the canyons of Wall Street, Ned had daydreamed about the important financial positions he would one day inherit. "I sometimes thought that it would be nice if mother would make me president of the Chemical Bank of New York. But I had vague ideas concerning the future," Ned told journalist James Morrow in a syndicated newspaper article published after Hetty's death.

If Ned's ideas were vague, Hetty's plans for the boy were anything but. She saw bank directorships in his future, but first, he would have to learn business from the ground up. It is to Hetty's immense credit as a mother—and, perhaps the most persuasive argument against the stereotype of her as uncaring or neglectful—that she never allowed him to use his bad leg as an excuse for inactivity or failure. Had she been a weaker or less attentive parent, she may have allowed Ned to wallow in self-pity as she went about her business. Not even Hetty's most ardent detractors produced evidence that Ned blamed his mother for the lost leg, and when Morrow asked him to name

Edward "Black Hawk" Robinson, Hetty's father. *(Used with the permission of the Board of Trustees of the New Bedford Free Public Library)*

Hetty Green at twenty-six. *(Used with the permission of the Board of Trustees of the New Bedford Free Public Library)*

*Sylvia Ann Howland*

The famous signature on Aunt Sylvia's will. Is it a forgery? *(Used with the permission of the Board of Trustees of the New Bedford Free Public Library)*

The old family farmhouse at Round Hill. *(Used with the permission of the Board of Trustees of the New Bedford Free Public Library)*

Abby Slocum Howland, Hetty's mother. *(Used with the permission of the Board of Trustees of the New Bedford Free Public Library)*

Sylvia Ann Howland, Hetty's Aunt Sylvia. *(Used with the permission of the Board of Trustees of the New Bedford Free Public Library)*

Hetty in old age.
(*Brown Brothers*)

Hetty with her
beloved dog, Dewey.
(*Brown Brothers*)

Hetty and her daughter, Sylvia. (*Brown Brothers*)

Hetty, Matthew Astor Wilks, and Sylvia, on Sylvia and Matthew's wedding day, 1909. (*Brown Brothers*)

Collis P. Huntington, Hetty's arch-enemy. (*Brown Brothers*)

The back of Hetty's Hoboken apartment building. She used the back basement doors to escape the press. (*Brown Brothers*)

Hetty Green in old age, in the garb that helped give rise to the name "Witch of Wall Street." (*Brown Brothers*)

Interior of the Chemical National Bank, 270 Broadway, when Hetty did her banking there. (*J. P. Morgan Chase Archives*)

George Gilbert Williams, Hetty's banker and friend. (*J. P. Morgan Chase Archives*)

Clerks at Chemical National Bank, 1894. These clerks would have dealt with Hetty regularly. (*J. P. Morgan Chase Archives*)

Colonel Ned Green's palatial home at Round Hill, South Dartmouth, Massachusetts, in a modern photo with an antique car in front. *(Photo by Barbara Fortin Bedell. Used with permission)*

Colonel Ned Green in his prime at Round Hill. *(Bachrach: Courtesy of Captain Noel Hill)*

The Tucker House in Bellows Falls. Hetty rarely paid for upkeep, and the house appeared in disrepair during much of the time she owned it. (*Used with the permission of the Rockingham Free Public Library*)

Hetty in her customary dress, sitting on the porch of the Tucker House in Bellows Falls. (*Used with the permission of the Rockingham Free Public Library*)

the most important lesson he had learned from his mother, he replied, without hesitation, "Self-reliance." That is, of course, a weighted term, and it comes from a man whose rise in business was liberally greased by his mother's money and influence, and whose moves she would often orchestrate. Nevertheless, he would have to prove himself to his mother in a long apprenticeship.

Ned's first job was as a clerk and handyman for the Connecticut River Railroad Company. Based in Springfield, Massachusetts, the Connecticut River Railroad provided regular service to Bellows Falls and offered express service for tourists between New York City and the White Mountains. Hetty was both a regular passenger and an investor. "She wanted me to learn railroading," Ned told Morrow, "and the only place to learn that business is on a railroad, down on the ground among the men." Artificial leg and all, Ned found himself patrolling a stretch of track for $10 per week, cutting weeds and helping repair track.

His next stint was with the Ohio and Mississippi Railroad, based in Cincinnati. In 1890, Hetty gave him a new assignment, in Chicago, helping look after her interests there. Among his early tasks was to manage some mortgages she held that had recently fallen in value. "Get the exact sum due on each mortgage, interest and principal, fixed in your mind," she told him. "If anyone is fool enough to offer you the full amount, take it. If you are offered less, tell the man you will give him the answer in the morning. Think the matter over carefully in the evening. If you decide that it will be to our advantage to accept the offer, say so the next day. In business generally, don't close a bargain until you have reflected upon it overnight."

As Ned left for Chicago, his mother gave him a package of papers, telling him to guard them on the train at all costs. Figuring that he was transporting some vast sum in negotiable bonds or other securities. Ned barely slept on the journey, keeping the package under the mattress in his berth as he lay

awake. When he reached Chicago and delivered the package to
the appropriate office, it turned out to contain wads of expired
fire insurance policies. The delivery was simply, Ned recalled
with a laugh, Mother's way of testing his reliability.

Ned's arrival in Chicago caused a stir far greater than most
twenty-two-year-old men could make. He was at once greeted
as an important figure, a player, a man who might leave a big
mark on the city of broad shoulders. He spent his days in an
office on the eleventh and top floor of the Owings Building, a
downtown skyscraper owned by his mother. Despite his youth
and lack of business experience, he was quick to make ties in
the new city, as visitors streamed in to introduce themselves.
Hetty was already well known in the city as a landowner. Ned
told people that he liked Chicago and planned to stay. His head
swelled with his first rush of importance as a man of affairs, a
man about town. Within a few weeks of his arrival he was gre-
gariously announcing big plans.

"Chicago will soon have a private bank, or rather a trust
company, backed by an immense amount of money," the *New
York Times* reported in a dispatch from Chicago in November
1890. "Mrs. Hetty Green, known widely as the richest woman
in America, and her son, E.H.R. Green, will be at the head of
the concern."

The article quoted Ned as saying, "Arrangements are practically completed for the new business, or rather the new form
of our old business." He added, "Ours will be a mortgage business. We will loan money on securities and nothing more. We
will loan it at a reasonable rate of interest and borrowers may
take up their paper at any time. Ours will be a sort of private
bank. It will be conducted on the principle of the Chemical
Bank of New York."

At twenty-two, Ned spoke like a seasoned professional. "My
mother and myself will have the controlling interest, for we
never invest in anything unless we have control over it," he
said. "Others interested will be the Chemical Bank of New-York

and Baring Brothers of London. San Francisco capitalists will also be interested. The nominal capital will be about $300,000, but the reserve will reach to about $150,000,000. The Chemical Bank of New-York is conducted on a similar plan. Its capital is small, but its reserve reaches about $30,000,000. This bank will be made, I think it is safe to say, one of the foremost financial institutions of America. Final details will be settled soon."

He finished this confident and boastful statement with a promise that must have warmed the hearts of civic boosters in Chicago. "We have decided to make the city of Chicago our home, and we will open an institution in keeping with the future high rank Chicago will hold as a financial centre [sic]."

It's not clear whether Ned spoke on Hetty's authority, or was simply indulging in grand dreams. Soon, however, the talk of the new bank quieted down. A gregarious young man, Ned loved to be quoted in newspapers, and genuinely liked reporters. By the next summer, he had begun to imagine himself as a budding newspaper mogul. The *New York Times* reported on July 16, 1891: "It was rumored to-day that E.H.R. Green, son of Mrs. Hettie [sic] Green, intended to buy a newspaper in Chicago." According to the story, three newspapermen—two from New York and one from Chicago, had approached Ned about the possibility of starting a large daily in Chicago. The paper would devote a page to New York news and a page to Boston news, in addition to local coverage. Ned did not identify the men, but said they were prominent journalists who were tired of drawing salaries and wanted to own their own paper. About the same time, an attorney had contacted Ned saying that someone could buy the *Chicago Times* for $300,000 to $400,000. "Whether the attorney was an authorized agent of that paper or not, I don't know. But if it is for sale, we shall make the paper a proposition," Ned said.

The newspapermen had asked Ned to put up sufficient funds to construct a building and furnish the presses, type, and staff. "I told them if they could show me that there was any money in the scheme I would go into it. The New-York parties have gone back East to see if they can secure aid. They will return next Saturday, and a meeting will be held in my office to see how the land lays."

Ned's high talk about becoming a newspaper mogul was at variance with the reality of his position as his mother's apprentice, and the plan quickly died. Hetty was determined that he would learn to economize. She kept him on a strict allowance—enough to live on but hardly more. She had suggested that Ned stay at the Auditorium Annex, where rooms cost six dollars per night. According to James Morrow, Ned's plan to put a little spending money in his pockets by moving to less expensive rooms at the Clifton House backfired when his mother learned of the move. She wrote to him: "I notice that you are not staying at the hotel I suggested. It is all right, but I have reduced your daily allowance $3. You are not to have any more spending money than the amount decided on originally."

Though Ned liked Chicago, liked the reception he received and the feeling of being an important man of affairs, Hetty had other plans for him. In 1893, she sent Ned, now twenty-five, down to Texas to see about some railroad matters. Specifically, it was time for her to exact some long-awaited revenge on Collis P. Huntington.

By the time Hetty and Collis Huntington had crossed paths during the Cisco crisis in 1885, Huntington was sixty-four years old and one of the most successful and feared businessmen in the United States. The sixth of nine children from a small town in Connecticut, Huntington set out for California in 1849 along with hordes of other gold seekers. But it didn't take him long to recognize that for every man who struck gold, thousands more came away with their dreams as empty as their pockets. Most came from the East without experience or equipment, and Huntington realized that, whether they were destined to strike it rich or, more likely, to fail, just about all of them needed

picks, shovels, boots, pots and pans, and tents. In the boom-
town of Sacramento, staging area for mining expeditions, Huntington took on a partner, Mark Hopkins, and opened a
hardware store that thrived from the start.

Surveyor Theodore Judah approached Huntington, Hopkins,
and California merchants Leland Stanford and Charles Crocker
in 1860 with a plan for a rail route pushing east from Sacramento across the mountains. The four became financial backers
of the new project. Eventually, they shunted Judah aside and
became known as the Big Four (a term used with equal parts
derision and respect) as they pushed the formation of the Central Pacific, the western portion of the transcontinental railroad.
Huntington, forceful, fearless, and ruthless, emerged as the Big
Four's leader. The transcontinental hookup was just the start. A
new railroad, the Southern Pacific, would, under Huntington's
leadership, spread across California and the southwestern states.
Huntington spent much of his time in Washington, D.C., alternately bullying and currying favor with congressmen to earn
extraordinarily favorable land rights that essentially turned
thousands of California farmers into vassal servants of the railroads—farming land deeded to the railroads, and paying usuri-
ous rates to ship their produce.

Novelist Frank Norris had Huntington in mind when he
wrote *The Octopus,* his classic novel about an all-powerful California railroad and its domination and abuse of the local population. For his climactic scene, Norris drew upon a real incident
known as the Mussel Slough Tragedy, in which a group of
farmers clashed with a coterie of railroad and government men
who had come to evict a wheat farmer from his land. When
the shooting stopped, seven men from both sides lay dead. Although Huntington was nowhere near the scene, enraged farmers and their sympathizers had no trouble in establishing the
true villains behind the violence—the Southern Pacific and its
ruthless leader.

A man who, tellingly, would identify himself only as "a citizen of California," submitted an open letter to Congress during the 1890s, calling Huntington "a persistent intermeddler without proper warrant in Government affairs, an unscrupulous dealer in threats and promises amongst public men, a constant menace to sworn servants of the people in their offices of trust, a tempter of the corrupt and a terror to the timid who are delegated to power, a remorseless enemy to wholesale legislation, [and] a constant friend to conspirators against the common welfare for private gain."

Unlike the villainous railroad agent in Norris's book, who suffocates in a loading car under an avalanche of wheat, Huntington just grew stronger as he moved from one scandal and controversy to the next. By the late 1880s, he had moved to New York, and was furiously working on pushing the Southern Pacific across Texas. Many men, strong and tough in their own right, hated Collis Huntington almost as much as they feared him. He was a physically imposing man, two hundred pounds, with a large head and piercing eyes. He knew he was intimidating and he used this quality to his advantage whenever it suited him. He was known as a vindictive man who never forgot a slight.

Hetty Green was not impressed. To Hetty, Huntington was no empire builder. He was the man responsible for the principal humiliation of her life, a time when she had come the closest to losing control of that which gave her life purpose and meaning. She blamed Huntington for mismanaging the Houston and Texas Central Railroad, and for the bond shenanigans that she felt had caused Cisco to go under. Because of Huntington, she had been forced to beg and plead before that impertinent Lewis May. Because of Huntington she had had to write out a check for several hundred thousand dollars, an act that felt like tearing a chunk out of her own flesh. If people thought Huntington could hold a grudge, they hadn't seen Hetty.

In the wake of the Cisco disaster, long before Ned began his apprenticeship, Hetty had bought as many of the damaged bonds of the Houston and Texas Central as she could. By 1887, she owned $250,000 in first mortgage bonds and about $1 million in general mortgage bonds, enough to be a thorn in Huntington's side for any plans he might have for the railroad.

As part of a reorganization plan, Huntington stiffed remaining bondholders. He proposed to exchange existing bonds with new ones that would pay 2 percent lower interest and run fifty years instead of five. Bondholders grumbled, cried foul, but had little practical recourse. They could give in, or, Huntington intimated, the Houston and Texas Central would fail outright, and the investors could use their bonds to paper the walls of their parlors.

One bondholder made it clear that she had no intention to go along with Huntington's proposal. "C.P. Huntington and his friends among the bondholders of the Houston and Texas Central Railroad Company had a meeting yesterday whereat a reorganization scheme was endorsed. Mrs. Hetty Green, however, was an absentee," the *Times* noted on December 16, 1887. "She owns something over $1,000,000 worth of the company's bonds and Mr. Huntington's offer doesn't suit her. The Huntington contingent say they do not care whether Mrs. Green assents or not; they can go right along and reorganize the company without her. Other big men have talked in just this way about Mrs. Green in times past, but somehow she usually contrives to come out ahead whenever the fighting notion strikes her."

Wall Street observers licked their lips at the prospect of a battle between Hetty and Huntington. "Wall street men, usually very gallant where women are concerned, have no very great liking for Mrs. Green and her close business methods," the *New York World* reported on May 27, 1887, "but on the other hand they are not particularly in love with Mr. Huntington, whose genius for driving a bargain is a matter of common fame; so they will watch this contest with impartiality, but with intense and lively interest."

A committee of increasingly nervous bondholders met over

several months to try to hash out a compromise that would earn better terms than what Huntington had proposed. Hetty sent as her representative William J. Quinlan Jr., cashier for the Chemical National Bank. The bondholders, not content to deal just with Hetty's representative, made several pilgrimages to see her at the bank, hoping she would join them in reaching a compromise before the railroad failed.

Whether Hetty gave her outright promise or merely intimated that she would go along, the committee members believed they had a unified front. They hashed out a compromise with Huntington, essentially going along with his demands. Amid rumors of the agreement, Houston and Texas Central stock rose to $40 per share, its highest level in ages. That was good news for Huntington, who had scooped up loads of shares at around $10. But no sooner had the bondholders announced the resolution, in May 1887, than Hetty made an announcement of her own. She had changed her mind. Was that not, she said sweetly, a woman's prerogative? If Huntington and his crowd wanted her cooperation, they would have to come directly to her.

As word spread of Hetty's refusal—presaging more months of haggling and delays—the stock sagged like a leaky balloon, back down toward $10. Huntington, who had broken more than a few tough men on his climb to success, watched in cold fury as the value of his securities sank and his broad plans for Texas stalled, all because of this . . . woman.

The bondholders, meanwhile, professed themselves to be stunned by Hetty's duplicity. "Members of the Committee . . . use a stronger term than 'changed her mind.' They say she 'deliberately broke her promise,' and while disinclined to make a public attack upon a woman, did not disguise their disgust at her conduct," the World reported the following Friday. "Her action, it was declared, was indefensible, and Mrs. Green's action two years ago in withdrawing her half-million-dollar deposit with John J. Cisco, which many believe was the immediate cause of the failure of that old-established house, was recalled."

What did Hetty care? If being noble and honorable meant getting swindled by Collis Huntington, the other bondholders could keep their nobility and honor. Edward Mott Robinson hadn't waited around, like other sentimental fools, while his fortune trickled away with the demise of the whaling industry. His daughter wasn't about to go down with the bondholders. Just as she had during the Georgia Central takeover battle a year earlier, Hetty had maneuvered herself into the position she wanted—the third point on the triangle, watching everybody sweat. She prolonged the negotiations with Huntington's representatives for another eleven months. At last, in April 1888, she consented to the reorganization. Just what Huntington was forced to yield was kept a tightly held secret. The *World* noted: "It was generally believed that she had carried her point."

But all of this had been merely a prelude. Now that Ned was full-grown and trained, he was ready to head for Texas. Together, they would make some real trouble for their adversary.

# TEN

# THOU SHALT NOT PASS

In December of 1892, a crowd gathered at a courthouse in Waco, Texas, for the federal auction of the Waco and Northwestern Railroad. As railroad properties went, the Waco and Northwestern was none too impressive—just fifty-four miles of poorly managed track connecting the small eastern Texas communities of Bremond and Ross. But this obscure property was a vital link in Collis Huntington's plan to control railroad traffic across the Southwest. In contrast with his Central Pacific's fairly straight line across the North, Huntington had no formal charter to cross Texas. His routes comprised a mismatched patchwork of large and small Texas roads that he'd been able to piece together. The Waco and Northwestern, in receivership since 1885, provided a crucial link. Huntington had just settled a long and nasty battle with financier Jay Gould, his principal rival in Texas. After racing one another across Texas in a furious battle to be the first to lay tracks to coveted cities, the two had settled on a truce to coordinate construction and pool freight traffic. Now, Huntington needed the Waco and Northwestern for access to Waco, and as a connection to the Texas Panhandle. As usual with railroads, this one came with a significant sweetener—nearly 500,000 acres of land deeded by the state.

Christopher Dart, a special commissioner appointed by the courts to handle the sale, called the gathering to order. In the crowd was Julius Kruttschnitt, the Southern Pacific's general manager for Texas and Louisiana, and Huntington's handpicked representative. Huntington had told Kruttschnitt he could bid as high as $1.25 million for the road. But nobody, least of all Kruttschnitt and Huntington, expected he'd have to go anywhere near that high. There was someone else in the crowd that day, a tall young man of about twenty-four. He was not a local man, and if anyone took notice of him it was perhaps because of his imposing frame and the contrast between the intense youthfulness of his face and his stiff, awkward gait.

Kruttschnitt opened with a bid of $800,000. He and a couple of other interested parties bid the price incrementally up from there. Then the young man spoke up with a bid of $1.1 million. Kruttschnitt realized too late that he was in a bidding war with a determined buyer. As he stood trying to balance in his mind Huntington's desire for the Waco and Northwestern versus his limitation of $1.25 million, the young man left him and the other bidders behind, with a winning bid of $1.365 million. It was all over in a matter of minutes. Commissioner Dart tapped his gavel and announced the winning bidder for the Waco and Northwestern Railroad—Edward Howland Robinson Green, on behalf of his mother.

The news, relayed by a sheepish Kruttschnitt, infuriated Huntington. And that, of course, had been the point. Huntington was quick to strike back. Using all of his considerable economic and political power, he and his associates magically produced liens against a large chunk of the land that went with the sale. Then, both local and state governments waded in, claiming that the land, all half-million acres, belonged to *them*. Through their lawyers, Ned and Hetty responded that they had believed in good faith that the land was included in the sale, pointing out that a railroad without any land was worth practically nothing. If the land wasn't included in the sale, they wanted out. Now Huntington filed a second motion, asking that the Greens not be allowed to with-draw from their bid. In essence, Huntington had decided that if the Greens wanted to jump into the Texas railroad business, he would make it an experience they would never forget. Let them watch their $1.365 million go down the drain as the railroad died.

Litigation over the Waco and Northwestern stretched on for three years. One effect of the battle was that it made Hetty a folk hero among California farmers who hated Huntington. A group of San Franciscans sent her as a gift a .44 caliber revolver, along with a holster, belt, and cartridges, and a note promising that if she ever came to visit, they would turn out ten thousand strong at the depot to greet her. For Hetty, accustomed now to being on the receiving end of unflattering articles about her personal idio-syncrasies, this was an unfamiliar gesture of embrace. She rel-ished it. She loved to tell friends about the gift, and also about the time, during the height of the battle, that Huntington came to see her at her office at the Chemical Bank. No doubt he went with the idea of intimidating her. During the course of the conversa-tion, he threatened that if she and Ned (who remained in Texas) didn't relent, he would see to it that Ned was tossed in a Texas jail. Hetty's eyes narrowed on Huntington. "Up to now, Hunt-ington, you have dealt with Hetty Green, the business woman. Now you are fighting Hetty Green, the mother. Harm one hair of Ned's head and I'll put a bullet through your heart!" She made a motion toward the revolver on her desk (perhaps the one sent to her from California). Huntington, surprised and alarmed, left the office so quickly that he forgot to take his silk hat. He sent an as-sistant for it the next day.

The dispute ended in 1865 with the court deciding that the land had not, in fact, been included in the sale, but that the Greens would not be held to the purchase. It was a muted vic-tory for both sides. Hetty got back the hefty deposit Ned had put up to secure the sale, and Huntington got his railroad. He paid $1,505,000, or, $255,000 more than his outside figure of three years before. Ned and Hetty asked to be reimbursed for $25,000 in lawyer's fees accrued during the case. A judge granted them half the amount. Huntington, showing he could hold a grudge as well as Hetty, sued, over a paltry $12,500, and had the decision overturned. Hetty, who hated to spend needlessly, probably considered the $25,000 in court costs some of the best money she had ever spent—if only to see Huntington squirm.

About the time the Waco and Northwestern imbroglio started, Hetty took over another obscure, run-down branch line. This was a fifty-two-mile branch line of the old Texas Central Railway Company (different from Huntington's Houston and Texas Central), connecting the towns of Garrett and Roberts, east of Dallas. When the Texas Central went through a financial reorganization, Hetty was faced with the prospect of turning in her $750,000 for a fraction of their value. Instead, she surrendered the bonds, plus $75,000 in cash to buy the spur line. This, she would turn over to Ned as the final test of his business abilities. Texas would be his principal home for the next sixteen years, a place big and wide enough to accommodate his bigger-than-life personality and appetites, and give him some of the happiest years of his life. It was there that Ned would prove himself as a businessman, not just an apprentice, with decision-making capacity and capital of his own. Ned would develop into one of the Lone Star State's most colorful characters, leaving his mark on politics, railroading, agriculture, sport fishing, and automobile racing.

In January of 1893, Ned arrived in Terrell, Texas, thirty miles east of Dallas, to assume his position as president of the newly christened Texas Midland Railroad Company. At twenty-four, Ned Green was terribly young and inexperienced for the grandiose title of president of a railroad. But then, the Texas Midland wasn't much of a railroad. It wasn't just the small length of track that made the railroad seem insignificant; it was clearly outdated and poorly maintained. The wooden bridges were sagging badly and required frequent jacking; the cars were old and worn. Passenger and freight service on the line were unreliable.

Terrell today is part of the Dallas metro sprawl, but in 1893 it was a small, out-of-the-way town. Ned's arrival, thanks to his mother's notoriety and wealth, created immediate excitement. He made a grand entrance at the American National Bank carrying a certified check for $500,000, to be used to whip the railroad into shape. The deposit amounted to twice the existing assets of the bank. When the bank officers got over their shock, and confirmed the identity of this tall, cheerful, young man, they immediately made him a vice president of the bank.

Though the money was Hetty's, when it came to decisions on what to do with a sagging railroad, she made it clear that her son was in charge. At first, for all of his confident bluster, Ned was terrified. When faced with a business decision, he told journalist James Morrow years later, he would immediately telegraph his mother in New York for advice. Her terse response: "You are on the ground. Mind your own business." He would have to make his own decisions. He became so frustrated at her obtuseness that he traveled to New York to see her.

She asked him, "Suppose I were not here?" She drew from her New Bedford past an old whaling parable about a captain with two sons. "His sons were his mates," Hetty said. "They wore uniforms and looked very spruce. But they didn't take their turn at the wheel or stand watch. Finally the captain died, and no one on board being competent to navigate the ship, it went on the rocks. I sent you to Texas to learn the railway business. I can't teach you by telegraph from New York. Go back and do the best you can."

Once he got over his nerves, Ned made the most of his opportunity. He made himself a student of railroading, studying schedules and timetables and statistics. He hired a staff of seasoned, capable railroad professionals and gave them sufficient license to revamp and rebuild. And he took a personal interest as well. He expanded the line to establish and improve connections to larger roads. He added three miles to the southern terminus of the railroad to improve its connections with other railroads. Then he pushed the northern end out by 14 miles, from the small hamlet of Roberts to the larger town of Greenville, and, finally, up to Paris, Texas, allowing for connections with large east-west railroads. Within four years, the Texas Midland's trackage had increased to 125 miles.

With his staff of experts advising him, Ned replaced the old wooden bridges with more durable steel, added heavier-duty track, replaced rotting ties. "No expense was spared in making the road the leading model of the Southwest," wrote S. G. Reed in his seminal volume, *A History of Texas Railroads*. "He was the first to use 'burnt gumbo,' a red brick-like substance baked from black waxy soil, as road ballast, because of its low cost and advantage of absorbing water without disintegration. His locomotives were of high speed type. The passenger equipment was the most luxurious in Texas. It included the first café lounge cars and observation sleepers to be operated in the Southwest, the equipment forming part of a through train between St. Louis and Galveston over the Frisco and [Houston and Texas Central]. Green also introduced the first locomotive electric headlights to be used in Texas, in 1894, and the first steel box car in 1900 and later, when the automobile had appeared, he was the first to adopt high speed gas-electric rail cars to meet that competition."

Ned was popular with his upper-level staff, because he was eager to learn, without being pushy, and because he readily agreed to most of their suggestions for improvements. He was popular with the rank and file as well, from the engineers to the immigrant laborers driving spikes, because he was affable, personable, and never seemed above sharing a jovial greeting or conversation, regardless of a man's rank or position. Nothing delighted him more than to board one of his own locomotives and ride the line in the cab beside the engineer.

Ned also showed a budding interest in science, one that would lead him into an incredible array of pursuits later in life.

The infestation of the cotton boll weevil from Mexico in the late 1890s threatened not only the cotton farmers, but the Texas railroads that depended heavily on cotton for freight revenues. As federal and state agriculture officials searched for a solution, Ned stepped in with an offer to build and outfit a demonstration farm to test possible remedies. The 400-acre farm, bought and outfitted for about $50,000, helped lead to new varieties of cotton more resistant to the weevil.

Hetty would never have spent this money herself, but she left him pretty well alone in Terrell. Still, Ned's reputation for being an affable soft touch concerned her, and when she learned that requests were pouring in from Texas politicians and others for free passes on Texas Midland trains, Hetty responded with characteristic wit. She printed up biblically inspired cards for Ned to pass out in response to the incoming requests:

> *Monday*—"Thou shalt not pass." Numbers xx, 18.
> *Tuesday*—"Suffer not a man to pass." Judges iii, 28.
> *Wednesday*—"The wicked shall no more pass." Nahum I, 15.
> *Thursday*—"This generation shall not pass." Mark xiii, 30.
> *Friday*—"By a perpetual decree it can not pass." Jeremiah v, 22.
> *Saturday*—"None shall pass." Isaiah xxxiv, 10.
> *Sunday*—"So he paid the fare thereof and went." Jonah 1, 2.

Ned's prominence naturally earned him invitations to the best Terrell homes and mothers plotted to fix their daughters up with him. But Ned preferred a more unrestrained life. He settled first in a hotel in Terrell, and then moved to the second floor of a two-story building. The large suite became known informally as Green Flats. Ned lived there with several other bachelors, and proceeded to build for himself a sort of backwater Xanadu. He threw frequent parties with women and drinking, and it was the sort of place that might well not have been tolerated in conservative Terrell if not for his prominent position and bankroll. During his early days in Texas, Hetty had kept Ned living on wages as slender as those he had drawn in Chicago. With his improvements the railroad prospered, and Ned was in a position to indulge and invest in his pleasures. At about the same time, a flame from the past—Mabel Harlow, the prostitute who had taught Ned the ways of life in Chicago—appeared, evidently by chance, in Texas. It was to lead to a long and colorful relationship.

About a year after moving to Terrell, Ned moved to Dallas. Dallas was close enough for him to keep tabs on the Texas Midland, but far enough away and in a large enough city that his arrangement with Mabel Harlow wouldn't raise too many eyebrows. He took rooms on the second and third floors of a brick building known as the Cullem and Boren Store, at the corner of Elm and Griffin Streets, in a business section of town. He outfitted the rooms as living quarters and installed Mabel Harlow as his "housekeeper" at $200 per month. While her skills with a duster and mop remain undocumented, Ned seemed satisfied with the arrangement, which they kept for years. It's not clear when Hetty became aware of Mabel Harlow. She disapproved of the relationship, but as it became obvious that Mabel was not going to be just some passing fancy, Hetty grew to tolerate her— coldly—referring to her as "Mabel Harlot." At least, Hetty reasoned, this extended fling would keep Ned away from the altar. Hetty may not have liked the idea of her son living with a prostitute, but it was better than having him married off to some respectable girl from Chicago or Dallas and giving her a legal claim on the fortune.

In the 1890s, the Texas Midland Railroad counted among its directors one somewhat surprising name—Edward Henry Green, Hetty's husband. Though Hetty had separated from Edward, the couple never divorced. From time to time, Sylvia and Ned visited him in New York and Bellows Falls and Hetty and Edward shared some holiday meals together. The Texas Midland directorship was a small bone for a man whose financial activities had once been so robust, and it probably served to help keep him paid up at the Union Club. Certainly, Edward had no money of his own left to invest with. He was broke, living out his once-grand life reading books in quiet studies and enduring one small humiliation after the next.

In September of 1893, at the time that Hetty and Ned were brawling with Huntington, Edward might have picked up a copy of the *Brooklyn Daily Eagle* and learned of his own demise. "Mrs. Green has been a widow for many years and her daughter is about 20 years old," the article stated. "Since the death of her husband Hetty Green has become a financier of unusual shrewdness. She has indicated by her actions that she has small faith in brokers and that if she wants anything done the best way is to do it for herself."

Even those who knew she wasn't a widow knew that Edward was out of the picture financially. In March 1889, the *World* noted that Edward "lost all his fortune in the crash of 1884, and since then he has received no assistance from his wife to rehabilitate himself. He is still 6 feet and 6 inches in height, but his financial figure has dwindled almost to nothing. He comes down on the Street two or three times a week, but his flyers are of the most modest description." Five years later, little had changed, except perhaps for girth, age, and lack of mobility. "Her husband sometimes assists her in a purely advisory capacity," the *Times* reported on Christmas Day in 1894. "He is seventy years old, weighs more than 250 pounds, and it is exceedingly difficult for him to get about. He spends most of his time at the Union Club."

While Edward sank ever deeper into obscurity, Hetty continued her surge into national prominence, aligning her fortunes with one of the nation's most powerful and visible banks. From its squat, columned, Greco-Roman facade to its roster of second- and third-generation blue-blood directors, the Chemical National Bank, located at 270 Broadway, bespoke solidity, security, and sober, conservative prosperity. These were all qualities that Hetty craved after the Cisco failure, and demanded of the institution she would entrust with the guardianship of her millions. Founded in 1824, the bank was an offshoot of the New York

Chemical Manufacturing Company, which a year earlier had begun manufacturing nitric acid, blue vitriol, refined camphor, and other industrial chemicals, as well as paints, dyes, and drugs.

In 1844, the bank was reorganized as independent from the manufacturing company, but retained the "Chemical" in its title. It prospered from the start. The shareholders list represented the cream of New York finance and society—Cornelius Vanderbilt, Anthony Drexel, Russell Sage, and a long list of Roosevelts were among the shareholders and depositors. Annie Leary, Hetty's closest friend, did her banking there. Like Hetty, the bank established a reputation for maintaining large cash reserves in good times and bad, and for keeping its head when everyone else lost theirs. When the financial panic of 1857 prompted banks to stop payments in gold, the Chemical earned national respect for being the only major bank that publicly vowed to continue using gold until its reserves ran out. After an initial run, the bank's reserves actually increased as depositors, impressed by the show of confidence, switched their assets to Chemical.

The cashier during the 1857 crisis, thirty-one-year-old George Gilbert Williams, was a rising young star who had started as an office boy. By the time Hetty made her first deposit in 1885, Williams had been an employee for more than forty years, and president for eight. By then, his personal reputation for hard work, thrift, and financial sobriety were so intertwined with the bank's reputation that many people looked on him as the physical embodiment of everything the Chemical National Bank was and wanted to be.

It required a special individual to deal with Hetty in any business or legal relationship, let alone to serve as her banker, and Williams was more than up to the task. Furthermore, Williams and Hetty seemed genuinely to like and respect one another. Williams exhibited a rare mixture of deference and toughness that Hetty found appealing. He was a dapper, fastidious man with a high starched collar, thinning gray hair, kindly eyes, and a Victorian beard-and-mustache combination that cascaded over the lips, reducing his mouth to a mere hint of a line. He was a man of firm and unchanging habit. Each day, regardless of the weather, he eschewed carriages and walked the several miles from his home on West Fifty-eighth Street to the Chemical Bank. Each summer he rented the same room at the same hotel in Manhattan Beach, Brooklyn (The Oriental), from which he emerged at precisely six o'clock in the morning for a swim in the ocean, before catching the ferry to lower Manhattan.

Like Hetty with her Robinson ancestors, Williams had descended from an old Rhode Island family, including Roger Williams, founder of the state, and William Williams, who signed the Declaration of Independence. But to Hetty, his greatest attribute was his unwavering, almost obsessive politeness. In his professional dealings, Williams exhibited a level of courtesy that even then was considered old-fashioned. To Williams, politeness was more than just kindness; it was sound business. "Politeness pays," he would tell his employees. "A grain of politeness saves a ton of correction. No institution is too important to ignore the laws of courtesy." Williams no doubt had his largest depositor in mind when he said, "I have observed that many a tattered garment hides a package of bonds and that gorgeous clothing does not always cover a millionaire."

Hetty was a shrewd enough judge of character to know the difference between those behaving out of conviction and those simply being obsequious in the presence of wealth. And because Williams, in essence, *was* Chemical National Bank, his insistence on comportment infiltrated every layer of the bank. "It is the invariable rule of the Chemical National Bank that every employee, from the humblest clerk to the highest official, shall be courteous to everyone," he said. This philosophy created a welcoming atmosphere for Hetty that went above and beyond merely stroking a major depositor. The employees at Chemical went out of their way to accommodate Hetty, and to avoid raising eyebrows at her unorthodox habits. They made no issue about her old clothes, or about her ways of economizing, which at times included arriving at the bank with a metal pail containing dry oatmeal, to be mixed with water and heated on a radiator for lunch, so as to avoid a restaurant tab.

The employees of the bank created a protective environment for Hetty. At times she used an office, but she declined offers for permanent office space for fear that the tax collectors would try to pin her to New York for tax purposes. Often she sat at a desk in the back and the tellers created a sort of shield for her from the prying eyes of the public and from reporters who more and more frequently came around in hopes of finding a story.

The bank also supplied Hetty with assistants to help with everything from clipping coupons as they came due, to supporting her in negotiations over securities, to simply keeping tabs on her ever-expanding holdings.

And this was important, for Hetty's wealth was rapidly becoming a financial empire. In addition to her heavy holdings in government bonds and railroads, she was becoming a real estate owner of epic proportions. She owned dozens of buildings in block after block in New York, Chicago, St. Louis, and Boston. Some of the property had come to her through her father's estate, but most she acquired through foreclosures on mortgages she held. This was a direct result of Hetty's large cash holdings, and her ability to act as a one-woman private bank. She rarely, if ever, bought a property outright on the open market. Once she owned a property, she held on to it. She rarely improved vacant lots with buildings, or improved buildings by renovating them. To do so would only add to her tax exposure, not to mention the cost of construction. It made more sense from her perspective to leave a property alone and wait for development to grow around it.

In Chicago, she owned property from the Loop to the northern suburbs, from the shores of Lake Michigan to undeveloped land southwest of the city. She owned the Howland Block at the southwest corner of Dearborn and Monroe, with nearly 200 feet fronting on Dearborn. The lone structure was a dated, five-story building, but the property was growing more valuable by the year. She also owned numbers 183 through 187 Wabash Avenue, another plot on Wabash near Harrison Street, and 80 feet of frontage on Michigan Avenue, and houses at 211 and 213 Monroe Street, and six apartment buildings on Sibley Street.

Among her largest holdings was a 480-acre tract southwest of Chicago in an area known as Gage Park. Hetty had acquired the property under foreclosure in 1877 for less than $200,000, and kept the land largely undeveloped. She leased some of it to truck farmers, who raised cabbages, cucumbers, and tomatoes for sale at local markets. Schoolboys from the area earned pocket money on vacations by helping farmers work Hetty's fields. One of these boys, Frank Mikulecky, recalled years later that the only building on the property was a lonely brick house sticking out like a sore thumb from the scraggly fields on South Western Avenue, the eastern boundary of her land. Mikulecky, remembered Hetty living "incognito" in this forlorn house when she visited Chicago.

She owned apartment buildings in St. Louis and Boston. Hetty owned mines in several states, including the famed Central Eureka Mine in Sutter Creek, California, which by itself earned Hetty some $12 million in gold and quartz production. She held mortgages on high-grade property. In New York, she held mortgages ranging from warehouses in lower Manhattan to mansions along Millionaire's Row on Fifth Avenue—where she herself refused to live. Among her holdings was a $400,000 mortgage on the Stern House on Fifth Avenue near East Sixty-seventh Street—one of the grandest homes in the district. One day, when Hetty visited a swank Fifth Avenue real estate office, a clerk looked at her unfashionable black dress and homely hat and figured she must be applying for a house-sitting job the office had advertised. "No more caretakers needed!" the clerk barked, preparing to usher her out. "I am Hetty Green," she said. "I came here just to talk over a loan of half a million dollars your firm wanted to borrow from me for a customer."

Municipalities around the country were coming to see Hetty as a reliable source of funding for civic improvements. In 1900, for example, the rapidly growing city of Tucson, Arizona, desperately needed to modernize and expand a water system that as recently as the end of the Civil War had relied on wagons carting water from nearby springs at five cents a bucket. The city turned to Hetty, who purchased the $110,000 bond issue—making possible a modern water and sewer system.

More than once she bailed New York City out of a pinch. It is staggering to think of a major city coming to a single person, hat in hand, but such was the scope of Hetty's fortune. Despite her reputation as a miser and a hard-nosed dealer, Hetty usually offered rates that were more than fair. Although she could be ruthless when dealing with an enemy, she rarely if ever took the opportunity to kick a borrower when he was down. That was bad business, she always said. In 1898, she lent the cash-strapped city $1 million at a rate of 2 percent, well below the prevailing rate of 3 to 3.5 percent. In 1901, she advanced the city another $1.5 million. "Hetty Green is smart," an anonymous New York finance official told a reporter from the *Times* in July 1901. "During the summer months there is not much demand for money in Wall Street. She loans New York City a million and a half, and just when the money market gets active in the fall the money comes back with good interest."

Hetty traveled frequently to survey her properties in cities around the country. Sometimes she traveled with Ned or Sylvia, but often she traveled alone, invariably by day coach rather than in a more expensive sleeper car. In an age when women rarely traveled unaccompanied, Hetty fearlessly traversed the country. She carried with her a black reticule that became the stuff of legend wherever she went. Reporters frequently speculated that the bag was ever stuffed with millions of dollars' worth of bonds, a claim Hetty denied. One item she did carry in the bag was a ring of keys, fifty or so of them—keys to many of her properties. They jangled in her reticule the way that charms might have jangled in the bags of other fifty-something women of the era.

# ELEVEN

# A LADY OF YOUR AGE

N o matter what anybody else called her, Hetty Green always saw herself as simply a woman looking out for her rights. When it came to struggles on Wall Street, she rarely lost a battle. In court, however, her record was spottier, as the case of Aunt Sylvia's will presaged decades earlier. Regardless, she could never resist a good legal fight. Her hatred of lawyers was surpassed only by her need of them. She went through batteries of lawyers during the 1890s, as complainant or respondent in dozens of lawsuits. She eagerly attended every hearing. Frequently one court case would spin off from another and yet another, like a fast-growing and pernicious vine of litigation. Sometimes she had to hire new lawyers to handle the case of an old lawyer suing to collect his fee from a previous case. And yet she obviously loved the process. Hetty would have been a formidable soldier. But women did not fight in wars. The courtroom was her battlefield.

Of all the legal cases she was involved with during the 1890s, whether as a plaintiff or a defendant, none occupied more time than her fight against Henry A. Barling, the trustee of her father's $5 million estate. Barling had worked as her father's clerk in New York shortly before Robinson's death. He was, by definition, the kind of person Hetty was predisposed to hate—yet another man appointed to handle money that was rightfully hers. She believed Barling had mismanaged the trust, allowing investments to languish and wallow while creating for himself a life of luxury. She had a point. The principal in the trust had barely increased in nearly thirty years. The $350,000 Hetty received each year was roughly the same amount that she had received the year after her father died. Hetty's lawyers charged that Barling squandered thousands of dollars each year in salaries for clerks, one of whom was Barling's son. They charged that Thomas Mandell, a cotrustee from New Bedford, had drawn $80,000 in fees over two years, without once setting foot in New York, where the trust was being managed. They charged that Abner Davis, another trustee, had continued to draw thousands of dollars in fees years after being committed to a sanitarium in Connecticut. Barling, collecting generous fees as trustee, emerged from his clerk's salary and New York flat to the life of a country squire, owner of a large house across the Hudson River in Highwood, New Jersey. Unfortunately for Mr. Barling, he spent much of his time in that fine home worrying about what Hetty Green might do next.

The dispute erupted in 1888, when the trustees decided to sell a 651-acre parcel of Chicago real estate Hetty's father had purchased during the 1860s. The trustees claimed the time was ripe to sell at a profit. Hetty's philosophy on real estate was simple, its wisdom borne out over and over in her experience. Hold on to property.

Hetty responded with a typically audacious move. In June 1889, when Barling was off on an extended vacation in Europe—paid for, Hetty no doubt fumed, with *her* money—she arrived at his New York office at 46 South Street in the company of several men from Chemical National Bank.

Hetty did all of the talking. She stood in the middle of the office and demanded that the clerks turn over all the securities on hand. As the clerks demurred, Hetty grew more loud and insistent. She had come for what was rightfully hers. With Barling gone, the clerks' resistance crumbled. They turned over stacks of bonds and stock certificates, worth a total of $3 million. Nobody said a word as Hetty and her companions stuffed the securities into several large bags and marched out the door to a waiting carriage. When Barling, in Paris, received the news by cable, he immediately cut short his vacation and returned to New York. He went straight to the Broadway offices of Chemical Bank and demanded that the cashier return all of the securities and papers immediately. "This the cashier did with due gravity, but promptly, and now the executor is once more in charge of the affairs of the Robinson estate," the *New York World* reported on June 9.

A reporter found Barling sitting on the verandah of his home in Highwood a day or two later, and asked if he intended to return to Europe to finish his trip.

"No," Barling said nervously. "I shall be obliged, the way things look, to remain on this side, for the present at least, and look personally after the interest entrusted to me."

All of that merely served as prelude to a series of suits and countersuits filed by both sides that became so entangled that a New York judge named H. H. Anderson was appointed to serve as referee, to attempt to straighten out the mess of accusations. For two years, the litigants filed into Anderson's offices at 35 Broadway for a seemingly endless series of hearings whose arcane minutiae were leavened only by Hetty's antics. Anderson didn't appreciate the show, but the reporters did.

In the winter of 1895, Hetty set the tone for one day's hearing by marching into the room, slapping Barling on the back, and exclaiming, in a hearty voice, "How d'ye do, Mr. Barling?"

Hetty's attorney began questioning Barling about Abner Davis and why he would continue to receive commissions while living in a sanitarium following a mental breakdown. Barling tried to put a positive spin on the situation, calling the hospital "a retreat for those who want a rest of mind."

"A place for howling lunatics," came a cheerful voice from the audience.

"Mrs. *Green!*" said Judge Anderson.

A couple of weeks later, Barling's attorney, J. Evarts Tracy, said Barling's books had always been open for Hetty and her lawyers to examine.

"No use lying," came the voice.

"Mrs. *Green!*" said Judge Anderson. "I do not like to speak to a lady of your age in this way."

"Oh, you needn't mind me," she responded. "I know I am in my second childhood, but you can't muzzle—"

"Mrs. *Green!*" Anderson snapped. "You must not talk. I *will* keep order, and you have your lawyers to talk for you."

When the proceedings were less lively, Anderson sometimes nodded off. Hetty, on the other hand, was always on alert, especially when reporters followed her out into the hall at the end of a long afternoon, looking for a quote. She rarely disappointed: "The referee on one day slept nineteen times, snored fourteen, and struck his nose on the desk three times. He wants me to stop talking, and I want him to stop snoring. He makes his noise with his nose, and I make mine with my mouth. It's nearly the same, ain't it?"

On June 14, 1895, as the lawyers, reporters, and others in the room organized their papers and headed for the door, Hetty quietly walked to a window, dropped to her knees, and folded her arms in prayer. The noise in the room stopped at once. Everyone seemed taken aback except for Sylvia, who often attended the hearings with her mother, and now looked on impassively.

Hetty stayed in that position for several minutes, moving her lips without uttering a sound. Then she got up, dusted off her dress, and headed for the exit. When reporters asked what she prayed for, Hetty declined to answer, took Sylvia by the arm, and left the room.

Hetty developed a particular distaste for Barling's lead attorney, Joseph Choate, a prominent New York attorney who would later serve as United States ambassador to Great Britain. She took to making public pronouncements against him, one of which almost got her into trouble the same month. "Did you ever see such a set of buzzards?" she reflected on Choate and other lawyers on his team. "Why, it is sad to think of poor Irene Hoyt. Choate and the other buzzards got hold of her, and she is in an asylum now."

Her words did not escape the eyes of Miss Mary Irene Hoyt, who on June 5 filed a $100,000 slander suit against Hetty. Editors, reporters, readers, and court observers could barely contain their glee at the prospect of a Hetty Green and Irene Hoyt squaring off in court. If Hetty was the most colorfully litigious woman in New York, Irene Hoyt probably came in second, having spent several years in a legal battle with trustees over the estate of her own father, steamboat magnate Jesse Hoyt. Choate had represented the trustees in the Hoyt case, so Hetty and Irene should have been sympathetic with each other's causes. But Hetty's mortifying statement put an end to any camaraderie.

The newspapers fairly licked their lips. "As both of these distinguished women are millionairesses, and as in times past they have demonstrated their undoubted capacity to make things interesting, a lively time may be expected when this slander suit comes to trial," the *New York Times* predicted. Three weeks later, reporters did not mask their disappointment when the suit was suddenly settled out of court, the details kept secret. "The trial had been looked forward to as one of the events of the age," the *Times* lamented.

Just when the Barling case looked as though it might drag out forever, Henry Barling obligingly dropped dead in April 1896. He had been handling the estate of Edward Mott Robinson for nearly thirty-one years A short time later, Hetty triumphantly solved the mystery of her public prayer that had perplexed the reporters: "What I prayed for was that the wickedness of that executor might be made manifest to New York," the New Bedford *Morning Mercury* quoted her as saying that August. "I'm a Quaker. In just a year after my prayer that executor was found stone dead in his bed."

At long last, Hetty was in a position to assume direct control over the fortune she had always considered rightly hers. Six weeks after Barling's death, Hetty persuaded a New York Supreme Court judge to name a more favorably disposed replacement for Barling: Ned Green.

Not all of Hetty's lodgings were cheap tenements. While she avoided the high-priced rent of fashionable Manhattan hotels, she wasn't altogether averse to comfort. Tops on her list of requirements were ease of access to lower Manhattan, and a management that respected her privacy. In December of 1894, she found both at Brooklyn's Hotel St. George. Built in 1888 and located on Henry Street in Brooklyn Heights, just a few blocks from the famous promenade overlooking the East River, the St. George was one of Brooklyn's newer and larger hotels, ten stories tall. In contrast to the Hetty legend of living in mean flats down dingy hallways, the St. George had a large, sunny dining room decorated by live pineapple plants—Hetty's favorite fruit. She and Sylvia occupied a fifth-floor suite. They registered under pseudonyms ("Mrs. H. Gray" and "Miss Gray"). The owner, J. W. Tumbridge, and the head clerk, Frank Niblo, went out of their way to protect their privacy, telling inquisitive reporters that Hetty and Sylvia had checked out when they hadn't.

Hetty was accustomed to getting around Brooklyn and into Manhattan using public transportation. With nearly a million residents spread throughout Brooklyn's horizontal vastness, the electrified streetcars were the most reliable and efficient mode of transportation. They squeaked, popped, and clanked across a network so intertwined that dodging the cars in the street became an unofficial pastime, and, as every baseball fan knows, gave the local professional team its name, the Trolley Dodgers, later shortened to the Dodgers. During that winter of 1894–95, the city came to a virtual standstill when the trolley workers went on strike. Drivers and conductors of the city's six trolley companies were looking for concessions that by today's standards are remarkable only for their modesty—a 24-cent-per-day pay raise on salaries that topped out at a meager two dollars per day, and a reduction in the shift length from twelve to ten hours. A sort of tense peace prevailed amid the eerie silence during the first couple of days of the strike. But soon moods turned as ugly as the January weather. Angry mobs threw stones, bottles, and garbage at the legions of scab drivers and conductors, who poured into Brooklyn from around the country. Most of the scabs were themselves desperate for work following an extended financial panic of 1893.

Charles A. Schieren, Brooklyn's mayor, took the side of management, calling out first the police and then the National Guard to quell protests and keep the trolleys moving. He said he just wanted to keep the peace. Critics noted that Schieren's New York–based company manufactured electric belts used by the trolley companies. An occupying force of some seventy-five hundred federal soldiers turned Brooklyn into an armed camp. Many strikers and sympathizers were arrested. Two men died; one, a roofer, was struck from his perch by an errant warning fired over the heads of protesters. A second man was shot after he approached too close to a car stable and ignored warnings to stop. In the face of overwhelming power, and with hungry mouths to feed, the strike petered out a month after it began, with the defeated drivers and conductors returning to work.

But the strike had succeeded in stirring up passionate sympathy among many observers. Theodore Dreiser, who covered the strike as a New York reporter, immortalized it five years later in his novel *Sister Carrie* through the eyes of a conflicted scab named George Hurstwood. Hetty, too, came out on the side of the strikers. This may seem an odd position for a famous capitalist to take, but Hetty never sympathized with management. While the public didn't quite perceive her this way, Hetty considered herself a populist.

"The poor have no chance in this country," she told a reporter for the *Brooklyn Daily Eagle* at the time of the strike. "No wonder Anarchists and Socialists are so numerous. The longer we live, the more discontented we all get, and no wonder, too. Some blame the rich, but all the rich are not to blame."

She added, "The law must be upheld, must it? Then why don't they begin at the right end? Who begins to break the law? The great railroad magnates. There is Huntington. He and his railroads and the men about him have been grinding wealth out of the poor for years and years and defying the authorities. But the militia are never sent against him. . . . Let the poor man break the law and see how soon he gets into jail."

Sylvia, Hetty's quiet companion during these years, was entering her mid-twenties, a period of life when, in those days, a young woman not busy raising her own family might inspire sympathetic comments from friends and relatives and panic on the part of the mother. Not so with Hetty. Hetty perceived protecting her daughter and protecting the family fortune as synonymous. And so Sylvia accompanied Hetty everywhere, to court, to Chemical National Bank, to one apartment or hotel after another. Hetty and Sylvia frequently spent their summers at Bellows Falls. They would stay at the Tucker House sometimes; other times, when Hetty had rented the house out, they stayed at one of the downtown hotels.

Sylvia loved Bellows Falls. It was the one place where she had friends and felt a certain degree of freedom. She loved the rural setting, loved riding horses. She hated when the fading summer carried the first faint chill of autumn. It meant it was time to return to some claustrophic room in Brooklyn. A batch of letters from Sylvia to her childhood friend, Mary Nims, survives. The letters are written on cheap, plain stationery. Some bear the return address of the Chemical National Bank, 270 Broadway. Those mailed from Brooklyn bear no return address, as if she wished to blot out that portion of her existence.

Sylvia writes to thank Mary for a bottle of perfume at Christmas, to send her regrets for not having stopped in to see her before leaving Bellows Falls. The letters are full of a sort of muted longing, and not a great deal of joy. "Please accept many thanks for the lovely photograph and calendar," she wrote from Brooklyn one January. "I would have thanked you before but have been sick in bed. I am just going down to my meals. . . . Papa is about the same. Mother as busy as usual. Ned is still in Texas, so you see we do not change much. Hoping this will find you all well. Do tell me what all of you are doing." She enclosed a photograph of herself, saying, "I hope to have some better pictures taken as soon as I get a little stouter. I have got so thin since I came down [to New York]. I wish I could stay in the country all the year round as country life seems to agree with me."

Despite her inherent awkwardness and shyness, and her mother's best attempts to keep predators at bay, Sylvia still attracted her share of admirers. The millions she stood to inherit sharpened her appeal for any number of suitors, legitimate, scheming, and lunatic. Articles about Hetty made their way overseas, and when one mentioning Sylvia and her presumed millions appeared in a Berlin paper, hundreds of letters arrived from would-be German suitors, about a quarter of whom directly proposed marriage. One persistent fellow, named Kaufman, claimed to be poor but well-born, a generational link or two removed from European royalty. If the Greens would but forward him a draft for 1,000 marks, this Prince Charming promised to board the next available steamship for New York and throw himself "at the feet of this esteemed angel, Sylvia." If Sylvia should fail to be duly impressed, Mr. Kaufman vowed (upon receipt of another 1,000 marks) to purchase a second ticket for a steamship bound in the other direction, thus to rid Sylvia forever of this heartfelt intrusion. The letters might have amused Sylvia or flattered her, had she read them; but Hetty took charge and turned some two hundred of them, unopened, over to her lawyers.

A bit closer to home, and more unsettling, was the case of one Thaddeus McDonald, who burst wild-eyed into a Washington police headquarters, claiming that Hetty Green was trying to break up his engagement to Sylvia, and had threatened to kill him. "I'm going to marry her daughter," McDonald told the officers on duty. "And the mother has conspired against me. She has men and women after me all the time." The man claimed to have written "a bushel" of letters to his beloved, although he conceded he had yet to receive a response. McDonald believed his life was in peril and demanded police protection. He turned out to have recently emerged from an asylum in Newark, New Jersey.

Not all of the suitors were frauds or lunatics. Hetty's friend, Annie Leary, attempted to bring Sylvia out from Hetty's shadow, to introduce her into society and free her from her seclusion. At her home on Fifth Avenue, and in Newport, Rhode Island, where Annie maintained a cottage, she continued to hold dinners and dances on behalf of Sylvia, inviting eligible sons of other wealthy families. Sylvia rarely spoke up or engaged the attention of potential suitors. Still, her family's money proved to be an aphrodisiac, even in circles where people had plenty to begin with. But Hetty, who trusted no one, trusted least of all the "idle rich," and would let young men get only so far before she clamped down.

The *New York Tribune* in December 1894 reported that an unnamed suitor, described as "a young man well known in fashionable clubs, the son of a conspicuous banker," had attempted to woo Sylvia. According to an "informant," the young man had shown a good deal of attention to Sylvia at Newport. The reporter described Sylvia as "plain, quiet, intelligent," and showing a "decided preference for the young man with whom her name has been connected recently."

Hetty, who had remained behind in New York, got wind of the budding Newport romance, and called Sylvia home, cutting her vacation short. When Sylvia arrived back at the Brooklyn hotel room that she and her mother called home, Hetty told her:

> I've found out something about the young man who has been waiting on you at Newport, Sylvia. I find that your young man is very nice and proper, but if it wasn't for his father, the world wouldn't know a thing about him. He has never earned a dollar and doesn't know the value of money. Now Sylvia, I've kept my eyes open all these years, and I want to say right here and now, that you shall never marry a society man with my consent. I want to see you happily married and in a home of your own, but I want you to marry a poor young man of good principles, who is making an honest, hard fight for success. I don't care whether he's got $100 or not, provided he is made of the right stuff. You will have more money than you'll ever spend, and it isn't necessary to look for a young man with money. Now you know my wish, and I hope I won't hear anything more about your young man at Newport, who knows just about enough to part his hair in the middle and spend his father's money.

The authority on which this remarkable speech was rendered, verbatim, in the *Tribune*, is unclear. The "informant" who provided the details would have had to have an incredibly keen ear and good memory, not to mention unusual access to what one assumes would have been a private conversation. And yet the words are Hetty through and through, from the matter-of-fact directness to the witty quip at the end, to the barely concealed contempt for a young man who had inherited a fortune and failed to seize the reins and increase the fortune through hard work, as she herself had done.

# TWELVE

# ACROSS THE RIVER

When the attention she generated in Brooklyn grew to be too much, Hetty began looking for another place to live. With Manhattan's high cost of living, the alternative to Brooklyn lay on the western banks of the Hudson River. Hoboken, New Jersey, where Hetty first rented an apartment in 1895, was an unpretentious town of immigrants, mainly of German or Irish descent. Hoboken was a rail and shipping center that since the eighteenth century had offered regular ferry service to lower Manhattan. For years, passengers had made the mile-and-a-half crossing over the Hudson aboard side-wheel steam ferries such as the *Morristown* and the *Montclair,* named for New Jersey towns. But forward-thinking Hoboken in 1898 had added to its fleet the *Bergen,* the world's first steam ferry with double-screw propulsion, a major advancement in speed and reliability over the plodding side-wheelers.

For Hetty, good ferry service was one of Hoboken's three main attractions. The other two were cheap rents and relief, if only temporary, from the tax collectors and reporters in Brooklyn. She liked the plain-spoken people and the hard-working, businesslike personality of her new town. Yet while Hoboken served as her primary residence for the rest of her life, she would continue to move restlessly about, from Bellows Falls to boardinghouses and hotels in Manhattan, Brooklyn, Long Island, Boston, and Morristown, New Jersey. She remained determined never to stay in one place long enough to be pinned as a resident. The annual city directory for Hoboken and neighboring Jersey City lists any number of Greens from the mid-1890s through 1916, the last year of Hetty's life. There is Abbie Green, a bookkeeper; Hannah Green, a tailor; Margaret Green, a widow; and Clayborne Green, a janitor. But nowhere does the name of the most famous Green appear.

And yet the residents of Hoboken became accustomed to the sight of Hetty on the streets. She rented several apartments over the years, mainly in two buildings located on the northern edge of the city. One was a large, six-story brick structure at 1309 Bloomfield Street. The second was two blocks closer to the river, along Washington Street. The flats Hetty rented were always modest, but the buildings were large, modern for their times, and well-built. Both are still in use. The building on Washington Street was and remains especially prominent, occupying an entire city block between Twelfth and Thirteenth Streets. Officially named The Elysian Apartments, it was more popularly known in Hetty's day as "Yellow Flats" because of the yellowish tint to the brickwork, or, sometimes, as "The Barracks," presumably because of the military-looking architecture, with parapets adorned with patterned brick.

To ward off the inquisitive, Hetty identified herself as "C. Dewey" on the name tag next to the electric buzzer at the entrance to Yellow Flats. This was her private joke. Dewey was the name of her pet Skye terrier; the "C" stood for "Cutie," one of the dog's nicknames. When reporters inevitably tracked her down in Hoboken as they had in Brooklyn, she frequently took the back stairs, ducking down the broad alleyway behind the building and slipping quietly onto the street.

Typical of her quarters during these years was a five-room, steam-heated apartment on the third floor of Yellow Flats, for which she was said to pay $23 per month. The apartment contained a small parlor, perhaps eight by ten feet, lit by one small window and a gas lamp that she kept at the lowest level that would maintain a flame. The room's mantle was decorated with a large bouquet of imitation American Beauty roses, made from dyed chicken feathers. Hetty proudly told visitors she had bought them in Chicago for a dollar. "I'd have to pay twenty times that for real ones, and they wouldn't last a week," she said. "These are good for ten years yet." Near the flowers were two photographs of Ned, a portrait of herself at twenty-six, and, on the walls, some pictures of dogs and cats. The furnishings were simple—a couch and three chairs arranged around a small table.

Hetty kept to a simple and predictable daily routine. Each morning she awoke early enough to eat a light breakfast in her apartment and make the short walk, rain or shine, to the ferry slip in order to catch the 7 A.M. ferry to Manhattan. She enjoyed the ferry ride—the water reminded her of New Bedford. From the landing at West Fourteenth Street, she rode a public streetcar to the Chemical National Bank offices on Broadway at City Hall Square. She was, invariably, among the first to arrive at the bank. She made her way back to a far corner of the narrow banking room, where she kept a desk near a window. As the bank began to fill up, the line of clerks created a Maginot Line of privacy between Hetty and the bank's everyday customers. Hetty spent her days cutting bond coupons that were coming due, speaking with representatives of the bank about her investments, and opening her mail, which she arranged to have delivered to the bank rather than her home. Requests for money from individuals and organizations invariably dominated the mail. She disposed of most of these immediately. "If I acknowledged them all," she told an interviewer, "I'd have almost as many cousins as I have dollars." When she left the bank to attend to business around Wall Street, she sometimes wore a thin black veil over the brim of her bonnet to avoid being recognized.

She ate a small and hurried lunch at any of several nearby restaurants where she was occasionally recognized despite her veil. Hetty sightings at restaurants became the stuff of legend. A businessman quoted in the *Times* claimed to have witnessed the following exchange while eating lunch at a downtown restaurant, when a shabbily dressed woman entered and sat down.

"Waiter, I want the best steak you can give me for thirty cents."

"We have no thirty-cent steaks, madam."

"No thirty-cent steaks! Haven't you something you can warm up for me?"

"No, madam."

"Well, how much is your tea?"

"Ten cents."

"Ten cents! Well, it isn't worth it. How much are your stews?"

"Fifteen cents."

"Can't you let me have a stew for less than that?

"No, madam."

"Well, you can bring me some tea, some toast without butter, and a stew."

When the woman had finished eating, she paid thirty cents for her meal (no tip) and walked off muttering that her dinner was worth at most twenty-five. The waiter walked in the other direction, grumbling, and the businessman felt compelled to ask the identity of the diner.

"Hetty Green."

Other encounters with waiters were equally colorful but less confrontational. When she heard a waiter complain of rheumatism, she offered her trusty cure: "dissolve two raw eggs, shells and all, in a pint of vinegar. Then add the same amount of alcohol and shake thoroughly. Apply to the part that aches and rub well." The waiter, Louis LaFranche, recalled the incident with fondness and humor years later, when he had become assistant manager at Boston's Hotel Lenox. LaFranche reported that the concoction worked remarkably well for his pains. He also reported dryly that the recipe came "in lieu of a tip."*

In the evening, Hetty was usually among the last to leave the bank. In the winter, she made her way back to a late ferry and ate dinner at 8 P.M. in her small dining room with Sylvia, or with only Dewey by her side. The dog ate well—rice pudding and beefsteak, rare.

Many of these intimate glimpses of Hetty's domestic life were recorded by an ambitious young journalist named Leigh Mitchell Hodges. In 1899, Hodges was a $50-a-week staff writer for *Ladies' Home Journal,* fresh from the *Kansas City Star.* Shortly after his arrival, the editor, Edward Bok, decided to test him with an assignment that he deemed impossible—an in-depth interview with the famous Hetty Green. While Hetty tended to be tolerant with reporters who tracked her down in the hallway of a hotel, or in a hearing room, she rarely granted more than a quote in passing. Hodges first attempted to see her at the Chemical Bank, where he announced himself, sent in his card, and received no reply. On the suggestion of a clerk, Hodges waited for Hetty outside the bank until the end of the day, then followed her to the ferry. He waited until she had taken a seat. He approached her and asked if she was Hetty Green. She stared at him and said nothing. He apologized and slunk away. Then he discreetly followed her to her apartment building in Hoboken. A dollar slipped to the janitor revealed the secret of "C. Dewey." Hodges rang the bell, and waited. There was no response. The dogged young reporter kept this up for a couple

---

* This vignette is preserved in an old newspaper clipping on file at the Kendall Institute, New Bedford, Massachusetts. The clipping does not identify the newspaper or the date.

of weeks, ringing at different times of the day. Finally, it dawned on him to try the building doorknob. It opened and he walked upstairs to "C. Dewey's" apartment and knocked.

Hetty, who opened the door, asked sharply, "Who are you and what do you want?" Hodges identified himself, expecting to be thrown unceremoniously out on his ear. Instead, Hetty invited him into her parlor. She respected his doggedness. Once they were seated, the genial reporter thawed her frosty suspicions. She patiently sat and spoke with him for more than two hours, recalling her childhood education in business at the knee of her grandfather and father, her time at finishing school in Boston, and her theories on investments and money.

During the course of the interview, Hodges sat on the couch—"a shabby haircloth sofa"—with Dewey sitting between him and Hetty. Hetty stroked Dewey affectionately during the interview, calling him "dearie."

Hodges was clearly enamored of Hetty and, like others aware of her fearsome reputation, surprised to find not the dour, sharp-faced woman he had expected, but an oddly youthful woman with a quick sense of humor and, when she let her guard down, a warm smile. "Her face is strong—quite masculine in its character—but her voice is low and womanly," Hodges reported. "Her deep sunken eyes are of steel gray, with a tinge of blue, and penetrate one as if they were sharpened points of metal. They lose nothing within range, and twinkle with a keen sense of humor that asserts itself more boldly in her conversation. They are as bright as the eyes of a child, and her cheeks are as rosy. If time and care had not drawn deep lines across her forehead and around her mouth one would not believe she was sixty-five years old."

Hodges asked Hetty why she avoided society when she might have been its queen. "As for society, I believe in it," she said. "When a young woman, I went out a good deal myself. I don't think society means what some rich people would have us believe. I'd get very tired of living in one of those great houses in

New York, going all night and sleeping all day. They don't have any real pleasure. It's intercourse with people that I like."

While Hetty could be ruthless with her financial enemies, she developed a reputation among many in Hoboken as a friendly neighbor. When a German woman living in the next apartment became ill, Hetty sat up with her at night and nursed her. She gave children in the neighborhood toy banks with a dollar inside. If, after a few weeks, the children brought the banks back with more than a dollar, proof that they were saving rather than spending their money, she would chip in another dollar. When a young couple wrote to her, saying that they had named their baby Hetty in her honor, she mailed the newborn as a gift a toy savings bank with a dollar inside.

She made friends with some prominent Hoboken citizens, including James and Michael Smith, Irish immigrants who had prospered as storekeepers. James Smith was city treasurer, and in time would serve as a witness to the signing of Hetty's will. Hetty in turn was willing to aid Michael Smith, who had a taste for expensive living. Michael outfitted his brownstone townhouse on Hudson Street with inlaid floors, engraved brass fittings, and molded plaster walls and ceilings. Exquisitely carved woodwork covered the length and breadth of the house, reaching a peak of opulence in the dining room, where a massive, hand-carved china cabinet covered an entire wall, and the ceiling was covered in carvings more exquisite still. Even in Hoboken, where there was a steady supply of inexpensive and skilled European labor, Michael Smith's spending habits left him in need of cash. Smith's checking records, found decaying in the attic by the current residents of the house, indicate that Smith repaid Hetty at least $1,600 in loans made over a period of several years.

As she had in Bellows Falls, in Hoboken Hetty became a part of the local lore. Perhaps the most enduring story about Hetty in Hoboken involves the time in 1903 when she left the town in a huff after being served a summons by the town recorder for failure to pay a $2 license fee for her dog. Hetty at first claimed that Dewey was licensed in New York and she therefore assumed she did not have to pay a fee in Hoboken. Next she claimed that the dog belonged to Sylvia, who stayed with her only infrequently. The recorder was unmoved. Faced with a maximum $25 fine, Hetty grudgingly sent an acquaintance named Charles Gahagan to the local Health Department to pay the $2. Irked by the incident, Hetty packed for a trip to Chicago, vowing to find another town when she returned. "Mrs. Hetty Green has left Hoboken, and, it is rumored, for good," the *Times* reported on April 4. "The experiences Mrs. Green had during the last month or so did not strike her as pleasant, and an intimate friend of hers said yesterday that she was not likely to return to Hoboken to reside." But distance mollified Hetty's anger, and return she did.

Three years later, as she boarded a Hoboken streetcar, she found herself short of the proper change. "I'll pay my fare later at the office," she told the conductor, according to the *Times* of January 21, 1906. "That letter carrier sitting opposite will vouch for me." When the postman nodded, the conductor paid Hetty's fare himself. The next day, Hetty arrived at the trolley company office with a nickel. She asked for a receipt. The conductor, George Krell, saved the nickel as a souvenir.

In their advancing years, Hetty and Edward found themselves drawn back together. Edward, well into his seventies when Hetty moved to Hoboken in the mid-1890s, was increasingly infirm. With Ned in Texas and Sylvia spending more of her time with Annie Leary in New York and Newport, Hetty turned her attentions to nursing him. Unorthodox as their marriage was, Hetty and Edward had been married for more than 30 years, and Hetty never fully severed the ties of family. Edward still spent much of his time at the Union Club in New York City, but he also from time to time occupied an apartment just above Hetty's in Hoboken, where she would visit and read to him in the evenings after she returned from New York.

Edward Green's final years were quiet and uneventful.

William Wallace Crapo, the New Bedford lawyer, politician, and businessman who spent much of his life tangled up one way or another with Hetty, saw the two of them together in New York one evening. Crapo had come from New Bedford for a meeting of the directors of a railroad. Hetty, staying temporarily at a boardinghouse in lower Manhattan, sent word to Crapo that she needed to see him on crucial business. Crapo promised to come by at the end of his business day. When he arrived, he found Edward seated quietly with Hetty in the boardinghouse's sitting room. As Crapo took his seat, Hetty launched into a by-now familiar diatribe against the late Edward D. Mandell, the late Dr. Gordon (Aunt Sylvia's physician and trustee), and various other New Bedford figures (all of them friends of Crapo's) whom she considered guilty of financial wrongs. Hetty held a bible and read underlined passages that she felt forecast divine retributions on her enemies. When Crapo realized that the "important business" he'd come for amounted to another chance for Hetty to vent, he settled in and listened patiently until she cooled down.

After a while, Crapo rose to go. Edward, sensing his chance to escape back to his club, rose also. In a few moments the two old men were heading down the steps and into the night. They walked east on Eleventh Street toward Broadway to catch their respective streetcars. As Green boarded his car, he turned to Crapo and said, "Women are queer." It struck Crapo that they were the first words Green had spoken all night.

William called after him, with a smile, "*Some* women."

Hetty and Edward spent the summer of 1900 together in Vermont, in the Tucker House. They were there when news that put a coda on Hetty's most bitter feud arrived. That summer, in August, Collis P. Huntington and his second wife, Arabella, boarded their private railcar for Raquette Lake, in the Adirondacks, where Huntington owned a sprawling summer home called Pine Knot Lodge, which he had built for $350,000. Still vigorous at seventy-nine and every bit as much a workaholic as

Hetty, Huntington spent the morning of August 13 doing business with his secretary, George Miles. In the afternoon, he walked around his property, then took several friends on a cruise aboard his motorboat, *Oneonta*. In the evening, the Huntingtons invited several guests from neighboring cottages for dinner. In the summertime, the health-conscious Huntington ate no meat (it was "too heating," he said). He never smoked and preferred tea to alcohol, often boasting never to have so much as tasted strong drink until after his fiftieth birthday. About eleven o'clock, Huntington bade his guests good evening and went to bed. A short time later, Miles and Arabella heard a groan and rushed to his room to find Huntington unconscious. He died shortly before midnight. The cause of death was a cerebral hemorrhage.

Huntington's funeral was held at his palatial Fifth Avenue home. The entire Southern Pacific system, every flatcar, passenger car, and locomotive, ground to a halt for seven minutes in his honor. Newport News, Virginia, which Huntington had transformed from a sleepy burg into one of the world's great shipyards, ceased operation for the day. Newspaper editorials spoke of Huntington's courage, perseverance, and energy, without reference to his duplicitous and often shady dealings with Congress, his ruthless tactics with competitors, shippers, and farmers. They praised his very real vision and steadfastness in directing an incredible project to completion.

At the Tucker House, Edward heard the news first. Then Hetty burst triumphantly into the room with a newspaper in her hand. "That old devil Huntington is dead," she said. "Serves him right."

Edward himself lingered for another two years, living part of the time with Hetty and part on his own. In the summer of 1901, with his health failing rapidly, Edward left for Bellows Falls for the last time. Ned sent his private railroad car from Texas to escort his father on this last journey in style. In Bellows Falls, where Edward was still remembered fondly, visitors streamed in as he lay quietly in bed, looking out his window at the green hills that gave Vermont its name, at the gentle sweep of the Connecticut River, recalling the time when the great Jack Adams fished him out of the canal.

In early October, Green suffered a severe attack of what doctors called inflammation of the kidneys. They gave him only a few days to live. Hetty arrived from New York, joining Sylvia, who had remained by her father's side for months. Ned came up from Texas and stayed for a few days before returning south, citing business pressures. Hetty, also reluctant to let her business concerns slip, summoned a Chemical Bank secretary and some clerks, who helped her conduct business from a room at the Tucker House. Despite the doctor's prediction, Green revived somewhat. Hetty traveled to New York when business demanded but mostly stayed on to nurse him. She did whatever she could to keep him comfortable. With the imminent reality of death hanging over the house, a sort of tenderness returned to Hetty and Edward's relationship. The terrific fights over money were long gone, if not entirely forgotten. They were two old people facing the end of time. Hetty would later recall the time as particularly stressful. Nearly two years after Edward's death, when a friend from Massachusetts wrote her to complain about her own illness, Hetty, in a letter postmarked January 5, 1904, responded: "Mr. Green's sickness & death & going up & down [from New York to Vermont] in storms and getting up three times in the night to see if the nurse was awake . . . I have had my troubles."

Green died peacefully on March 19, 1902, a Wednesday. He was eighty-one years old. The examiner, A. L. Miner, determined the cause of death as chronic nephritis and heart disease. He was buried the following Saturday afternoon in the little graveyard of Immanuel Church, a stone's throw from the Tucker House, where he joined several generations of Greens. His pallbearers included four local men and his New York doctor. Ned, still on business in Texas, did not attend his father's funeral. Hetty was escorted by Frank Green of Boston, one of Edward's cousins. There were many bouquets from well-wishers, but none was more striking than Hetty's; she had splurged on a large circle of laurel and Easter lilies. Among the other tributes was a pillow from Sylvia and Ned bearing the word "Father."

Considering how harsh, strenuous, and limited life could be in the nineteenth century, Green had lived better than most people from Bellows Falls. Town folk who died during the same part of 1902 as Edward included a seventy-one-year-old laborer who broke his spine in a fall and a seventy-five-year-old mason who keeled over from exhaustion while working; along with three children under sixteen and five babies who died at birth. And yet for all the ease and longevity he enjoyed, there was an undeniable melancholy of having lived his life in reverse, making his fortune early and then losing everything by agonizing degrees, until he barely seemed to exist.

At the time of his death, Edward had a little over $5,500 in cash. His estate consisted of a small family house and land in Mandell, Massachusetts, his father's hometown, valued at $1,500. Other small properties included those taken by foreclosure, most likely by Hetty, in Edward's name. There was a watch and chain and some rings, valued at $300; and, most poignantly, an oil painting of his mother, valued at $200. In the final tally, Edward Green, who had once boasted a fortune of $750,000, was worth $24,509.75.

The *New York Times* obituary ran under the headline:

HETTY GREEN'S HUSBAND DEAD

"Excepting for his distinction as the husband of the richest woman in the world, Edward Green was a figure of whom the public knew little," the obituary noted. "He had been an invalid for many years and lived in retirement at the Green home in Bellows Falls, Vt. Even there people knew little and saw less of him, as all business relating to the household was transacted by his wife."

In May, less than two months after Edward's death, Hetty, back to business in New York, walked into the Leonard Street Station of the New York Police Department, accompanied by a clerk from Chemical National Bank, and some of the ever-present cadre of reporters who followed her movements. She announced her desire for a permit to carry a pistol. She had long owned the revolver given to her as a gift by the Californian, but now she wanted to arm herself as she walked the streets.

"I am a rich woman and some people want to kill me," Hetty told the surprised desk sergeant, Isaac Frank.

When Sergeant Frank asked her if she believed that carrying the pistol would protect her, Hetty replied, "Certainly. And I want everyone to know I have one. Those who have any knowledge of me will not doubt my ability or courage to use it."

She added, "I can take care of myself under ordinary circumstances, but there have been so many murders of rich people that I feel I ought to be constantly on my guard."

Hetty then completed an application form. Sergeant Frank was skeptical of Hetty's need to bear arms; nonetheless, Hetty Green left the Leonard Street Station on May 8 the owner of pistol permit No. 13,854. The *Times,* which wrote of her application the next day, pointed out that it was rare in New York for a woman to be granted a permit to carry a revolver.

A *Times* reporter had followed her back to Chemical Bank, where she said, simply, "Yes, I have a revolver. And I know how to use one. I have often been threatened. People know I have money, and think I can be scared out of it. But I can't."

As the reporter took notes, Hetty spun out some of her more bizarre claims of threats against her life. She claimed to have been approached in New Bedford by a drunk who demanded $100,000 or would "send me out of town feet foremost as my father had been," and outside the Hotel St. George in

Brooklyn, by a man who later shot and killed a bank president. "If he had acted in the same way toward me I would have driven a hatpin through his brain," she said. To this she added perhaps her oddest claim to date: that Edward, six weeks dead, had been murdered. "I am satisfied that he was given an over-dose of mercury," she said. Just why someone would want to kill a dying eighty-one-year-old man with hardly any money under his own control, she didn't say, other than to suggest that "people wanted him out of the way."

Editorial pages took a dim view of Hetty's permit. The Brook-lyn Daily Eagle, which had always been among the kinder news-papers in its treatment of Hetty in the past, suggested on May 9 that her permit was symptomatic of an overgunned and slightly screwy city. "The unlawful carrying of pistols, which resulted yesterday in one murder and two suicides in this city, is winked at by the authorities," the Eagle stated. "If there is a form of penalty for carrying them, there is perfect freedom to buy and sell them, and any thug or burglar can arm himself as heavily as he pleases. Mrs. Hetty Green . . . has applied for and obtained permission to carry a revolver, with which to shoot lawyers who may become obstreperous in her presence, or to kill people who suspect her of carrying money and jewelry about the streets. The permit should not have been issued.

"Mrs. Green is well on in years. She is suspicious and hos-tile. Her attitude toward the world is that it is envious and re-sentful, and will try to take away the wealth she hoards so earnestly. It is the wrong attitude, of course, for the world re-gards her merely as a curiosity. But so thinking, she is liable to put a false construction on the words and actions of her fellow creatures, and the impulse to shoot may become ungovernable."

The editorial concluded: "This woman who believes that her father was killed and her daughter injured by lawyers, yet who constantly resorts to the law and so wearies the patience of courts that she must be regarded as a confirmed litigant, is not the kind of person who should be intrusted [sic] with firearms."

The *Times* took a similar, if somewhat more lighthearted tone, with an editorial ending: "The applicant did not set forth that she was an expert markswoman, although she left no doubt of her determination to use upon suitable occasions the weapon which she asked to be allowed to wear. It is rather to be hoped that the Sergeant, before he issued the permit, satisfied himself that the pistol would not go off."

Edward's death was followed in May 1903 by the death of George G. Williams, the courtly president of Chemical National Bank, one of the few men of finance whom Hetty liked and trusted, and who liked and understood *her*. He died of a heart disease at his home on West Fifty-eighth Street. He was seventy-seven. The death of Edward and Williams left her feeling increasingly isolated. Hetty had always feared that people were after her money or her life.

She had first vented the fears publicly during the Barling fight nearly a decade earlier. A *Times* reporter had followed her down Pine Street in December of 1894 and waited for her to finish doing business in a bank. He asked her plainly if the rumors were true, that she feared for her life.

"Yes, it is true," Hetty said.

"Have you ever been approached or threatened in the street?"

"Yes, many times," she said. "I am no enemy of the poor people—the people one ordinarily meets in the streets. They would never attack me. I could go everywhere unmolested, at all times, if it were not for the devices of people who have an interest in annoying me."

These people, she made no secret, were "the hostile executor and trustees of my father's estate."

She added, "The newspapers have printed no end of stuff about my going around with a little black bag with a million or two in cash and securities in it. I am convinced that those stories were set afloat by the people I refer to, in expectation that I should be attacked or murdered for my money."

With that, Hetty opened her fabled black bag.

"You may see for yourself that it contains nothing but letters, the accumulation of correspondence that I get in my business affairs during the day. I always attend to my own correspondence. As a matter of fact, I never carry more than a dollar or two about with me."

Now, these fears seemed more real to her than ever. Hetty began to suggest openly that her father had been murdered, and her aunt Sylvia as well, all by greedy manipulators after a piece of the family fortune. Her fears peaked when she visited New Bedford, home, as it was, to a high concentration of heirs-in-waiting. When Hetty visited on business she usually stayed at the home of Benjamin Irish, one of the few people she trusted. Irish had been a clerk at the old Isaac Howland Jr. and Company whaling firm. Sylvia had left Irish $15,000 in her will. After the deaths of her aunt and father, and the dissolution of the whaling company, Hetty kept Irish on as her business agent in town, looking after her real estate there. She trusted his honesty and integrity and, significantly, his home was one of the few places in town where she felt no fear in eating a meal. On one occasion in New Bedford, Hetty visited with a friend and distant relation, who subsequently asked her to stay for dinner. Hetty demurred, saying the Irishes were expecting her. She then described for her friend some of the fears and suspicions she had about eating at various homes of relatives around town.

"I'm one of those heirs," the friend said. "Hetty, you don't mean to insinuate I would poison you, do you?"

When Hetty tried to smooth her friend's ruffled feathers, the friend replied, "Humph. I'm going to get only a few hundred dollars out of that old will. If I was going to get thousands, I would consider a proposition to poison you."

---

# THIRTEEN

# IF MY DAUGHTER IS HAPPY

conomics is complex enough to fill a thousand fat textbooks and as simple as the law of supply and demand. Through the ages, whether the commodity was tulips in Holland, gold in California, or cash on Wall Street, speculation has made millionaires and paupers, created and destroyed fortunes in the blink of an eye. But the most secure fortunes have always belonged to those with the discipline and foresight to stay out of the fray, those who supply speculators with the tools of their glory or ruin.

Stock values soared during the first years of the twentieth century, as the United States transformed itself from an economy based on agriculture and thousands of small, mostly local manufacturers to one driven by a new creature—the Large Corporation. In 1901, J. P. Morgan paid Andrew Carnegie nearly $500 million for Carnegie Steel—the highest price ever paid for a company—laying the cornerstone for U.S. Steel. The purchase set off a wave of mergers and acquisitions as would-be Morgans bought up strings of mills and factories to form one national colossus after another, with names such as United States Spinning, International Weaving, and American Steel and Wire. Some of these corporations were based on sound financing. But in many cases the deal-makers simply financed their acquisitions by issuing huge amounts of watered stock—stock whose value on paper vastly exceeded the actual assets of the company.*

In their optimism, investors eagerly snapped up even the most heavily watered shares of major corporations, believing, as would Internet investors nine decades later, that values were destined to continue rising forever. With the exception of a brief downturn in 1903, the mania continued unabated until early 1907, when reality set in. It wasn't just individual investors who were caught unprepared when the bubble burst. Many banks and trust companies had been speculators themselves, and had made reckless loans secured only by still more shares of inflated stock. Stocks began to slide in March, but the real catalyst for disaster came several months later, on October 21, when word spread that the venerable Knickerbocker Trust Company, one of the city's largest, was in deep trouble. The next day, after a furious run, Knickerbocker shut its doors for good, leaving many of its seventeen thousand depositors searching in vain for their $35 million in deposits. Panic spread—within a week, six banks with combined deposits of $57 million were closed, and many more teetered precariously on the brink of failure. And the panic soon spread beyond New York, jeopardizing banks nationwide.

Hetty had avoided any temptation to join in the speculative fever. During the height of the boom, in November 1905, she told a *New York Times* reporter, "I buy when things are low and no one wants them. I keep them, just as I keep a considerable number of diamonds on hand, until they go up and people are

---

* The term "watered stock" came originally from a deception of a different sort—during the 1830s, cattle baron Daniel Drew kept his animals thirsty, then allowed them to gorge on water just before reaching the market scales. In the new economy, watered stock referred to radically overvalued shares.

anxious to buy. That is the general secret of business success." She added, "I never speculate. Such stocks as belong to me were purchased simply as an investment, never on a margin." Her words must have seemed hopelessly stodgy and archaic to speculators riding the crest of the wave. But by 1907 the wisdom of her investment methods was painfully clear.

When the bottom fell out, she expressed sympathy for hapless investors caught in the panic, telling a *Times* reporter during a trip to Boston that fall, "Can't you see that watered stock is in everything? It's ruinous . . . I mean the middle class. They've got a lot of this watered stock, and the water has been squeezed." While others watched their fortunes float way on rivers of all but worthless stock, Hetty had the comfort of real assets—the bricks and mortar of her buildings, secure bonds, and tens of millions of dollars in cash that she was prepared to lend to buyers who met her standards.

In mid-1907, with the crisis drying up city coffers, New York mayor George McClellan announced a freeze in the hiring of new police officers, a halt in new government construction projects, and a freeze on salaries for the street cleaning department. As she had done several times before, Hetty came to the rescue, writing a check for $1.1 million, drawn on her Chemical Bank account, in exchange for short-term revenue bonds, paying 5.5 percent. Her money helped keep the government running.

This crisis in particular showcased Hetty's ability to remain coolheaded while others panicked. Banks, which until recently had been passing out loans like party favors, now indulged their own deepest fears, often refusing loans even to sound, well-run companies needing cash for expansion. When they did lend, they accepted stock as collateral only at rates far below the stock's actual market prices. After all, the banks reasoned, in these uncertain times the stock could collapse, leaving them holding scads of worthless paper. Faced with a Hobson's choice of doing without needed loans or mortgaging themselves to the hilt to get them, many companies simply folded. Hetty remained one of the few sources consistently willing to lend money at or near the market value of the stock.

One such company was the Delaware, Lackawanna and Western Railroad, which hauled coal east and west from Pennsylvania and carried seagoing passengers from the Great Lakes at Buffalo to the mouth of the Atlantic at Hoboken. In addition to its choice routes, the DL&W was a forward-thinking railroad—among the first to power its locomotives with cleaner burning anthracite (as opposed to soft bituminous) coal, ensuring its passengers a relatively soot-free ride. Hetty no doubt considered these factors as she extended loans to the company during the panic. On October 19, 1909, two years after the crisis ended, the *New York Times* singled Hetty out for levelheadedness that had helped save the railroad. "So great was her confidence in the intrinsic worth of the stock that she was willing to take the chance of wide fluctuations occurring during the panic. That she was right about the stock has been shown since the panic, for Lackawanna since October, 1907, has advanced several hundred points."

J. P. Morgan, whose purchase of Carnegie Steel had helped touch off the wave of mergers, eventually played the lead role in bringing the panic of 1907 to a close. Shortly after the Knickerbocker closing, two of the city's largest trusts—the Trust Company of America and the Lincoln Trust Company—appeared on the verge of collapse. Morgan stepped in, organizing one of the most extraordinary meetings in the history of Wall Street. With his private library on East Thirty-sixth Street as headquarters, a furious, daylong series of negotiations ensued, drawing around thirty of the nation's leading bankers and industrialists. Calling themselves the Committee of Trust Companies, they hashed out a plan to rescue the two companies. Negotiations with the directors of the two trusts stretched on into the night. At midnight, a wagon from the Waldorf Hotel pulled up in front of Morgan's library, and six hotel workers carried in a catered supper and urns of coffee. George B. Cortelyou, President Theodore Roosevelt's treasury secretary, waited in a hotel nearby. Although Cortelyou did not participate directly in the meetings, the Treasury, at Morgan's request, had deposited some $35 million in national banks for the specific purpose of bailing the distressed trusts out.

Finally, at 3 A.M. on November 6, the Committee of Trust Companies announced a plan to save the trusts by assuming control of their stock. The bankers also decided to make millions of dollars available from the New York Clearing House (set up to clear checks drawn on the city's largest banks) specifically to bolster banks during the threat of a run. The meeting marked the first step toward what would become, six years later, the Federal Reserve banking system, providing a measure of stability for the banking industry. The gathering included a lone woman. The *Times* reported that a woman wearing a black veil entered Morgan's library at 6:30 P.M. and stayed for several hours. Although the woman was never positively identified, reporters were convinced that the woman was Hetty Green. Hetty was known to wear a black veil on the streets at times to give herself a measure of privacy. Perhaps Morgan and the other bankers invited Hetty to gauge her interest in the 6 percent bonds they planned to issue to establish the Clearing House fund. She would have been a logical buyer. At any rate, it is difficult to imagine any other woman of the time being called in by J. P. Morgan and his associates to discuss a national financial crisis.

As her financial power reached its zenith, so did the popular impression that Hetty was, despite her money, a desperately unhappy person. Her customary black dress, accented at times by the veil, gave her a witchlike appearance as she walked the streets of lower Manhattan. Some took to calling her the Witch of Wall Street. This notion of her unhappiness owed itself in part to the tenor of the times. How could a woman be happy whose thoughts were so dominated by business and finance? Her preoccupation with money must be covering for some huge gap in her domestic life. Certainly, nothing Hetty said supported the notion that she was unhappy. Virtually every public comment she made regarding her own life reinforced the idea of a woman living her life contentedly, according to a few simple rules. "I really have nothing to say," she told a *New York Times* reporter in November 1905, "further than to be thankful for my continued health and interest in general affairs. I know of but very few people who are busier than myself or who are better trained to combine business with pleasure." Asked if she planned to retire, Hetty responded, "Why should I give up work? I was never more capable of handling my affairs."

In the end, her principal crime seems to have been that the rules she chose to live by were her own rather than society's. One of the more cutting portraits came in January of 1908, when *Broadway* magazine published a particularly long and unflattering article describing Hetty as the "least happy woman in New York."

The article, by a writer named Mabel Potter Daggett, began: "If you have been a part of the hurrying throng that daily jostles down lower Broadway, you may have seen her. Such a lonely little figure! A withered leaf, it seems strangely tossed in the great financial current. Follow this little old woman in rusty black and see her enter the Chemical National Bank. She is not the scrubwoman. The scrubwoman has no clothes of such ancient date as hers, the alpaca gown that has weathered many seasons, the black woolen cape that has shaped itself to the shoulders as they have bowed through the last ten years, and the tousled bonnet with its little bunch of flowers that faded with the millinery of many summers past."

Daggett continued: "The shabby little old woman who has just passed from view is worth $60,000,000, even $100,000,000, some estimates say. She is Hetty Howland Robinson Green, greatest mistress of finance the world has ever seen. Seated atop of her huge yellow millions, a wrinkled old woman, the financial limelight of a continent plays about her as she directs the destinies of men and of corporations. There is power in the

pen stroke of her aged fingers, the thin old fingers that are busy,
busy all day long cutting coupons and signing checks. She has
more ready money at her command than any other one individual. Wall Street waits on her coffers. To the old-fashioned
mahogany desk comes a procession of bank presidents, hat in
hand, railroad magnates, bowing low, and rich directors humbly
making obeisance. Even the city of New York in need has
brought its plea to her, its richest citizeness."

Yet for all of her power, Daggett wrote, "Hetty Green is
really a bankrupt to-day, bankrupt in desire! With money to
buy all that the world has for sale, it holds nothing that she
would like. She has mortgages strewn in acres from Boston to
San Francisco. She owns railroads and steamboat lines, copper
mines in Michigan, gold mines in Nevada, iron mines in Mis-
souri, telegraph and telephone securities and government
bonds, and in her safe is locked a pint of diamonds and one of
the finest collections of pearls on earth. Yet the girl stenogra-
pher who takes her dictation probably has a lighter heart under
a new spring gown, the butcher from whom she buys chuck
steak at twelve cents a pound has a better Sunday dinner, and
her neighbors in a Hoboken flat, when they go on a Coney Island outing, brighten the monochrome of existence with more
of color than varies her drab days."

Although Hetty had lived her entire life as a repudiation of
what others thought or expected of her, she was not entirely
immune to their barbs. She may have had Daggett's description
of her as a "shabby little old woman" in mind when, in a re-
flective moment, she turned to her friend Annie Leary one day
and said, "Oh, Annie, am I really as awful as they say I am?" It
could be, too, that Leary's influence was rubbing off just a few
of Hetty's hard edges. Like Sylvia, Hetty was a periodic guest at
Annie's Fifth Avenue home, where she no doubt chided her
friend for her extravagant living. Hetty and Sylvia had visited
Leary in Newport in October of 1907, when Leary held a dinner in Hetty's honor, inviting twenty-six guests. Her friend

seemed determined that Hetty should enjoy her money more, live a little among the community of her peers.

Whatever her motivation, Hetty made news one spring day in 1908 by walking, not into another bank or brokerage house, but into an establishment altogether different: a beauty parlor. The salon she chose was on Fifth Avenue and was described by one newspaper as "a Mecca for dowagers with waning charms."

She stepped cautiously into the salon where, beyond the reception room, women surrendered themselves to treatments such as mud masks, steam baths, and facial massages with exotic, scented oils. As Hetty glanced cautiously about the room, the attendant looked with equal caution at the odd woman wearing a long, worn, black dress and unfashionable bonnet.

"What do you do here?" Hetty asked. The attendant, quickly assessing the woman's needs, offered a program of twenty-one sessions, stretched across several weeks.

Hetty said, "What do you charge?"

"Three hundred dollars," the attendant said.

Hetty may have reached for a chair for support as the calculations whirled in her head: Three hundred dollars . . . how many months' rent in Hoboken or Brooklyn? How many rides on the ferry? She considered for a moment. Then she lifted the skirt of her dress, reached into a pocket, and produced a wad of bills. She counted out six $50 bills and handed them to the surprised attendant.

"I'll pay for this now," she said.

Minutes later she was being whisked to a backroom, where she held her face before a steam bath as long as she could stand it, then sat still as thick layers of black mud were applied. The attendant advised her to relax her muscles and let all of her thoughts and cares drift away.

But there was another reason for Hetty's sudden awakening to personal refinement—Sylvia, at last, had a beau whom Hetty considered worthy of her daughter's hand in marriage. Hetty had been through a number of scares regarding Sylvia's suitors over the previous several years. A procession of Europeans with impressive-sounding titles had come looking for a union that would exchange lineage to this or that royal house for cold American cash.

In early April of 1900, Sylvia had been briefly linked with one Francesco Serrano y Dominguez, otherwise known as the duke de la Torre. The duke had traveled from his native Spain in order to study American military methods. Annie Leary introduced Sylvia to the duke, and within six weeks rumors were spreading around town about a romance between the two, with open speculation that Sylvia was on her way to becoming a duchess. "The Duke is tall and distinguished looking," the *Times* reported on its front page on March 19. "He speaks English badly." Despite his lineage, the duke was said to get by on an income of about $4,000 per year—hardly enough to support an ambitious young man in a style befitting his title. The newspaper reported that the duke was planning a trip to Mexico, during which he would stop off in Texas and pay his respects to Ned, in advance of a June wedding.

Both Sylvia and the duke discreetly declined to answer any questions about their reported romance. Hetty, clearly annoyed with the whole idea, did not decline to comment. "This is the first I ever heard of such a thing. It's just one of them lies they are always starting about me and my children," she told a reporter who knocked on her door in Hoboken.

A year later, in the spring of 1901, Sylvia was linked romantically with one Charles Francis Seymour, earl of Yarmouth, who, despite that fancy title, was hungry and unemployed and seeking his fortune as an actor when he arrived in the United States in June 1899. The earl, who went by the stage name Eric Hope, had parlayed his title into introductions at Newport to the Astors, the Vanderbilts, and other leading families—and it was at Newport that, again through Annie Leary, he met Sylvia.

The newspapers pegged the earl for a gold digger, and one day a particularly strident article appeared in the *New York Tele-*

*graph,* including the following line: "Speaking of Dukes and such things reminds one that the Earl of Yarmouth is in dire straits these days. The Earl is hard up." The article also intimated that any young American heiress in search of a title might pick up the earl at a bargain rate.

The earl sued for $25,000, claiming that the article "caused great damage in his profession and brought this plaintiff into public scandal and ridicule in his said profession." An unrepentant *Telegraph* responded that "it was generally understood in the United States of America that Earls and other English noblemen without means had been fortunate by reason of their titles in marrying rich American heiresses, and that by reason of the conduct of said Earl, it was the general belief that he was in search of an heiress." The defendants added that the earl "then was and still is shopworn and damaged in reputation."

Sylvia was subpoenaed by the defense, apparently to confirm the newspaper's allegations that the earl was aggressively seeking to marry an heiress. But she was never called to testify. The earl, whom a sympathetic jury awarded $2,500, publicly apologized for having indirectly involved Sylvia in the case. The earl later married an heiress in Pittsburgh, bestowing on her a royal title in exchange for a life of leisure, thanks to an industrial fortune.

Having thus been linked romantically to a duke and an earl, all that remained was for Sylvia to find herself a handsome prince. This came about three years after the earl had left the scene, in the person of Prince Don Giovanni del Drago, of Rome. Here's how the *Times* explained the prince's claim on the Italian throne: "The del Drago family is an ancient one of Rome. They are related collaterally to royalty, as the great-grandmother of Prince Giovanni was the daughter of Maria Christina, Queen of Spain, by her second husband, the Duc de Rianzares. Consequently Prince Giovanni is a cousin several times removed of the present King of Spain, whose great-grandmother was also Maria Christina, he descending from the

King, Prince Giovanni, from the Duc." But this romance proved to be just as short-lived as the others, and in 1909 the prince married American Josephine Schmid, the widow of a beer magnate, whose husband had left her some $10 million. At the time of the wedding, Josephine was fifty, the prince, twenty-seven.

In 1908, Sylvia was in her late thirties, at the time an age of confirmed spinsterhood. By then, even the newspapers had pretty much stopped speculating on possible matches for her, and potential suitors had drifted away. It was generally assumed that she would spend the rest of her life—and the millions she stood to inherit—alone. It was then that she met (again, through her angel, Annie Leary) a man so painfully proper, so mild, so inoffensively correct, that not even Hetty Green could object. His name was Matthew Astor Wilks. Wilks was a great-grandson of John Jacob Astor, who had made a fortune in the fur business. Matthew Astor Wilks was a relatively minor heir, and not one who showed any particular ambition or skill in business—he "has never done any very active work," a newspaper reported. But he had enough of a fortune (about $2 million) that he could not rightly be suspected of gold-digging. When not at the family compound in Galt, Ontario, Wilks lived in fashionable comfort at 440 Madison Avenue and was a member of most of the best clubs, including the Knickerbocker, Metropolitan, Turf and Field, Fencers, Badminton, and the New York Yacht Club. He spent much of his time at Edward Green's old haunt, the Union Club. Moreover, he was fifty-seven years old—two decades Sylvia's senior, so it was highly unlikely that one of Hetty's worst fears would be realized—that one of her children would marry, and die before the spouse, sending all those millions of hard-earned dollars into the greedy arms of another family. If the odds played out, Sylvia would outlive her intended by years.

Hetty did put up a bit of a fight when word of the romance began to leak. She claimed to know nothing about it. But by the spring of 1908 she was clearly growing resigned to the fact that her only daughter would soon be wed. Perhaps at Sylvia's insistence, in early May Hetty surprised everyone by abandoning her Hoboken apartment and taking up residence across the river in a spacious second-floor suite at the Plaza Hotel, overlooking Central Park. Perhaps Sylvia and Annie Leary, working in tandem, convinced Hetty that Hoboken was no way for the mother of a millionaire bride-to-be to live. In May, Hetty even hosted an elegant dinner for twenty in honor of Sylvia and Wilks at the Plaza. The ten-course meal, with wine, was served in a special suite known as the "state apartment"—a large drawing room, a dining room decorated in green and gold, flanked by a series of dressing rooms. When Hetty stood with Sylvia to receive their guests, she wore, not her customary frumpy black dress, but a black satin gown trimmed with old point lace. Sylvia wore a gray dress that set off a string of pearls. The party was widely seen as confirming the engagement between Sylvia and Wilks, although no announcement was made. Guests took home their embossed place cards as souvenirs of one of society's rarest events—a party thrown by Hetty Green.

Guests, hotel staff, and curious reporters were as stunned by Hetty's appearance as they were by the fact that she was splurging on a party. By June, though, she abruptly checked out of the Plaza, tiring, perhaps, of the expense or of the attention that her comings and goings always drew. She and Sylvia moved into a modest but decent two-room apartment in a boardinghouse on Madison Avenue. They would stay just a month or so, before joining Annie Leary in Newport, and then heading on to Bellows Falls for a summer visit.

In August, Hetty returned to Hoboken, taking another apartment in the same building at 1309 Bloomfield Street where she had lived before. Rumors of the impending marriage between Sylvia and Wilks grew and swirled through the fall. Hetty, Sylvia, and Wilks continued to guard the plans like a state secret, but their reticence only fueled the speculation. In early

February, Katherine L. Wilks, Wilks's sister in Ontario, sent an announcement to family friends:

Mrs. Hetty Green, New York, announced the engagement of her only daughter, Miss Sylvia, to Mr. Matthew Astor Wilks of New York, eldest son of the late Matthew Wilks of Cruickston Park, Galt, Ontario.

But Hetty herself made no public announcement to her own acquaintances, and when this one inevitably made the society columns, Hetty's only response was to vigorously deny it and to question where the Wilks family was getting its information. Reporters camped outside her building at all hours, determined not to be scooped. At one point, the city posted a police officer in front of the building to keep reporters at bay. Rumors flew regarding the date and location of the wedding, and whether, perhaps, the couple had already been married, in secret. These rumors were in part fostered by Hetty herself, who, for all of her stated dislike for reporters, seemed to enjoy the cat and mouse game, and brought her customary wit and ingenuity to it.

Hetty knew that reporters were plumbing her neighbors in the building for information, and that neighbors were natural gossips and could not resist spreading information, especially if reporters were offering cash for tips. The building's dumbwaiter was a natural conduit; the women of the building would exchange gossip with those on other floors. Hetty, aware of this, began holding informal daily briefings near the dumbwaiter, to be sure that her messages were spread around.

"Mind you, although I say I'd like to kill all reporters, I wouldn't murder them. But, oh! I would like to pull their hair a little bit now and then." That comment duly made the papers, as did her answer when a neighbor asked when the wedding might occur.

"When? Now, I will tell you a secret, and you mustn't

breathe it to a soul," Hetty said. "Just to spite some people, Sylvie and Mr. Wilks and I went over to Morristown last Wednesday and—exactly! It was our own business and nobody else's. My, but Sylvie looked fine in her new gown, but she caught a dreadful cold wearing it."

The *New York Times* reported on page one the following day, under the headline "Wilks Already Wed to Silvia [sic] Green?":

> According to neighbors of Mrs. Hetty Green, reputed to be the richest woman in the world, who lives at a flat at 1309 Bloomfield Street, Hoboken, Mrs. Green confided to them yesterday that she had outwitted the newspapers in concealing from them the fact that her daughter, Miss Silvia [sic] Green, had already married Matthew Astor Wilks, great-grandson of the original John Jacob Astor.
>
> The ceremony, according to the statement attributed to Mrs. Green, took place in Morristown, N.J. last Wednesday. Mrs. Green said her daughter wore a wedding dress upon which they had been at work for several weeks, and had caught cold as a result. Mrs. Green also described the cake of which the wedding party partook after the ceremony. Efforts to confirm this yesterday were unsuccessful owing to Mr. Wilks's reported absence from town and Mrs. Green's reticence.

The newspapers sheepishly recanted their stories a couple of days later when they re-reported Sylvia's wedding, this time for real. The scene was, in fact, Morristown, New Jersey, where Hetty and Sylvia had occupied a boardinghouse during one of their frequent moves. To keep the actual date as secret as possible, they had sent no formal invitations. Just before nine o'clock on the morning of February 23, a cab pulled up in front of the building. Hetty and Sylvia emerged and dashed for the cab without a word. Reporters and other curious onlookers scrambled to follow the cab on the short ride to the railroad station, where at precisely 9:20 a special reserved car took them and other members of the wedding party on a short trip to Morristown. Sylvia and Wilks were married at noon at St. Peter's Protestant Episcopal Church. The simple ceremony, performed by the Reverend Philemon F. Sturges, included no bridesmaids. Curiously, Ned does not appear in the newspaper accounts. Perhaps Hetty had told him to stay away, in order to put off speculation. The wedding party was small, not quite filling the front pews of the church. If anything, they were outnumbered by the reporters and curious onlookers who filled the back pews.

During the ceremony, Hetty sat in the front pew, near the center, wearing a black silk gown with white point lace. Sylvia did not wear a traditional white wedding gown. Instead, she wore a rather plain brown dress, festooned with a white feather boa wrapped around her neck, and a hat with a sheer black lace veil, and a white flower and feathers on top.

After the ceremony, there was a reception at the Morristown Inn.

"Mrs. Green, despite the many stories to the effect that she did not altogether approve of the match, seemed in excellent spirits," the *Times* reported on February 24. "Even though she would not make any statement about the marriage, she did not seem to object when newspaper photographers shot the wedding party in front of the hotel. She stood in the front line with Mr. and Mrs. Matthew Astor Wilks."

A formal picture from the wedding survives. It appears to have been taken outdoors, perhaps on the porch of the inn. Except for the bridal bouquet gripped in Sylvia's white-gloved left hand, it might have been taken at any function. Little about the clothing bespeaks the nuptials that have just taken place; but more, the camera betrays almost no trace of emotion, of joy, at the occasion. Hetty, to the left of the camera, sits straight-backed and fully upright, her hands by her side, her head thrown back and chin raised, a stony expression on her face. Wilks stands in the background, wearing his formal dark coat, a hand on the back of either chair, his distinguished-looking

face framed by a bald dome on top and bushy mustache hanging over his unsmiling mouth, and the only pictorial evidence
that he is the groom rather than the father of the bride is the
slight tilt of his head toward Sylvia. Sylvia is the only one who
betrays any emotion, but barely; there is a ghost of a smile on
her face. Under the veil and her spectacles one sees, not a full
smile, but something in the eyes that indicates a sort of happiness. The picture seems a symbolic as well as actual portrait of
this odd family—Hetty, proud, stoic, strong; Sylvia, wan, with
some emotion struggling to escape, an expression not of outright joy on her wedding day, but of contentment.

For Sylvia, the transformation from Miss Green to Mrs.
Wilks would mean an end to the cheap flats of Hoboken and
Brooklyn, listening to her mother's carpings on the foolish expenditures of others, an end to day coaches, pinching nickels,
suffering through her mother's hagglings, and empty hours at
the Chemical National Bank. She had missed several stages of
marriage—the happy optimism of newlyweds, when the whole
world is bright and full of promise; the chaos of children; and
the solidification of a marriage from a giddy romance into a
partnership. Instead, Sylvia and Wilks entered into matrimony
by going straight into the comfortable if slightly dowdy stage of
marriage, where long silences are tolerated without worry, a
time when retiring comfort displaces romantic expectations. For
Sylvia, still two years shy of forty, the marriage to the fifty-
seven-year-old Wilks would always be middle-aged. There was
no question of children.

When asked on her daughter's wedding day whether the
marriage made her happy, Hetty replied: "I am happy if my
daughter is happy." Only on Hetty's death seven years later
would a final piece of the puzzle regarding this marriage be put
in place. The revelation came through her will, which bestowed
$5,000 on Wilks for having agreed to sign a prenuptial agree-
ment disavowing any claim on the fortune.

---

# FOURTEEN

# THE HAT WAS "HETTY" GREEN

Hetty never minded being alone. In a way she had lived her entire life courting solitude. Independence was her pride and her strength. She had distanced herself from New Bedford, from Fifth Avenue, and for many years from her own husband. But that had been her choice. Now, in her mid-seventies, she found that she was not simply alone, but lonely. By 1908, Edward had been dead for eight years and Ned had been living in Texas for fifteen. Now Sylvia, her constant companion, had moved across the river to Manhattan and a life of quiet comfort with her new husband.

Mr. and Mrs. Matthew Astor Wilks lived at 440 Madison Avenue, his home, and spent their summers in Newport, Saratoga, or Bar Harbor. Their names appeared frequently in society columns; generally in lengthy roundups of the seasonal comings and goings of the rich. Hetty, long accustomed to the dominant hand in her relationship with Sylvia, now missed her company more than she would have guessed. In the months following the wedding, Hetty took rooms at the Plaza and the

St. Regis Hotels, prompting speculation in the newspapers that she planned to move to Manhattan to be close to Sylvia. But each time, after a brief stay, she returned restlessly to Hoboken and her modest flat. In 1910, she suffered another loss with the death of her Skye terrier, Dewey. Dewey had been her companion for years—it was one of the few relationships in her life in which love could be freely given and accepted without the looming specter of money. The loss of this companion sent her into a tailspin of sadness that lasted for weeks.

At about the same time, Hetty began to acknowledge that she was growing old. All of her life she had considered herself physically indestructible, and her remarkable constitution generally supported this conceit. She attributed her ability to function into her seventies with the energy and sharpness of someone half her age to her prudent habits—moderation, frugality, and self-denial. Illness and health to Hetty had always carried a moral component—people who were sick were probably overindulging their desires, becoming soft, or else spending money they did not have and driving themselves to an early grave over worry. But maintaining her customary work pace was getting to be more and more of a challenge. In the spring of 1910, she turned to her son, asking him to tie up his affairs in Texas and come back to New York to help her with the business.

In Texas, Ned had become a big man in his own right. He had started with huge advantages, of course—but he had prospered, with imagination and style. A couple of thousand miles away from Hetty's watchful eyes, Ned had developed into one of the most colorful characters in a state that never lacked for colorful characters. In fifteen years, his influence and persona had spread far beyond the relatively minuscule strip of track that constituted the Texas Midland, far beyond the town boundaries of tiny Terrell, or even Dallas. He was famous in

Texas, not simply as Hetty Green's son, but as Ned Green. He was a civic booster, political wheeler-dealer, playboy, business-man, and world-class sportsman. If he could never escape en-tirely from the shadow of his mother, Texas was the one place he could come closest.

In politics, he had thrown himself into the state's Republican Party. In Texas as across most of the South, Republicans were vastly outnumbered by Democrats and were still widely re-sented as the party of Lincoln. Much of the white population viewed Republicans with a combination of disdain and suspi-cion, as the party of Yankees and blacks. It was the only party open to African Americans, who formed a large faction known as the Black and Tans. In opposition to them stood an all-white faction known as the Lily Whites, and power struggles within the Republican Party could be raucous. But the very underdog nature of the Republican Party created a perfect opportunity for an ambitious, affable young man with money to rise quickly within its ranks. He could circumvent the years of dues-paying and back-scratching that might be required to make his mark as a Democrat.

Ned aligned himself with the Black and Tan faction. In 1896, at twenty-eight, having been in Texas just three years, Ned was named state chairman of the Republican Party. Despite the party's poor reputation in Texas, the position gave him a chance to flex his muscles nationally at political conventions, at which he arrived in style aboard his private railroad car. With a Re-publican, William McKinley, in the White House, the associa-tion with Republicans gave him the opportunity to rub shoulders with national forces in politics. "Texans at the Wal-dorf-Astoria say there is no more popular man in the Lone Star State than Edward H.R. Green, son of Mrs. Hetty Green, who is accounted the richest woman in America," the *New York Times* reported on August 29, 1899, during a national Republican gath-ering at the New York hotel. "Mr. Green, who is one of the

Texas contingent at the Waldorf, is reported to have high political ambitions, and people from that state say he is spending money liberally in the hope of reaching the United States Senate via the gubernatorial chair."

To help grease the skids of his political ambitions, Ned built a lavish and exclusive fishing club on the Gulf Coast, known as the Tarpon Club, around 1898. The club was situated on a flat, sandy island a few miles from Corpus Christi, one of a string of islands that forms a natural bank with one side facing open sea and the other forming a narrow, shallow inland waterway. A grand clubhouse rose off the flat sand on pilings and, at night, was a beacon that boaters could see for miles around. The house sat high enough that windblown sand would whip under the house rather than into the faces of members enjoying cocktails on the verandah after a day of hunting or fishing.

Guests shot ducks in the winter, and fished for tarpon, channel bass, jackfish, alligator gars, and kingfish year-round. If they didn't feel energetic enough to venture out for their sport, members might simply sit on the verandah of the spacious clubhouse and pick off crabs with a .22 rifle. The large common rooms were decorated with a 175-pound trophy tarpon and other game fish, ducks, and game birds. The club was an immediate success, counting among its three hundred members President McKinley, ex-president Grover Cleveland, a host of senators and other politicians, and millionaires from as far away as New York, St. Louis, and Ohio.

Ned served on the board of directors of the Texas World's Fair Commission in 1903, assigned with devising the state's entries for the St. Louis fair. Ned and another commissioner abruptly resigned in protest when the commission decided on a star-shaped building for the Texas pavilion, which Ned considered tacky and playing to the stereotype that outsiders held of Texans. Ned said he could not be part of "a building that portrays Texas as a freak," according to an article in the *Times* April

13. He added, "I want a building that will impress those who see it with the idea that Texas has dignity. This state has outgrown its shooting and cutting and sombreros and high-heeled boots. Caricaturists have hurt us by their exaggerated picturings. Stars belong in the heavens, to be looked up to, not on the ground, to be walked around in order to see what they are. It is a waste of money to erect such a building."

In 1899, Ned had made what is widely considered to be the first car trip in Texas—a rugged trip across dusty horse trails from Dallas to Terrell. By 1905, he was an enthusiastic promoter, financier, and participant in the rapidly growing sport of auto racing. He had poured thousands of dollars into racing cars and was widely regarded as the most avid racer in Texas. On a cold, raw day in early 1905, three thousand spectators turned out, despite the weather, to watch five cars battling in the first 100-mile automobile race in history. Green was not just an organizer of the event—he was one of the five drivers. Using his one good leg to operate the pedals, he held a lead through much of the race. At the seventieth mile, with Green and competitor A. B. Wharton running neck and neck, a bolt on Wharton's car broke and Ned cruised to victory. Two weeks later, the American Automobile Association recognized Ned's time of 2 hours, 6 minutes as a new record for 100 miles. Crowds flocked to him at a car show at Madison Square Garden in New York that same month. He had attended the show in part to meet with a manufacturer to make a custom racer he hoped would be among the lightest and fastest in the world. "I want a racing car that will weigh within 1,400 pounds," he told reporters. "What horse power? Well, that is immaterial to me. If the car is built for me I shall only stipulate that it be made to go fast, the faster the better, and I will leave the horse power entirely to the manufacturers."

Ned's crowning honor came when Governor O. B. Colquitt bestowed on him the honorary title of colonel. Ned wore the title proudly for the rest of his life. Colquitt was a Democrat, but he was a Terrell native and he and Ned had become good friends. At Colquitt's inauguration, Ned proudly appeared in a uniform adorned with gold braid. Wherever he traveled, people called him Colonel Green or, simply, "The Colonel."

And, finally, there was the rather sticky situation of Ned's live-in "housekeeper," Mabel Harlow. Mabel's true role in Ned's household was an open secret that Ned's friends and associates accepted with equanimity because of his overall affability and his generosity to the state and its citizens. Hetty had long known about Mabel, but as long as Ned remained in Texas he and his mother could quietly avoid the subject. For Ned, returning to New York meant the added headache of trying to keep Hetty and Mabel separated. He would not risk his mother's wrath by marrying Mabel, but neither could he break with Mabel and end a relationship that had mellowed with the approach of middle age from one of purely sexual attraction (on Ned's part, at least) to one based on mutual affection and need.

Nevertheless, at forty-two, Ned was nothing if not a dutiful son; when Hetty called, he and Mabel packed up and headed to New York. In July of 1910, Ned arrived aboard his private railcar and settled into a deluxe suite at the Waldorf designed especially for him, with living quarters and office. As workmen put the finishing touches on the suite in the stuffy summer heat, Ned stood in his shirtsleeves under an electric fan, talking to reporters. When they asked about his mother, Ned was characteristically kind, the *Times* reported. The decision to come to New York had been a natural one, he said. "I just dropped everything in Texas when mother wrote for me to come and relieve her of some of her financial cares," Ned said. "Of course, I can't look after all of her interests, they are so immense, but I can do my part in looking after some of the details."

"My mother has improved wonderfully in the past few

months," Ned added. "After we have had several long talks she will go to Bellows Falls, Vermont, for a well-earned rest. I am very proud of my mother. She is one woman in ten thousand, although she will insist on working despite her years. I am big enough to do her share and mine, too."

Having Hetty in Vermont would keep Mabel out of his mother's field of vision. It would also absorb the shock of being back within shouting distance of his mother after so many years of relative autonomy. But as Ned acknowledged in his comment, it was wishful thinking to assume that Hetty would ease into some sort of sunny retirement of rocking in a chair and knitting doilies in Bellows Falls.

Hetty, in fact, continued her daily ferry ride across the Hudson to Wall Street, but gradually, with Ned's gentle insistence, she began to slow down. In 1911, Ned and Hetty began discussing forming a trust company to handle her affairs. Ned would oversee the trust, which would relieve Hetty of much of the overwhelming burden of keeping tabs on all of her vast and far-flung empire. They called the trust the Westminster Company, after the Vermont county where Bellows Falls lies.

Among Ned's first acts as managing director of the Westminster Company was to help Hetty shed some of her vast real estate holdings, either through outright sale or by ninety-nine-year lease. In particular, Hetty began unloading her substantial Chicago properties. By now, she owned some ninety separate pieces of property in the city, worth at least $6 million. The lots, scattered around the city, were increasingly difficult for Hetty to keep track of. Most of the lots remained largely undeveloped, because of Hetty's long-standing policy of keeping the taxes low while allowing the property values to rise. By the early twentieth century, Chicago was on its way to becoming one of the world's great cities, and was bursting at the seams. Property Hetty held that had been quasi-rural scrubland was now close to the downtown and developers and residents clamored for the space. Her tactics had endeared her to few people—save for the farmers who tilled her vacant lots—but her policy held true to her financial convictions.

Among the first major sales was the 480-acre tract southwest of the city in Gage Park. Ned negotiated a sale price of nearly a million dollars for the land. Cobe and McKinnon, the buyers, immediately announced plans to develop the area as houses, apartments, and businesses to meet the city's swelling needs.

Then, Ned found a buyer for an 11-acre lot in the northern lakeside suburb of Winnetka, for $80,000. Over the next several years Hetty, through Ned, disposed of numerous properties through sale or ninety-nine-year lease. Developers, including her Chicago real estate agent, R. F. Lowenstein, snapped up the long-dormant property. In July of 1912 she sold the six apartment buildings on Sibley Street for $140,000.

Among her downtown holdings, worth a total of around $3.5 million, the Howland Block at the southwest corner of Dearborn and Monroe was particularly valuable. The lone structure on the property was a dated, five-story building, but for years, developers had been pursuing Hetty, through her Chicago agents, to sell or lease the land for development. Acquired through foreclosure some thirty years earlier, the lot remained untouched, rising in value to $1,625,000 by 1911, according to the Chicago Board of Review. A developer leased the property from Hetty long-term at $65,000 per year. In short order she sold or leased numbers 183 through 187 Wabash Avenue, valued at $325,000; the plot on Wabash, near Harrison Street, worth around $200,000; the lot with 80 feet of frontage on Michigan Avenue, worth an estimated $1 million; and the houses at 211 and 213 Monroe Street, worth $157,000.

The headquarters of the Westminster Company consisted of three offices on the sixth floor of the Trinity Building at 111 Broadway in Manhattan. Administrators of the estate of millionaire Russell Sage operated in a suite in the same building. Sage, who died in 1906, had been a friend of Hetty's. Hetty still put in full days. She occupied a Spartan office furnished with an old roll-top oak desk and three chairs. Often her days consisted of sitting next to enormous piles of coupons for bonds coming due. Patiently, steadfastly she worked her way through mound after mound of coupons, cutting with a pair of large shears. She kept a grindstone nearby for sharpening the shears when they became dulled by the ceaseless tide of her wealth. Ned appeared regularly at the offices, as did Walter Marshall, his personal secretary from Texas, whom he had brought to New York. Keeping track of daily office operations was a small, wiry man named Wilbur Potter, who dutifully and quietly supervised a small staff of clerks.

Hetty still appeared at the offices early in the morning and stayed until evening. Her millions in cash and her willingness to lend made her a sort of one-woman Federal Reserve, whose decisions on interest rates were followed the way investors today await word from Fed chairman Alan Greenspan. "Hetty Green Cuts Rates," the *Times* reported on January 7, 1911, when she made a loan of $325,000 at 4.5 percent to the Roman Catholic Church of St. Ignatius Loyola on Park Avenue, between East Eighty-third and Eighty-fourth Streets. "This is the lowest rate of interest at which a real estate mortgage has been made in this city for many months," the article stated.

In fact, Hetty often lent money to more than thirty churches at rates well below the going market. These churches benefited from the low rates, but Hetty would not give them a free ride. Several years earlier, in 1903, the Fifth Presbyterian Church of Chicago defaulted on a $12,000 loan. The pastor made the mistake of trying to shame Hetty into forgiving the loan. He arranged for pastors at other Chicago churches to denounce Hetty from their pulpits as a ruthless financier, and wrote to Hetty threatening that she would not get into Heaven if she foreclosed. Hetty wrote back: "As long as you're in a threatening mood, you had better climb up on your cornerstone and pray for my soul because I am going to foreclose." A number of pastors leapt to Hetty's defense. The Reverend M. P. Boynton, of Lexington Avenue Baptist Church in Chicago, told reporters, "To expect the holder of a church mortgage to cancel it upon the grounds of Christianity, after the money has been lent in good faith, is nothing less than a hold-up." The *New York Times* agreed on its editorial page of February 29, 1903: "If churches . . . see fit to borrow money in the regular way from persons who make a business of lending it, there is no imaginable reason why they should not pay their debts." Within a year the site of the Fifth Presbyterian was being occupied by the Trinity Methodist Episcopal Church.

Lending money to churches at a low rate of interest is not the same thing as an outright gift, of course. If she did give portions of her vast wealth away, she did so anonymously. "One way is to give money and make a big show. That is not my way of doing," she told her friend, C. W. deLyon Nicholls, in a *Business America* magazine profile in May 1913. "I am of the Quaker belief, and although the Quakers are about all dead, I still follow their example. An ordinary gift to be bragged about is not a gift in the eyes of the Lord."

There was another reason, of course, for keeping any acts of generosity a secret—if word got out, she would be besieged by requests for more. She was not alone in this fear. A *New York Times* article on anonymous philanthropy in November 1913 stated: "Often the donors are controlled not by modesty but by a desire for self-protection against the thousands of letters that follow widely heralded public giving. The same article identified Hetty as the likely anonymous donor of $5,000 for relief efforts for victims of major floods in Dayton, Ohio, the previous spring. "In this connection the question has been raised if Mrs. Hetty Green is not accustomed to give generously in secret."

Breaking her own rule of talking about one's gifts, Hetty told Nicholls: "I have done one deed of which I am proud. I have helped a school for boys to the extent of between three or four hundred thousand dollars." Hetty told Nicholls the unnamed school was in New York State, and that she had bought the land during the panic of 1907, at a steep discount. "The buildings were put up at a time when the poor urgently needed employment."

When confronted with reports of charitable acts, she was quick to deny them. In 1904, rumors surfaced that Hetty had given $500,000 to the Nurses' Home in New York City, and another $50,000 for a nurses' settlement home. When reporters arrived at the Chemical National Bank seeking comment, she sent a terse written reply out to them: "It's a chimera; it's absurd; there is not a scintilla of truth in it; it's all a dream." When Annie Leary announced plans to build an art school on Fifth Avenue, opposite Central Park, newspapers reported that Hetty would donate $500,000 to pay for the site. Neither Hetty nor Annie ever confirmed the reports.

In 1911, Nicholls organized a contest among society ladies to trim Easter hats to be given to poor girls. The women gathered at the Madison Avenue home of a wealthy woman named Mrs. George Kemp, a friend of Hetty's. Hetty was not only a sponsor, she helped judge the entries. Among her favorites was a wide-brimmed hat with a spray of flowers and a large green bow—a color that the contest participants christened as "Hetty green."

In the annals of philanthropy, a hat-trimming contest is a minor event, to be sure. But Hetty's participation made it news. Just as everything she did made news. By now, she was so familiar to Americans that she was becoming a popular icon. She seemed to be everywhere. Her name cropped up in popular songs, one of them, written in 1905 by Sidney S. Toler, titled "If I Were As Rich As Hetty Green" (*Each day I'd give the poor a thousand dollars / A diamond ring to every little queen— / O you bet your life that I would go to the limit / If I were just as rich as Hetty Green*). Another song, "At the Million Dollar Tango Ball," written in 1914 by

James White, included the lines: *Given by the millionaires at Wall Street Hall / John D. Rockefeller sold the tickets by the score / Andrew Carnegie was taking tickets at the door / Hetty Green was Dancing Mistress of the floor / Vanderbilt was playing every rag encore.*

In 1912, a trotter named Hetty Green finished sixth in a field of seven at the Detroit's Grand Circuit horse races. That same year, a wealthy slumlord in New York, Mrs. Pasquale Spinelli, was murdered. She had been known as "the Hetty Green of Little Italy." At the Thirty-ninth Street Theater in Manhattan in 1914, in a play called *Too Many Cooks*, a character named Albert Bennett told his fiancée that he loved her and not another character named Minnie, with these words: "If Minnie was as beautiful as Lillian Russell and as rich as Hetty Green . . . I'd laugh in her face." A few months later, the *New York Sun* reported (erroneously, as it turned out) that Hetty planned to buy the Chicago Cubs.

To the public, Hetty was ageless and timeless—people could not remember a time when Hetty could not be seen bustling along the streets of lower Manhattan. It seemed as if she might live forever. And she was determined to give that impression, working long days and weekends, ever minding her fortune. But she was beginning to contemplate her death, and in a quiet way to make preparations. In 1911, she made up her will, a straightforward document passing everything along to her children. A year later, she made another arrangement. One Saturday in July of 1912, Hetty spent the morning, as was her custom, in the offices of the Westminster Company. She worked until a man, the Reverend Augustine Elmendorf, arrived at the building. Ned was there, too. The three of them got into Ned's chauffeur-driven car, and Ned ordered the driver to take them across the river to Jersey City, where the Reverend Elmendorf was rector. Jersey City was the next town over from Hoboken. When the car arrived at the church, located at the corner of Arlington and Claremont Avenues, the little party entered the rectory. The occasion had been kept a strict secret, to keep the ever-curious reporters away.

Here, in the rectory, with only her son as witness, Hetty was baptized in the Episcopal church. She had not, however, undergone a conversion of faith or become suddenly devout. Her reasons were more practical, and perhaps more touching. The little burial ground in Bellows Falls where her husband lay interred only Episcopalians—and that is where she preferred to be buried, next to Edward, when the time came.

# FIFTEEN

# I'LL OUTLIVE ALL OF THEM!

Among the many properties Hetty had acquired through foreclosure in New York, the old loft building at 74 Broad Street, just off Wall Street, was perhaps the most homely and unprepossessing. It stood empty of tenants, except for a lunchroom on the ground floor, which Hetty leased because the rent covered her taxes on the building. The building was old and cobwebbed, with shaky wooden stairways leading to floor upon floor of dustbound, grime-streaked gloom. The dirty windows, nailed shut to discourage intruders, allowed only miserly streaks of light that did little to illuminate the interior. And yet this old building was perhaps Hetty's most valuable possession, for personal if not proprietary reasons. Tucked away on the sixth floor of 74 Broad Street was a trove of treasures so guarded that Hetty was willing to keep the entire building vacant for years so as to discourage the curious. She examined the contents of this repository several times a year, in the company of Walter Marshall, Ned's private secretary.

There was something ceremonial about the process, with

Marshall following Hetty through Wall Street and Curb Market staying twenty feet behind, on her instructions, so as to avoid attracting attention. Upon reaching 74 Broad Street, Marshall would light a borrowed lantern to guide their way up the dim staircase. On the sixth floor, Hetty pulled out the load of keys from her black reticule and stopped in front of a large room whose door was secured with a padlock. Before opening the lock, Hetty always knelt and ran her finger under the double door. She had secured a black thread running from a nail in the door to another nail in the floor.

"This is my safeguard—this black thread," she told Marshall. "If anybody else ever goes in here, I'll know it because the thread will be broken." Satisfied that her treasures had not been tampered with, she unlocked the door.

"When we finally got into the room beyond that door, grotesque shadows arose above a great clutter of objects stored there," Marshall later recalled. "A gray film of dust covered everything. I saw an ancient sleigh with a buffalo robe in it, office and household furniture in various stages of decreptitude, a dressmaker's dummy, a grandfather's clock with no hands, a tall beveled mirror with a crack across the top, several trunks and many heavy wooden boxes, a bunch of leather-bound account books, a lot of framed pictures, and a ship's figurehead—a painted mermaid. When I brushed the dust off that with a piece of newspaper the colors appeared faded."

This inner sanctum was even more airless than the close and airless building around it. Marshall felt faint. Hetty, dressed in layers of black garments, with rubbers on her feet, did not appear to notice the heat. She chewed a raw onion and advised Marshall to take small breaths if the heat disturbed him.

"This sleigh was my father's," Hetty said. "I used to ride with him behind a black horse that beat anything on hoofs in New Bedford. Black Hawk Robinson's daughter was the envy of all the other girls in town." Inside the sleigh was the buffalo robe under which she'd sat, snug on winter rides. On one visit, when she picked up a corner of the robe it began to deteriorate in her hand. Tears filled her eyes.

Other boxes opened other memories. There were dresses she had worn as a young woman, including the white gown with the pink sash that she had worn to dance with the Prince of Wales.

"She might have been a magician pulling surprises from a hat as she showed me various mementoes dating back across the long stretch of her life. There were silken shawls and wall-hangings which some sea captain had brought her from China; pieces of jewelry, some in fantastic design; specimens of fine old glassware, shoes and slippers, dance programs, opera tickets, an ocarina that her father had played, baby shoes that Sylvia and Ned had worn, photographs of Hetty as a young woman."

Hetty observed wistfully, "People said I was good looking then," and the words lingered for a while and died in the hot thick air.

But for each of the pleasant memories of balls and parties and sleigh rides, there were sterner memories that reminded Hetty of her life's great struggles. Rummaging through one chest she came across a pile of newspaper clippings she had saved about Collis P. Huntington. "That old Hyena thought I'd die before him," she said. "But he's long in his grave." Then she named other financiers, part of the endless gallery of enemies. She signaled to Marshall it was time to leave. She bent down and refastened the black thread that was her bulwark against prying eyes. She got up and shook her fist in the gloom.

"They'll never murder me! I'll outlive all of them!"

As she entered her eighties, Hetty began conducting much of her business from a four-story brick house at 7 West Ninetieth Street, near Central Park. Ned was living next door, at 5 West Ninetieth. Both homes had been owned by Hetty's father, and left to her as part of the estate. She visited Ned, Sylvia, and Annie Leary frequently at their respective New York homes, but she refused to move to the city herself. On May 10, 1915, the *Jersey Journal* reported that Hetty was living in Hoboken as a guest of Jacob Van Twisk and his family. Van Twisk was the janitor of the Yellow Flats Building, and lived nine blocks south of the building. "The noted woman financier is positively incognito," the article stated. Even so, Hetty couldn't help but be recognized, the reporter added. A young girl approached her and asked, somewhat impertinently, how to become rich. Hetty looked at the girl's fancy dress and replied, "The first thing, don't spend so much money on your clothes."

She returned to New York for her eighty-first birthday, in November, which she spent quietly with Ned and Sylvia. On November 22, 1915, the *New York Sun* ran a brief account of Hetty's day:

> Mrs. Green came to the city early from her residence "somewhere in Hoboken" and took a Madison avenue street car. She transferred to the Eighty-sixth street crosstown branch and journeyed over to Central Park West. With brisk strides, apparently with the fourscore years resting but lightly upon her, Mrs. Green walked north to her son's residence.
>
> In the afternoon she went motoring through Central Park and returned about 6 o'clock to her daughter's residence in Madison avenue. Of course there was nothing ostentatious about the party. Mrs. Green's birthday parties never are. She took this one so much as a matter of course that hardly any one knew she was having a party at all.

On April 17, 1916, while staying on Fifth Avenue with Annie Leary, Hetty suffered a stroke. Ned would later say that Hetty had had an argument with one of Leary's cooks—a woman given to drink. Hence the legend, handed down through the years and given permanence by the *Guinness Book of World Records*, that she "died of apoplexy in an argument over the virtues of skimmed milk." Whether the stress of that argument actually contributed to Hetty's stroke is unclear. But the stroke left her partially paralyzed on the left side. Hetty was taken to Ned's home on West Ninetieth Street to recuperate.

When newspaper reporters caught wind of her illness, Ned denied there was anything seriously wrong with his mother. On April 26, nine days after the initial stroke, he told the *New York Times* that Hetty had suffered a cold, but was quickly cured by "simple remedies." "Mother was rather brave last Sunday and went for a ride," Ned dissembled. "As a result she contracted a slight cold. When she came back home, hot-water bags were put to her feet and she was given a glass of hot toddy. If we had given her a larger glass it would not have been necessary even to call a doctor. As it was, she was up yesterday attending her usual heavy routine of business."

The reality of the situation at 5 West Ninetieth Street was more serious. After the first stroke, Hetty suffered a series of additional strokes that left her unable to walk. Ned hired nurses to attend to her around the clock. He instructed them to wear plain clothes rather than uniforms. Her doctor, Henry M. Painter, visited regularly. Nurses wheeled her up to a window overlooking Central Park. Through the trees she could see crowds of park visitors and the shimmering waters of the large reservoir. The city was coming to life with the spring.

In May, to be closer to her mother, Sylvia, with Matthew, bought a four-story house at 7 West Eighty-first Street. When Hetty's condition seemed to improve, attendants lifted her into Ned's car for a drive through the park. She still met daily with Ned, who recounted for her the financial reports of the day, just as Hetty had done for her own father and grandfather decades ago.

A reporter from the *New York Sun* caught Ned leaving the house early in the evening on June 25.

"Does your mother attend to her own business now?" the reporter asked.

Ned chuckled. "Well, if you heard her put me over the jumps every day, you'd think so. She scolds me for the way I handle her affairs and says she surely made a mistake in my education or I would be doing things better."

But by the time Ned uttered these words, Hetty was already bedridden, and Ned admitted that she had suffered "a slight stroke." Dr. Painter, dutifully holding the family line that Hetty's illness was a minor one, told the *Times* on June 25, "Mrs. Green is not as well as she was ten or fifteen years ago, but that is to be expected. During the last few days she had been a little worse than usual, and I advised that she remain in bed, as she had taken cold. It is not true that Mrs. Green had a stroke of paralysis, though the presence of the nurses may have given rise to the rumor." The doctor continued, "In fact, after I saw her yesterday morning I gave Mrs. Green permission to sit up in an arm chair, and in the course of a day or so I feel sure that she will be quite well again."

Privately, Hetty was less sanguine. Sensing that her time was drawing near, she called Sylvia and Ned together for a final talk about the subject that so defined her life—money. She assured them that each would receive an equal share of her estate.

On the morning of July 3, Hetty ceased to respond to her nurses. They immediately called for Ned and Sylvia, who, in turn, called for Dr. Painter. It was still just seven-thirty in the morning when Dr. Painter said that while Hetty's condition was very bad, she would most likely survive through the day. The doctor left, with a promise to return. A half hour later, with her son and daughter by her side, Hetty Green died. She was eighty-one.

July 3, 1916, was a particularly heavy news day. In the Great War, advancing French and British troops launched a major offensive against the Germans along the Somme River. In North America, tensions between the United States and Mexico were running at a fever pitch following alternating raids by Pancho

Villa into Texas and General John Pershing into Mexico in search of Villa. Nevertheless, Hetty's death still made front-page headlines in New York, Los Angeles, Chicago, Denver, Boston, St. Louis, and dozens of other cities.

The *Los Angeles Times* ran a large drawing, in profile, of Hetty in the top center of the front page, under the words "World's Richest Woman Dead." The *Chicago Tribune* ran a photograph of Hetty as an elderly woman, with her long black dress and her bonnet covered in a black veil. "Was Wizard of Finance," the *Tribune* headline read in part. Underneath the picture was a roundup of "Anecdotes of Hetty Green" including this quote of hers on society women: "Fashionable women pass their time playing bridge, smoking cigarets, drinking pale tea and strong whiskey."

Many of the newspapers used the same Associated Press article, a long piece that stated, in part: "Hetty Green was the World's most remarkable mistress of finance. The fortune she has left is close to $100,000,000. The richest woman in America, she lived almost as frugally as a shop-girl. Her home was wherever she chose for a time to hang her little black cape and bonnet, often in the hall bedroom of some cheap boarding house, or in some remote and modest flat around New York."

Most articles were respectful in their assessment. The *New York Times* quoted Ned at some length. He described her as a woman who had been largely misunderstood, hardly the miser that people made her out to be:

> Mother held herself aloof because there was nothing else she could do in her position. When it becomes known that a person has money to lend you have no idea of the requests that come for it—bona fide offers to borrow, begging letters, and letters from unbalanced people. In recent years she had moved her office many times and had finally taken up quarters in the Ninetieth Street house to avoid these money seekers.
>
> For the same reason, mother never told of her charities, though they were many. The sums of $500, $1,000 and $10,000

she gave away were many and there was a list of about thirty
families who received regular incomes. These were mostly members or descendants of families who had been associated with
our family for many years.

Writing in the *Boston Sunday Globe* on July 9, six days after
Hetty's death, A. J. Philpott stated: "In point of fact, it is a question if Hetty Green—in a financial sense—wasn't the greatest
woman that ever lived." Among the newspapers seeing Hetty's
life as a cautionary tale against greed and miserliness was the *St.
Louis Post-Dispatch*, which offered the opinion that Hetty's behavior was only natural for a woman. Under the headline "Hetty
Green, Feminine Croesus," the article stated: "The familiar type
of masculine multimillionaire who has piled up great accumula-
tions through unsocial methods turns naturally to ameliorative
philanthropy when his years lengthen. He becomes as intem-
perate in the making of gifts as he once was in the making of
money. He even tries to regain the esteem of his fellow man by
inventing and endowing new forms of benevolence.

"Womanlike, however, Mrs. Green, disillusioned as to all
other things, pursued her one remaining phantom to the end
without faltering and without betraying qualms of conscience,"
this odd editorial stated. "Almost every town, even small
towns, have women like her. The only difference is that she devoted the same sort of mean sacrifices in a narrowed life to
conserving and increasing tens of millions that they may devote
to conserving and increasing only thousands."

A more balanced and thoughtful assessment came two days
after her death in an editorial in the *New York Times*, which
noted that Hetty hardly would have come in for the criticism
she did had she been a man. "If a man had lived as did Mrs.
Hetty Green, devoting the greater part of his time and mind to
the increasing of an inherited fortune that even at the start was
far larger than is needed for the satisfaction of all such human
needs as money can satisfy, nobody would have seen him as

very peculiar—as notably out of the common. He would have done what is expected of the average man so circumscribed, and there would have been no difficulty in understanding the joys he obtained from participation in the grim conflicts of the higher finance," the editorial stated. "It was the fact that Mrs. Green was a woman that made her career the subject of endless curiosity, comment, and astonishment." The most perceptive assessment may have been this: "Probably her life was happy. At any rate, she had enough of courage to live as she chose and to be as thrifty as she pleased, and she observed such of the world's conventions as seemed to her right and useful, coldly and calmly ignoring all the others."

The *New York Sun* struck a similar theme, praising Hetty for her independence and courage: "If Mrs. Hetty Green was not the richest woman in the world, as popular fancy delighted to regard her, she was one of the most sensible. What common report said of her she disdained to notice. If her frugality was painted as miserliness, well and good; if she was depicted as moving 'twixt days to escape taxes, she refused to reply; she had her life and dared to live it without compromise or concession. And this is sensible, because no person, rich, poor, miser or spendthrift, can extract comfort, to say nothing of happiness, from the effort to live according to another's prescription."

On July 5, two days after her death, Hetty took a ride in luxury that she would not have afforded herself in life. For her long, last journey to Bellows Falls she rode not in a day coach, as was her custom, but in a private railroad car provided by Ned. Ned, Sylvia, and Matthew Wilks accompanied the body on the train, as did Mrs. Herbert Bancroft, an old friend of Hetty's from Bellows Falls, who had lived for many years in New York. Out of respect for his mother's feelings, Ned's wife, Mabel Harlow, did not attend the funeral.

The train bearing Hetty's body from New York arrived in the late morning, about an hour after schedule. It was loaded onto a horse-drawn carriage for the solemn procession up the hill from the station, within view of the shuttered windows of the Tucker House, to the Immanuel Episcopal Church. About two hundred people attended the service. They included acquaintances from years past and curious onlookers. The rector, Alfred C. Wilson, presided over a traditional Episcopal service. The plain coffin was covered with broadcloth, upon which lay a mantle of white carnations. The choir sang two nineteenth-century hymns, "There Is a Blessed Home" and "I Heard the Sound of Voices." In the latter hymn, the choir sang:

> *I saw the holy city*
> *The New Jerusalem*
> *Come down from heav'n, a bride adorned*
> *With jeweled diadem;*
> *The Flood of Crystal waters*
> *Flowed down the golden street;*
> *And nations brought their honors there,*
> *And laid them at her feet.*

It was a simple ceremony, as plain and unostentatious as the wooden coffin that contained Hetty's body. Annie Leary, who was unable to attend due to her own advancing age, sent a spray of lilies and orchids. On the day of the funeral, all trains along the Texas Midland Railroad line stopped for five minutes in tribute, and businesses in Terrell, Texas, ceased operations for an hour. The body was moved outside to the shady spot where Edward was buried. She was laid alongside him; they were together for eternity as they had not always been through years of turbulent marriage. They share a tombstone—a modest-sized obelisk. In death, on the memorial stone, she accepted a subordinate position to Edward that she rejected during her life. There is no mention of her financial prowess or fame. Only this, beneath Edward's name: "Hetty H. R. Green. His Wife."

# SIXTEEN

# HIGH TIMES AT ROUND HILL

Because of the ever-shifting market value of real estate and securities, putting a precise dollar value on Hetty's total estate was difficult or impossible. Hetty further complicated the guesswork by including no inventory in her will and specifically declaring that the trustees (Ned and Sylvia) not be required to file an inventory or appraisal in order to divide the spoils. The most conservative estimates put her net worth at $100 million, the highest at $200 million. According to an estimate cited by William Emery, the Howland family's genealogist, Hetty's holdings of New York City real estate mortgages were worth $30–$45 million; industrial and mining securities, $40–$60 million; railroad and bank securities, $15–$25 million; farming tracts, oil properties, and other real estate in the Southwest, $10 million; and assorted other real estate in Chicago, Boston, St. Louis, and other cities, $10 million.

The will was admitted to probate, without contest, in Bellows Falls on July 22. Hetty, who had spent her life avoiding classifying

herself as a resident of any city, town, or state, in death designated herself a resident of Vermont. There was more than sentimentality toward Bellows Falls in her decision—the state levied
only paltry inheritance taxes. The will was dry, unsentimental,
concise, and tight. Hetty bequeathed a total of $25,000 to people
other than her children. There was $5,000 to Mrs. Herbert Ban-
croft of Bellows Falls, $10,000 to Amory Lawrence of Boston,
who had served as a trustee of Aunt Sylvia's estate (and was one
of the few trustees of any sort for whom Hetty felt affection); and
$5,000 to Ruth Lawrence, a New York friend. The most interest-
ing of these bequests was $5,000 put aside for Matthew Astor
Wilks, Hetty's son-in-law, in thanks for his having signed the
prenuptial agreement. Hetty left nothing to charity, a fact that
newspapers were quick to point out.

Everything else that Hetty owned went evenly to Ned and
Sylvia. She gave the remainder of her father's estate to Ned and,
as a compensation to Sylvia, set up a ten-year trust using railroad and mortgage bonds worth a total of $4.2 million. No val-
uation was given for Edward Mott Robinson's estate, but if
Sylvia's compensatory trust fund is any indication, the trust of
Hetty's father had barely increased in value in all those years.
Hetty's own money, meanwhile, had exploded in a literal em-
barrassment of riches. All of her remaining fortune was to be
divided equally between Sylvia and Ned, and Ned served as
sole executor of the estate.

Within days of Hetty's death, New York and New Jersey both
announced they would fight to have her declared a legal resident,
entitling them to inheritance taxes that New York's comptroller
estimated at up to $5 million. But Hetty hadn't been playing res-
idential cat-and-mouse all those years for nothing. Lawyers for
both states quickly learned the difficulty of proving that the elusive Hetty had lived anywhere, except as a transient.

As the battle wound through one courtroom after another,
New Jersey flinched first, dropping its claim in March 1917.

The state received as consolation around $60,000 in transfer taxes on securities Hetty held in New Jersey companies. New York, stirred by the prospect of perhaps the biggest inheritance tax windfall in state history, fought on. After three years of legal wrangling, the case made its way to the United States Supreme Court. In 1919, the court sided with Hetty's estate in declaring her a resident of Vermont, the state which, ironically, had shown the least interest in claiming her. The reason for the indifference became clear when the estate in February of 1920 doled out Vermont's cut of just under $58,000, per the state's lenient tax code. Defeated in the residence battle, New York turned next to Hetty's business dealings. In May 1920, an appellate court awarded the state $1.5 million in transfer taxes, based on an estimated $38 million in investments she controlled there. In the absence of federal inheritance taxes, the estate paid out a little over $1.6 million to the three states (or, less than 2 percent of the estate), ensuring that the vast fortune Hetty had protected so jealously would pass to her children virtually intact.

With Hetty's death, one other matter was to be cleared up at long, long last—disposition of Aunt Sylvia's trust fund. Now the descendants of Gideon Howland would receive their share of the fortune. The original would-be recipients had, of course, long since died, and their descendants were scattered across the map. Instead of the several dozen relatives, mainly concentrated in southeastern Massachusetts, there were now 439 descendants in line to receive a share of a pie that had scarcely increased in value in the fifty-one years since Aunt Sylvia's death. Descendants lived in Paoli, Pennsylvania, and Rochester, New York; in El Paso, Texas, and Paris, France; in Englewood, New Jersey, and Saginaw, Michigan; Richmond, Virginia, and Jet, Oklahoma. As the appointed genealogists set about to determine the rightful heirs, anticipation built among both legitimate recipients and schemers. Letters arrived from around the world from people claiming Howland blood. Some people, misinterpreting the source of the money, wrote to the trustees claiming relationship with the Green family of Bellows Falls. A woman from Chile sent a picture of herself, claiming her face showed the stern lines of the Yankee Howlands, and she must therefore be related. A memorial monument designer wrote in hopes of getting a contract to design a magnificent stone memorial for the deceased, unaware that Aunt Sylvia had been dead and buried for more than half a century.

As it turned out, the hubbub was over an amount of money that, once divided, was in most cases modest even by the standards of the day. The estate was valued at $1,030,040.55, and each recipient received a portion carefully calculated according to his or her proximity on the family tree to old Gideon Howland. Newspapers reported that H. A. Merrill of Michigan, "a cobbler in a dingy, dirty backroom shoe repair shop," was to receive $100,000 from the will. Unfortunately for Mr. Merrill, the reports exaggerated his take. There was, indeed, a Horace A. Merrill of Michigan listed among the recipients. But he would get only 1/1440th of the estate, or $715. Maria E. Strobeck, of Worcester, New York, received a 1/8640th share, or $120. Ned and Sylvia received a 1/90th share each, or around $11,500 apiece, which they most certainly did not need. At last, the great debate and fight over the estate of Aunt Sylvia could be put to rest. The largest shares, 1/45th, went to a half dozen Howland descendants and amounted to just under $23,000 each.

The matter of Aunt Sylvia's fortune livened up the *Boston Transcript*'s normally staid genealogy column. One letter writer, identified only by the initials J. E. W. B., said: "If it could be supposed that Mrs. Green had a sensitive soul it must have wrung her heartstrings to think that she was the only person in the world every year of whose prolonged life added to the natural hatred and envy of a constantly increasing number of people." But, of course, that had been the very nature of Aunt Sylvia's gentle revenge.

Ned was always respectful toward his mother after her death. He did what he could to protect her reputation, praising her in interviews with reporters as a financial genius, and expressing gratitude for the things she had taught him. Yet almost from the moment of her death, he embarked on a spree of spending that seemed calculated to repudiate everything Hetty Green had held sacred regarding thrift and saving. If Hetty had tried to save her way to happiness, Ned would test the opposite course.

On July 10, 1917, a year and a week after his mother's death, Ned stepped out of the Blackstone Hotel, his favorite stopping point in Chicago, and journeyed by hired car to Highland Park, a suburb a few miles from downtown. There he exchanged wedding vows with Mabel Harlow, his housekeeper of twenty-four years, the former prostitute who had introduced him to sex when he was in his early twenties. In their wedding photo, they look like a prim, proper couple, well beyond their prime. Mabel is wearing a dress that appears to be white, and holding a large bouquet. Ned, just shy of forty-nine, wears a long black jacket, high starched collar, and bow tie, with a flower stuck in his lapel.

The wedding—a conventional consummation of a highly unconventional relationship—seems to have been an act of genuine devotion for both parties. Ned, who never concealed the relationship, showed that he didn't fear social condemnation. And Mabel finally earned the recognition and right to call herself "Mrs. E. H. Green."

As a wedding gift, Ned presented Mabel a trust fund for $625,000. That was her reward for cooperating on another matter—her signature on a prenuptial agreement giving up any further claim on the family fortune.

The newlyweds celebrated their union with an extended cruise aboard Ned's newly purchased yacht, *United States,* a former Great Lakes steamship that was the first great indicator of the life Ned was to enjoy after his mother's death. At 255 feet in length, and with renovations totaling more than $1 million, the *United States,* with its crew of sixty-one, was widely regarded as the largest private yacht in the world. Stripped of its utilitarian furnishings for transporting freight and passengers, and reincarnated for pure luxury, the yacht contained no fewer than forty-eight staterooms, including nine master chambers, each with its own bathroom. Ned's stateroom was decorated in Georgian style with walnut furnishings, gold-colored drapes, and silver fixtures. Mabel's stateroom was outfitted in the style of Marie Antoinette, with light gray walls, gold fittings, and three full-length mirrors. The library was paneled in rich oak, waxed to a shine, and filled with maroon leather furniture. A living room on the main deck was furnished from the Jacobean period, with a large stone fireplace, a Welte Philharmonic self-playing organ, and a piano. The carpeted floor displayed a lion skin rug.

Ned and Mabel sailed from New York, down the Atlantic coast and around to the Gulf, stopping at ports along the way and making a stir wherever they landed. In Charleston, reporters tried in vain for interviews. In Galveston, the Greens picked up friends from Texas and Chicago and spent a week fishing and cruising. Ned and Mabel had used the *United States* for barely two years when it met its doom in perhaps the least violent shipwreck in history. Anchored in the tranquil waters of Padanaram Harbor, near Round Hill, the old Howland estate at South Dartmouth, Massachusetts, the ship swung slowly around and struck a rock. The hull filled with water slowly enough to allow passengers to leave the sinking ship unharmed. Most of the furnishings were saved, but the ship was lost, lying like a dying whale on its side in sixteen feet of water. The wreck of the *United States* barely registered on Ned's balance sheets. Already his restless imagination was leading him to other pursuits.

Ned had spent little time in New Bedford and South Dartmouth before he was in his fifties. And Sylvia had never shown much interest in family history, either, but now Ned decided to return to Round Hill, the old family estate. He had no desire to occupy the historic but by now dilapidated farmhouse. Instead, he set about planning and building an immense mansion and estate, costing $1.5 million, set on the 110 acres he'd inherited from his mother. Sylvia, who by rights owned half of the estate, did not object, but showed about as much interest in developing Round Hill as she did in her own family history. Ned acquired an additional 140 acres in the area, giving him 250 acres to play with.

The house, completed in 1921, was an enormous limestone-and-marble palace, three stories high, with sixty rooms. Just to the left of the tiled entranceway was an elevator, and in the center a large, curved hallway. Ned filled the house with the fruits of a breathtaking collecting spree. He collected with abandon, with unrestrained zeal, as if he were trying to buy his way to happiness. He bought shelf after shelf of books from Goodspeed's Book Shop in Boston. That fortunate seller routinely alerted Ned to rare and valuable volumes available. Ned was an avid buyer but not indiscriminate—the surviving correspondence between Ned and Goodspeed's shows him buying heavily in books on the history of New Bedford, whaling, and New England, returning books when Goodspeed sent him an incorrect volume. He paid $110 for a first edition of Samuel Johnson's great *Dictionary of the English Language;* $962.50 for a 151-volume, blue-cloth-bound set published by the Hackluyt Society, devoted to maritime exploration, covering 1847–1923; and he paid $1,000 for a volume on Sir Francis Drake, published in 1626.

He collected jewelry by the bin, more than Mabel could have worn in a thousand lifetimes. A surviving appraisal of his jewelry purchases covers dozens of ledger-sized pages. There was a double bracelet with a half-moon diamond, for which he paid $18,000; a 6.86-karat ring for $28,000; a solitaire pendant purchased for $15,200; a diamond necklace and brooch for $2,700; and the list goes on and on. He collected rare stamps and coins by the thousand. To this day, Ned remains something of a legend among stamp collectors for purchasing the original 100-

stamp sheet of perhaps the most famous and rare misprint ever, the 1918 upside-down biplane known as the "Inverted Jenny." They are worth about $150,000 per stamp today. Ned broke off most of the sheet individually and sold them to friends, but he had one placed in a locket for Mabel. Coin collectors know him for owning all five 1913 Liberty "V-Nickels."

But his interests didn't end there. He owned a large collection of erotic pictures, many of them on glass negatives, and the enormous dried penis of a whale, which he displayed prominently at the entrance to the mansion, where it loomed over guests who, to Ned's delight, had no idea what it was. A statue of a naked female stood in the foyer, clutching a fishing pole whose line dangled into the cavity of a gold spittoon.

Despite all of his spending, Ned did not, as is sometimes suggested, blow through his mother's fortune. In fact, he proved to be a fairly able custodian of the principal that she left to him and to Sylvia. He did not double, triple, or quadruple the money, as his mother would no doubt have done. It was perhaps among his graces that he realized enough was enough. He lacked Hetty's burning drive to acquire money, and was instead interested in finding ever more creative ways to spend it. But he was careful not to squander the principal. The several million dollars he received in annual interest was more than enough income to cover even his most expensive hobbies and interests. Wilbur Potter, in the offices at 111 Broadway, continued to handle investments for Hetty's estate, but he cleared purchases of securities through Ned.

Correspondence between Ned and his New York brokers, R. L. Day and Company, reveals him to be an active investor. He stayed true to his mother's formula of maintaining conservative investments and copious reserves of cash, and was able to navigate the Great Depression more or less unscathed. During the Depression he bought stock, in keeping with Hetty's dictum to buy when everyone else is selling. R. L. Day sent him detailed reports on blue-chip companies such as Otis Elevator and AT&T. On a single day in June of 1930, eight months after the stock market crash, Ned spent more than $250,000 for 295 shares of AT&T, 500 shares of Chase National Bank, and 1,400 shares of Southern Pacific, the company once owned by his mother's mortal enemy, Collis P. Huntington. In 1928, Ned had sold his beloved Texas Midland Railroad to Southern Pacific. His financial timing was impeccable, a trait that was clearly passed on to him from his mother and grandfather, Edward Mott Robinson. Shortly after the sale, Walter P. Allen, his old banker from Terrell, wrote to tell him that new, hard-surfaced roads were sprouting all over the state, carrying an influx of trucks and passenger buses along the same route as rail tracks. "I think you sold the Midland just in time," Allen wrote. The union of the Midland and the Southern Pacific added a final coda to the long feud between Hetty and Huntington.

Ned also continued to use the Round Hill property to explore a spectacular array of interests, sometimes to the chagrin of neighbors. He had a keen eye for emerging technologies and developments. In 1923, he took out a license to operate a radio station on the property. He lavished money on the enterprise, turning it into one of the most technologically advanced stations in the country. Just to the right of the mansion, he built a studio with a fully equipped music room. The station generated a signal strong enough to be picked up by radio operators in England. For the benefit of the many people who did not have radio in those days, Ned had radio features broadcast by amplifiers around the property, and invited the public to come listen. They arrived in droves. As many as 15,000 people turned out on September 14, 1923, to hear an announcer describe boxer Jack Dempsey's pummeling of Luis Firpo. Cars jamming Smith Neck Road at the entrance to the estate created what historian Elliott Burris Knowlton called "one of the greatest traffic jams in South Dartmouth history."

Like Jay Gatsby, Ned loved to throw open his gates to the public. They flocked to his beach in the summertime. Knowlton quoted a grounds superintendent describing the typical scene: "The noise was awful, between blast of music from WMAF, Klaxons honking, kids screaming, and hawkers selling hot dogs, balloons and Bon Ami. They used the Bon Ami to sprinkle on car windows so that they couldn't be seen when they got undressed to get into their bathing suits."

With his combination of inquisitive mind and unlimited resources, Ned threw money at everything that interested him. In 1929, he paid $8,400 for a custom-made Rauch and Lang Electric Brougham, which he ordered through a Boston car dealer. The car had an extra-tall passenger compartment—it stood a full six inches higher than Ned's head, with tall doors that made it easy for him to get in and out without stooping. He rode about the estate in this car, greeting visitors and checking on various operations. But his fascination with cars was already giving way to a new passion: aviation. Though not a pilot himself, he built a large airstrip and hangar near the beach. He set up a training school for pilots and for years operated one of the most modern and well-equipped airports on the East Coast. It was among the first airports with lit runways for night landings. Round Hill attracted visits from aviation luminaries ranging from Charles Lindbergh to the original Goodyear blimp. He built a hangar capable of sheltering the blimp and several airplanes at once.

Ned built large greenhouses to provide his mansion with fresh flowers and exotic plants. He invited scientists to the estate and funded experiments in aviation, radio, and early television. Engineers used WMAF's powerful transmitters to communicate with Admiral Richard E. Byrd during his Antarctic expedition of 1928–30. From 1925 until Ned's death eleven years later, scientists from the Massachusetts Institute of Technology lived and worked at Round Hill. In the early 1930s, MIT professor Robert J. Van de Graf built a prototype "atom smasher" at Round Hill. The device couldn't, as it turned out, split the atom, but it did generate prodigious electricity. On November 27, 1933, a large crowd gathered to watch as the machine generated 7 million volts of electricity. "No Fourth of July fireworks exhibit ever approached this in spectacular, indescribable splendor," the New Bedford *Standard-Times* gushed the next day.*

When Ned learned that the famous whaling ship *Charles W. Morgan* was falling into disrepair, he bought it, restored it, and put it on display at Round Hill. Launched in 1841, the *Morgan* had been owned by his great-grandfather, Isaac Howland Jr., proprietor of the whaling company. During its storied, eighty-year career, the *Morgan* had completed thirty-seven voyages. Ned opened the ship to tens of thousands of tourists each year. Five years after Ned's death, in 1941, the *Morgan* would be towed to Mystic, Connecticut, where it remains a featured attraction of the Mystic Seaport Museum.

The great Round Hill circus, with its endless cacophony of sound and light, airplane motors, atom smashers, screaming bathers, floodlit runways, music, the *thwack* of boxing gloves amplified by a dozen loudspeakers and made audible for miles around, was all too much for the wealthy owners of nearby summer estates. They had come for the peace and quiet of shore summers, for sanctuary from the heat and noise of Boston and New York. And, it must be said, they were accustomed to seeing local residents mainly when they arrived to trim the hedges, paint the portico, or deliver groceries—not as hot dog–eating, Bon Ami–sprinkling fun-seekers frolicking in the sun. Weren't there public beaches for them . . . elsewhere? Owners of nearby summer homes complained at public hearings and signed petitions trying to enforce some quiet at Round Hill.

The Colonel made a few token concessions—airplanes would fly no lower than 1,000 feet over neighboring houses—but mainly the complaints delighted him. He never cared much for stuffed

---

*In 1956, MIT donated the two-story-tall generator to Boston's Museum of Science, where it has been on prominent display for decades.

shirts, anyway. "It's just another sport—complaining about me," the *American Magazine* quoted him as saying in 1933. "In the morning they swim, in the afternoon they play golf, and at night they talk about Colonel Green."

For a warm-weather retreat, the Colonel built a fabulous, $600,000 estate at Star Island, in Biscayne Bay near Miami Beach. He had first come to Florida on the advice of a physician. He lived in hotels and, later, on a magnificent houseboat docked next to his property, until the house was completed in 1927. That part of Miami was attracting more and more conspicuously wealthy people, some of them notorious. Just across the water from the Colonel sat the compound of gangster Al Capone. The Colonel and Mabel became familiar figures in Miami, throwing lavish parties and motoring around town in a chauffeur-driven car. They spent about four months of each year there, but the Colonel never established residency in Florida. He followed his mother's example of moving about frequently, as a way of thwarting tax collectors. He never established residency in Massachusetts, or in New York, where he frequently stayed. When pressed, he continued to claim Texas as his legal home, though all he kept there was a rented room containing a pair of pants and a vest. It was enough to maintain his voting rights in Texas. At Star Island, the Colonel maintained his habit of inviting the public onto his property. His Easter celebration became an annual event, to which hundreds of local children came to hunt eggs hidden all over the property. The Colonel personally supervised the hiding of the eggs by his staff. He handed out baskets to the children, gave them the signal to start, and laughed in delight as they tore over the property in their search. Ned shrugged off the inevitable complaints from neighbors, just as he did at Round Hill.

The Colonel's acts of philanthropy were never terribly focused or sustained. He liked to quote his mother's adage that paying people to work was more honorable and better for the recipient than simply giving money away. His endless projects at both Round Hill and Star Island provided hundreds of jobs throughout the Depression and pumped millions of dollars into local economies that needed them. Despite Hetty's dictum, the Colonel did give money away, but it was sporadic and spontaneous. In 1932, he donated $5,000 for a children's ward at Jackson Memorial Hospital in Miami; when he learned that a trip to New York for the Miami Boys Drum and Bugle Corps had been canceled when the Junior Chamber of Commerce ran short of funds, Ned wrote out a check for $3,000 to cover it. In 1926, he chipped in $2,000 to the New Bedford Community Fund. He also enjoyed playing the white knight when banks ran into trouble. In 1921, he stopped a run on the Security National Bank in Dallas by depositing $100,000. A few months later he saved the First National Bank of Terrell in more dramatic fashion, placing $250,000 in cash on a table in the middle of the lobby and paying depositors until the panic subsided.

The largest single act of philanthropy by the Colonel was also one of the more intriguing. Over the years, Ned and Mabel informally adopted a series of young women, mostly the daughters of acquaintances, who cruised with them on their boats and, later, stayed with them at Round Hill. The women came to be known as the Colonel's "wards." Among the many things Ned did for these women was to pay for several of them to enroll at Wellesley College outside of Boston. Given the unconventional and unorthodox atmosphere that prevailed wherever the Colonel went, there were inevitable stories of sexual relations between Ned and the girls. But these rumors were never substantiated, and the girls themselves insisted Ned's behavior toward them was proper and avuncular. Indeed, Ned was already suffering from mounting health problems, and in 1921 had undergone an unsuccessful operation to reverse impotence. It is difficult to imagine him taking advantage of the situation even if he had wanted to. Ruth Lawrence Briggs, who graduated from Wellesley in 1925 (she was the only one of the wards to actually graduate), wrote an article for the college alumni magazine in 1988, when she was eighty-five years old. "I guess Uncle Ned took a fancy to me," she wrote. "I don't mean in any wrong way." Uncle Ned bought Ruth a horse, and a car. And when Briggs was married, Mabel bought rugs for her house. Briggs's portrait of Ned and Mabel is of a doting, older couple who, childless themselves, enjoyed having young people around.

Because of this connection with Wellesley, Ned in 1923 talked his sister into joining him in a $500,000 donation to the college. They agreed to give $50,000 each per year for five years, toward the construction of an administration building. The building, with a tower rising 185 feet high from Norumbega Hill, was constructed of brick and Indiana limestone; it was and remains the most prominent building on campus. It also bears the distinction of being the only edifice or monument to Hetty Green. It is called Hetty H. R. Green Hall.

For all of their vast differences in personality and temperament, Ned and Sylvia cared for one another. Letters between these two wealthy, childless siblings are playful and affectionate, passing along trivial details of daily life. Ned signed letters to his sister "Your affectionate brother," or "Your loving brother." He addresses Sylvia, whose first given name was Hetty, as "Hetty B."

The day after Christmas 1927, Sylvia wrote: "Many thanks for the electric clock you so kindly sent to Greenwich. I have put it in the library under George Washington's picture. It is with good company." In 1935, he sent her another gift, a case of three dagger rum, "which I think is about the finest on the market. I have found this rum to be an excellent sleep producer, and this is how you fix it up: Put some cracked ice in a glass; then squeeze in half a lime; then put in a little over an ounce of rum and gradually increase it until you have two ounces in; then add a little sugar and drink it just before going to bed."

Sylvia owned a dog named Prince. Ned had two, Stella and Beauty. In the summer of 1928, Sylvia sent a dog bed for Stella. Ned wrote back to "Dear Auntie" from "Your affectionate niece," as though Stella was Ned and Mabel's child, writing a thank-you note to her Aunt Sylvia. This conceit amused Ned; he used it on several occasions. Once, he sent a Western Union telegram to Prince, Sylvia's dog. It read: "Wishing your mother and you many happy returns of the day. —Stella and Beauty." It is impossible to miss the pathos between the lines, of the aging brother and sister, both childless, exchanging gifts and notes for their dogs instead of their children, writing in the voices of their pets, the closest either of them ever came to producing heirs.

Sylvia, a widow since the death of her husband in 1926, shared her mother's contempt for Mabel. Ned and Mabel tried their best to thaw Sylvia's feelings toward her sister-in-law. Ned refers casually to "Aunt Mabel" in some of the letters, and sends love from both of them. But Sylvia wasn't buying any of it. To Sylvia, she would always be "Mabel Harlot," the interloper after the family fortune, as she had been to Hetty. In 1930, when Ned fell ill at Round Hill, Mabel sent a seventy-two-word telegram to Sylvia: "Connection over the phone was so bad could not talk to you as I wanted to. While Ned is getting along fairly well, I would like you to come down and see for yourself. Dr. Pascal advises blood transfusion, will probably be Thursday. You could understand things much better if you were here. I could meet you at Providence if you will advise me time of arrival there. Love from us both. Mabel." Sylvia responded with the chilly, aloof politeness of someone turning down a dinner invitation from a social inferior: "Regret cannot make a trip at present. All best wishes. Sylvia Wilks."

Mabel's note to Dr. Henry S. Pascal, Ned's New York doctor, and the reference to the blood transfusion in a letter to Sylvia, reveals Ned's state of health. Because he was so tall and heavy, weighing between 250 and 300 pounds for most of his adult life, his good right leg took a tremendous amount of wear and tear. By his fifties, Ned was suffering from advanced arthritis, which made getting around on his own difficult. He frequently trav-

eled in a wheelchair as the condition worsened. He took copious amounts of Bromo-Seltzer for his stomach, which caused,
according to Dr. Pascal, acetanilide poisoning. He suffered from
anemia and heart disease. For several years he included stops in
Lake Placid, New York, on his regular circuit between Miami
and Round Hill, seeking rest and treatment at the Lake Placid
Club. He was there in June 8, 1936, when he died. He was
sixty-seven years old. The coroner listed the cause of death as
myocardial failure.

The Colonel was transported back to New Bedford, where a
procession of local dignitaries followed him out to Round Hill
for the funeral services. But Ned was not to be buried at his
beloved Round Hill. Shortly after the funeral, Ned, the lover of
trains, took his final ride up into the hills of Vermont. Although
he had little personal connection with Bellows Falls, he was
taken up to join his mother and father in the cemetery of the
Episcopal church.

For the Greens, money and litigation always went hand in
hand, and Ned's death prompted two spectacular court cases.
In the first, Mabel tried to invalidate the prenuptial agreement
she had signed forswearing any claim on the fortune. She tried
to prove that the Colonel had been predominantly a resident of
Texas, which had one of the nation's strongest community
property laws. She wanted half of Ned's estate. But Ned had
signed his will in 1908, when his mother was still alive. He left
everything to Hetty and, should Hetty be dead, to his sister.
The fact that he had not felt compelled to update it during the
remaining twenty-eight years of his life speaks to the closed circle that the family fortune had become. The fortune must stay
in the immediate family. He would not violate that trust. Mabel
hired a prominent Philadelphia law firm to handle her case. But
she was outgunned by an opponent—Sylvia—who had more
money, more lawyers, and who had spent much of her formative life in courtrooms observing her mother in action. For
Sylvia, the idea of sharing the fortune with Mabel was unten-

able. She felt, as keenly as her brother, the importance of keeping the money within the nuclear family, even if that number had now dwindled down to one lonely widow of sixty-five. She was prepared to do whatever she had to do, even if it meant calling up private details from her brother's life.

Sylvia's lawyers traveled to Texas to dig up dirt on Mabel, which, by implication, involved digging up dirt on Ned. They paid a call on a man named Dan Quill, the son of Ned's early secretary at the Texas Midland. The elder Quill had written an unpublished memoir allegedly detailing wild times in Terrell in Ned's early days there. On September 30, 1936, Dan Quill wrote a letter to Mabel in Port Henry, New York, where she was staying. Quill promised Mabel that he had not shown the memoir to the lawyers, but he *had* contacted New York agents about the possibility of publishing it. He would, of course, withhold publication should he find some other means by which to take care of his aging mother. "I wish to sincerely state there is no disposition on the part of the Quill family to in any way injure your cause of action in the Courts, and you have our assurance that nothing will be done in this matter until advice is received from you." It is not known how Mabel responded to this unctuous letter, or if she responded at all. In any case, Sylvia hardly needed Mr. Quill's memoirs to prevail. Ned's will was sound, as was the prenuptial agreement Mabel had signed. In the end, more than a year of litigation resulted in a settlement in which Sylvia, gritting her teeth, agreed to pay Mabel a nuisance settlement of $500,000 to get rid of her. Mabel went off to live on Long Island, not so wealthy as she hoped but wealthy enough to live out her once riotous life in comfort.

The second court case developed as a battle among four states—New York, Texas, Florida, and Massachusetts—over estate taxes. Each of the four states sought to have Ned declared a legal resident. In the end, although he had never voted in Massachusetts and had avoided paying state income taxes by claiming to be a resident of Texas, the courts found him to be a resident of Massachusetts. For its efforts, the state received some $5 million in taxes, the largest single estate payoff it had ever received.

So now Sylvia, having rid herself of the annoyances of greedy widows and bureaucrats, gathered the fortune into her arms. Within a few weeks of Edward's death, Mabel had been evicted from Round Hill, and the house was largely empty. Through her attorneys, Sylvia announced that she would no longer pay to heat Ned's beloved greenhouses through the winter, and directed that the plants be sold off. Curious residents, accustomed to liberal access to the property, now found the entrance padlocked and guarded by a hired policeman. In South Dartmouth, it did not take residents long to realize that the Colonel's fabulous party was over; the era of Sylvia clamped down like a January frost.

# SEVENTEEN

# SCATTERED TO THE WIND

In May 1940, two demolition workers from George W. Donahue and Son, of Rutland, Vermont, climbed to the roof of the Tucker House in Bellows Falls. Stepping carefully along the slope, they tied lines around the southeastern chimney. With the lines secured, they stepped back a few paces and gave the signal to workmen on the ground to start pulling. The chimney did not surrender easily. The house had been built to last. The mortar and bricks were as sound and tight as on the day they were laid 134 years earlier.

Eventually, the chimney ceased its protest. It keeled over, fell in silence for a moment, and crashed with a dull thud. The demolition of the Tucker House had begun. Within a few weeks, every vestige of the Green family's ancestral home, with its magnificent views of the Connecticut River and Mount Kilburn, was gone. Crews leveled, graded, and paved the property, leaving in place of the house that most prosaic footprint of human development: a parking lot.

The demolition came on the express orders of the property

owner: H, Sylvia Ann Howland Robinson Green Wilks, who donated the property to the town. The parking lot was her idea. The symbolism of her choice is inescapable. The woman whose seven-word name paid homage to every branch of her family tree seemed to want nothing more than to eradicate the place where she spent summers dutifully by her mother's side; the place where her father died. It was as if she believed a layer of steaming asphalt might adequately seal her past away forever.

Round Hill held equally little interest for Sylvia. In 1948, she donated her brother's grand estate to the Massachusetts Institute of Technology, which had conducted so many experiments there during the Colonel's lifetime. MIT used the property for radio experiments. Scientists erected dozens of broadcast towers and antennas and sent signals into deep space. One dish antenna, a relic of those days, sits on a promontory overlooking the ocean, and is a well-known landmark for local boaters. The Institute used the property until 1964, when it became a Jesuit retreat. The property has since been developed and is dotted with private homes. The mansion has been converted into luxury condominiums.

Sylvia spent most of her time in New York City, looking after the fortune that had concentrated in her hands. She spent far less money than her brother had, and she made good, sound business decisions. With her mother, brother, and husband dead, Sylvia lived a quiet and solitary life, shuttling between her New York apartment at 988 Fifth Avenue, and her home in Greenwich. In Connecticut, she studied the birds that flitted about her garden. Human visitors were more rare—they included a few old friends from Bellows Falls. One was Helen Guild, who had befriended Sylvia half a century earlier at the suggestion of her mother, who told her that Sylvia "hasn't had a happy girlhood."

As old women, Helen and Sylvia walked along Sylvia's small stretch of private beach in Greenwich, about a mile from her house, watching waves and picking up shells. They toured

Greenwich in Sylvia's chauffeur-driven Lincoln, stopping for ice cream at a local parlor, or ducking into a dress shop, where Sylvia instructed her friend to choose seven or eight dresses for herself.

Sylvia also remained in touch with Mary Nims Bolles, her old friend from Bellows Falls. Mary visited Sylvia in Greenwich occasionally, and the two exchanged letters and gifts at the holidays. When Mary sent Sylvia some fruit from Florida in 1946, Sylvia replied, "My dear Mary. Many thanks for the oranges & grapefruit— Sorry to hear your eyes are not behaving well. We all have some trouble one way or another." Sylvia did not, as a rule, send out Christmas cards. But one Christmas, Mary did receive a thin, plain envelope. The envelope, almost overlooked amid the profusion of boxes and presents, contained no card or note, just a check from Sylvia for $500.

Sylvia died in a New York hospital on the evening of February 4, 1951, at the age of eighty. Obituaries noted that Sylvia died without heirs, and that her passing had put an end to the strange and fabulous saga of Hetty Green. And they remarked on Sylvia's unusual upbringing. "Sylvia was grudgingly permitted to enter New York society in 1897–98 and occasionally visited friends in Newport, but these sorties were timid, reluctant, and accomplished very little beyond the finding of a suitable husband," the *Times* noted. The obituary added: "As time wore on, she developed many of the frugal characteristics of her mother in a gentler way. Few friends graced her life, nor did she derive much apparent enjoyment from the wealth at her disposal."

The *Herald Tribune* wrote that "Mrs. Wilks, a tall, austere woman, shunned publicity and pursued privacy with almost the intense devotion that fired her famous mother." The article continued: "Even her estate managers seldom saw her, although she continued to be active in the management of her vast financial affairs, and always made major financial decisions herself."

The *Bellows Falls Times* noted somberly: "Despite Mrs. Wilks' bitterness over the kind of life her mother led and imposed upon her children, she evidently was unable to escape living a life that was much like her mother's in its dedication to money. Even though she may have hated her mother's influence, she could not escape it."

While Ned's burial had drawn fifteen hundred people to the New Bedford train station, just to observe the procession, Sylvia's arrangements were as quiet, restrained, and understated as her life. After a small service at a funeral home on Madison Avenue, her body was transported to Bellows Falls to join those of her mother, father, and brother. A small group of New Yorkers joined about fifty local residents standing graveside on a bitter cold day. The New Yorkers included two executives from Chase National Bank, where Sylvia kept more than $31 million in a single cash account; her lawyer; and her chauffeur.

The four Greens—Edward, Hetty, Ned, and Sylvia—lie in the same few square feet of soil next to the church. The children's names appear on the same obelisk that bears Edward's and Hetty's. Ned's wife and Sylvia's husband are buried elsewhere.

Sylvia's will, directing the distribution of around $100 million, was found stashed with four bars of soap in a cabinet in her New York apartment. It named sixty-three individuals and institutions as beneficiaries. There seemed to be little overall plan to the bequests; they were scattered willy-nilly, sometimes to people who pleased her from afar. Sylvia left $10,000 to Robert Moses, New York City parks commissioner, "in appreciation of his work creating public parkways." Moses had been the mastermind behind the Hutchinson River Parkway, the leafy thoroughfare connecting New York City with her home in Connecticut. The Boston Public Library received a half-million dollars, because one of her father's cousins had been a trustee there.

She divided $1 million of her estate evenly among ten distant relatives—all, like herself, descendants of Gideon Howland. Most barely knew Sylvia, if at all, and were shocked to learn of their inheritances. Henry A. Loomis, an eighty-five-year-old retiree living in Rochester, New York, was perplexed. "I won't be able to use much of it. I'm too old," he told reporters. "I'm going to continue to live simply—and wear old clothes—as I have been doing for the last forty years."

The lion's share of Sylvia's estate was divided into 140 shares, worth more than $600,000 each. These she doled out to some of the nation's most elite and least needy universities and private schools—Yale, Harvard, Columbia, Groton, and Vassar—despite having little personal connection to any of them. Some of her bequests were personal. She left money to some friends, such as the now-elderly Mary Nims Bolles. She left money for the construction of a new hospital in Bellows Falls, and for the library in New Bedford. It was the same library to which her namesake, Aunt Sylvia, had given money in her own will.

The great fortune that Hetty had spent her lifetime acquiring, saving, and guarding against interlopers real and imagined slipped quietly out of the family's grasp. Time and death did what no Wall Street shark, meddling trustee, or tax collector could—it dispersed the great fortune among people and institutions who were strangers to Hetty. Hetty, who had set out to win at a man's game, and played it ferociously, courageously, brilliantly. Perhaps, she had played it a bit too well.

# ACKNOWLEDGMENTS

In my parents' home outside of Boston, there is a silver tray and a porringer that, according to family legend, were given to an ancestor of mine by Hetty Green. When my mother, Carolyn Slack, showed me the items a couple of years ago, with the suggestion that I consider writing a book about Hetty, I had only the vaguest idea of who she was talking about. I half recalled something from the *Guinness Book of World Records* about "world's greatest miser." Unfortunately, the tray and porringer contain neither inscription nor initials, and must remain the stuff of family legend. But the story was enough to set me on my way to writing this book, and I have become even more of a believer than before in the wisdom of that simple phrase: Listen to your mother.

My research began where Hetty's life did, in New Bedford, Massachusetts, and several people and institutions helped me. Edie Nichols is a small business owner who has worked diligently over the past decade to keep Hetty's name alive in her hometown through public appearances and a privately run museum, the Hetty Green Historical Society. The museum is an essential stop for anyone interested in learning more about Hetty and her family. When I first called Edie, she might have dismissed me as an interloper. Instead, she greeted me warmly, introduced me to people and resources, and even gave me a guided tour of the city.

Dr. Stuart M. Frank and the staff at the Kendall Institute (part of the New Bedford Whaling Museum) gave me time and space to examine their remarkable collection of whaling books; their thick, bound volume of the Howland will trial; Howland family records; and other materials. At the New Bedford Public Library, then-archivist Ernestina Furtado directed me to books, papers, and maps that helped me to re-create the New Bedford of Hetty's childhood, and to fascinating documents related directly to Hetty and her family. Paul Cyr of the library staff located and copied several of the photographs that appear in this book.

Llewellyn Howland III, an author, editor, and publisher who is an indirect relation to Hetty Green, shared his extensive knowledge of the New Bedford Howlands and his thoughts on Hetty, and pointed me toward several crucial books and other sources. He also introduced me to two people in South Dartmouth, Massachusetts (home to the Greens' Round Hill estate), who were particularly helpful. Captain Noel Hill, the son of Ned Green's Round Hill caretaker Bert Hill, invited me into his home and gave me unrestricted access to his remarkable collection of papers, photographs, and other documents related to Colonel Green and Round Hill. Barbara Fortin Bedell, a resident of one of the homes on the Round Hill estate, shared her knowledge of the Colonel, much of which is collected in her excellent book, *Colonel Edward Howland Robinson Green and the World He Created at Round Hill.*

In New York City, I owe thanks to the staff of the New-York Historical Society, where I spent a great deal of time scanning microfilm copies of New York newspapers and poring over books on New York history. The New York Public Library was another vital resource for period newspapers and journals, as well as several hard-to-find books. The Museum of American Financial History is a small gem located on lower Broadway, a stone's throw from the site of the old Chemical National Bank and Hetty's other Wall Street haunts. I found many helpful books, bank records, and other materials in the museum's library, with the help of assistant director Meg Ventrudo. Shelley Diamond of the JP Morgan Chase Archives Department in lower Manhattan located and copied historical information on Chemical National Bank, including lists of depositors from Hetty's time, photographs, and so forth.

In Bellows Falls, Vermont, Chris Burchstead of the Rockingham Free Public Library pointed me to thick files of clippings on Hetty and her family, and allowed me to examine original letters and other items in the library's second-floor museum. Local historian Robert Ashcroft gave me a tour of Bellows Falls. Thanks also to Rockingham town clerk Doreen Aldrich, and Wanda Blanchard of the Westminster Probate Court for their help in locating and copying birth and death records, wills, deeds, and other records.

Robert Foster, of the Hoboken Historical Museum in New Jersey, showed me around Hoboken, helped me visualize the town as it would have appeared during the late nineteenth and early twentieth centuries, and shared his bountiful knowledge of local history. In neighboring Jersey City, I owe thanks to Joseph Donnelly and Bruce Brandt of the Jersey City Library.

Thanks also to James McCord of the Terrell Heritage Society in Terrell, Texas; Helen Nichols Battleson of Urbanna, Virginia, a descendant and genealogist of the Robinson family; and to the Historical Society of the town of Greenwich. The American Antiquarian Society in Worcester, Massachusetts, Harvard University Law Library, Harvard's Widener Library, the Library of Congress, and the Trumbull Public Library in Connecticut all opened their doors to me.

I owe immeasurable thanks to my wife, Barbara, for her constant support and encouragement through my highs and lows, and to my daughters, Natalie and Caroline, who make life so sweet, and to JoAnn and Anthony DiPanni. Among those who read the manuscript and made valuable suggestions are my father, Warner Slack, physician, teacher, and author, whose steadfast support and encouragement continue to amaze me; Dean King, who has shown me by his example how to be a professional writer of books; and Claudio Phillips, a trusted friend and wise reader.

I must also thank my agent and friend Andrew Blauner, a wise and gentle guide for the past seven years. Julia Serebrinsky, my editor at Ecco Press, took enthusiastic interest from the start, and her careful editing of the manuscript improved it greatly. And thanks to her assistant, Gheña Glijansky, for her cheerful competence throughout.

# SOURCE NOTES

There have been two previous mainstream nonfiction books dealing with Hetty: *Hetty Green: The Witch of Wall Street,* by Boyden Sparkes and Samuel Taylor Moore, published in 1935, and *The Day They Shook the Plum Tree,* by Arthur H. Lewis, published in 1963. The Sparkes and Moore book, first published in 1930 as *Hetty Green: A Woman Who Loved Money,* and reprinted in 2000 by Buccaneer Books, was well researched, and the authors were able to interview some acquaintances of Hetty's who by now are of course no longer living. In a few cases I have used anecdotes that could only have come from their interviews, and I have cited these instances in my chapter notes. The Lewis book dealt mainly with the fortune as it was handed down to Hetty's children. The author's research papers, on file at the Temple University archives in Philadelphia, yielded many magazine articles, newspaper articles, and other leads.

## PREFACE

John Steele Gordon's concise and highly readable history of Wall Street, *The Great Game,* was a great help to me here and elsewhere in terms of understanding the evolution of finance in America and placing Hetty in the context of her times. Other useful books included Charles R. Geisst's *Wall Street: A History,* and Charles P. Kindleberger's *Manias, Panics, and Crashes.*

## CHAPTER ONE: NEW BEDFORD

For presenting the history of New Bedford and of the Howland family, I drew on many resources, ranging from whaling books and old city directories to a physician's handwritten diary from the cholera outbreak in 1834, the year of Hetty's birth. But two volumes deserve particular mention. The first is William M. Emery's *The Howland Heirs,* a monumental genealogical work written in 1919 by the historian who after Hetty's death was assigned to untangle the enormous list of Howland descendants in line for a portion of Aunt Sylvia's trust fund. More than just a genealogical table, *The Howland Heirs* is loaded with family history and colorful anecdotes, and was a constant reference guide for me during the writing process. The second is Leonard Bolles Ellis's *History of New Bedford and Its Vicinity,* an enormous, kitchen-sink history that always seemed to yield just the fact or detail I needed.

## CHAPTER TWO: AUNT SYLVIA

Outside of trial lawyers, historical researchers are among the few people who think litigation is great. Old court records, when you can find them, yield wonderful details. Records of the 1867 lawsuit filed by Hetty against Aunt Sylvia's estate are especially revealing. Lengthy testimony by Aunt Sylvia's domestic staff helped me to re-create in Chapters Two and Three the atmosphere of her lonely life in New Bedford and at Round Hill, and the tumultuous impact that Hetty had when she visited. Given the animosity between Hetty and the servants, it is not surprising that much of their testimony casts Hetty in a negative light. Hetty's own testimony mainly concerns the making of the wills rather than domestic details. The servants also had a financial interest in seeing Hetty lose the case, because the will Hetty was contesting included bequests to them. Still, the servants' testimony comes off by and large as plain, straightforward, consistent, and believable. Many of the scenes of Sylvia's domestic life are re-created from their testimony.

The account of Hetty dancing with the Prince of Wales on page 19 is adapted from the unpublished memoirs of Walter Marshall (see notes for Chapter Fifteen).

### CHAPTER THREE: A TEST OF WILLS

Information on the capitalists who became known collectively as the robber barons came from various biographies of the men, and from *Webster's American Biographies*. Another good source was Gustavus Myers's polemical classic, *History of the Great American Fortunes*, first published in 1907. Myers's book is an unabashed, 700-page slam against big money in all forms, and must be read as such. He can find barely a redeeming quality in any of the people he writes about. Still, his research was enormous, and the book sheds fascinating light on the origins of the wealth of some of America's richest families.

### CHAPTER FOUR: ALONE IN A CROWD

The two letters from Edward Green I cite are in the collection of the New-York Historical Society. The description of the trial came almost entirely from the voluminous court records. The expert testimony of Agassiz, Holmes, and others represents one of the most exhaustive scientific examinations of the issue of forgery. Although the judge ironically never considered forgery in rendering his decision, the case was studied closely by attorneys in subsequent forgery cases because of its clinical treatment of this emerging science.

## CHAPTER FIVE: SELF-IMPOSED EXILE

When I was looking for a description of the London neighborhood where Hetty and Edward lived, the Internet paid off. I found a copy of *The National Gazetteer of Great Britain and Ireland* for 1868, offering detailed descriptions of St. Marylebone. Thanks to British genealogist Colin Hinson, who painstakingly transcribed the *Gazetteer* onto his Web site, and who gave me permission to quote from it.

## CHAPTER SIX: PRIDE AND PAIN

Bellows Falls, Vermont, is a village within the town of Rockingham. Among several local histories I consulted, Lyman Simpson Hayes's 1907 *History of the Town of Rockingham, Vermont* was especially helpful in providing information on the village as well as on the Green family. Even better was an unpublished paper by Hayes, called "Hetty Green at Home: Reminiscences of Her Neighbors at Bellows Falls, Vermont," on file in the Rockingham Free Public Library. Hayes interviewed many town residents and recorded their impressions of her as well as some of the more delightful and colorful stories from her times there. The Arthur Lewis papers at Temple University contained a typescript of memoirs by Mary Nims Bolles, the lifelong friend of Hetty's daughter, Sylvia. These memoirs contained many interesting details about Hetty, Edward, and the children.

## CHAPTER SEVEN: HETTY STORMS WALL STREET

The Cisco bank failure was widely covered by the New York newspapers, and Hetty figures largely in the stories. The *New York World* and the *New York Daily Tribune* were especially exhaustive in their coverage, and for much of the information for this chapter I owe thanks to those un-bylined reporters of yesterday.

## CHAPTER EIGHT: THE VIEW FROM BROOKLYN

The New-York Historical Society was an excellent resource for information on the extraordinary wealth accumulating in New York during the Gilded Age—the lives the wealthy led and the homes they built. Robert Stern's *New York 1900* offered detailed description of the fabulous pleasure palaces these lightly taxed captains of industry erected for themselves along Fifth Avenue. Stewart Holbrook's *The Age of the Moguls,* with its section on "What They Did With It," was also useful. Alexander Noyes's *Forty Years of American Finance (1865–1907)* was extremely helpful in describing, on a year-by-year basis, the prevailing economic conditions of America during the years when Hetty was most active.

## CHAPTER NINE: GROOMING A PROTÉGÉ

The exact details surrounding the loss of Ned's leg are vague, and separating the myths from the reality is difficult at best. A search for records of Dr. McBurney's operation at Roosevelt Hospital unfortunately came up empty. Assessment of the popular myth that Hetty caused her son to lose his leg out of miserliness and spite must therefore fall into the area of educated guesswork. Hetty's behavior with doctors was certainly unattractive. But, based on her obvious love for her son, and her many unsuccessful efforts to correct his condition over several long and painful years, it is inconceivable to me that she would have allowed her son to lose his leg out of fear of paying a doctor's bill.

## CHAPTER TEN: THOU SHALT NOT PASS

Hetty's acquisition of the Texas Midland Railroad, and Ned's subsequent improvements, are recounted in S. C. G. Reed's authoritative *History of the Texas Railroads.* The story of Hetty's pistol-packing confrontation with Collis P. Huntington comes from the Sparkes and Moore book, *The Witch of Wall Street*. Most of the information regarding the Chemical National Bank and its president, George Gilbert Williams, came from files in the JP Morgan Chase Archives in New York. A 1902 profile of Williams by Edwin Lefevre, author of the Wall Street classic *Reminiscences of a Stock Operator*, was particularly helpful. The clipping does not identify the journal in which the article appeared.

### CHAPTER ELEVEN: A LADY OF YOUR AGE

Hetty's interminable legal battles with her father's appointed trustees were given extensive coverage in the newspapers. The *New York Times* was my primary source in re-creating the fight. Sylvia's letters to her friend, Mary, survive under a glass case at the Rockingham Free Public Library in Bellows Falls.

### CHAPTER TWELVE: ACROSS THE RIVER

For the information about Hetty's friendship with James and Michael Smith, I must thank Hoboken resident Lisa Conde. Lisa and her husband, Tom, live in Michael Smith's old house, and happened to come across records detailing Hetty's loans to him. Lisa showed me around the house and shared information she has collected on the brothers. The incident involving Hetty, Edward, and William Crapo at the New York rooming house is drawn from Henry Howland Crapo's *The Story of William Wallace Crapo*. The book contains a delightful chapter on Hetty. The story of Hetty's reaction to news of Collis P. Huntington's death first appeared in the Sparkes and Moore book, *The Witch of Wall Street*. The story of Hetty's fears of being poisoned in New Bedford, at the end of the chapter, comes from William Emery, the official Howland genealogist, who described her fears in an article for the New Bedford *Standard-Times*, June 13, 1948.

## CHAPTER THIRTEEN: IF MY DAUGHTER IS HAPPY

The causes of the panic of 1907 were legion, and my description is by necessity greatly simplified. Alexander Noyes's *Forty Years of American Finance (1865–1907)*, published just as the country was emerging from the crisis, offers an excellent view of the crisis as it unfolded. More modern perspective can be found in John Steele Gordon's *The Great Game*, and Charles P. Kindleberger's *Manias, Panics, and Crashes*. The solution to the crisis, worked out by J. P. Morgan and others including, apparently, Hetty, was supposed to stabilize the banking system by ensuring a flow of cash to forestall panics. The ensuing establishment of the Federal Reserve system did, in fact, stabilize the banking system, but not so much as Morgan and the others had hoped. A little over two decades later, of course, the markets collapsed again and hundreds of banks failed, leading to the Great Depression. The story of Hetty's beauty treatments was detailed in the *New York Times* of May 28, 1908. The description of the Earl of Yarmouth lawsuit appeared in several *Times* articles in 1901.

## CHAPTER FOURTEEN: THE HAT WAS "HETTY" GREEN

According to popular legend, Hetty's beloved dog, Dewey, is buried in the Hartsdale Canine Cemetery in Westchester County, New York. Founded in 1896, it claims to be the nation's oldest pet cemetery, and its roster of departed dogs includes many owned by entertainers, politicians, and other celebrities. Given Hetty's love for Dewey, she might well have splurged on a fine resting place for the animal. Unfortunately, the cemetery's roster of permanent guests includes none named "Dewey." Even with Hetty's penchant for secrecy, it is hard to imagine her burying the animal under a pseudonym. And so Dewey's final resting place, like many other Hetty legends, remains an intriguing mystery.

CHAPTER FIFTEEN: I'LL OUTLIVE ALL OF THEM!

Walter Marshall, Colonel Ned Green's personal secretary in Terrell, came with Ned to New York in 1911. It's safe to say that Marshall liked his New York job less well than the Texas one—a major reason being his rather contentious relationship with Hetty. Marshall's unpublished memoirs include a chapter detailing his trips with Hetty to her locked vault containing her prized possessions. Barbara Fortin Bedell, who at this writing is preparing Marshall's memoirs for publication, shared with me a chapter describing Marshall's trips with Hetty to the locked vault.

CHAPTER SIXTEEN: HIGH TIMES AT ROUND HILL

It is difficult to spend much time around Colonel Ned Green and not be impressed with his insatiable curiosity, his scale of living, his humor, and, in his own way, his large heart. Condensing his later years into a single chapter was a difficult task. The Noel Hill collection, referenced in my acknowledgments, yielded many interesting details, including correspondence between Ned and Sylvia, a list of items at Round Hill and cars kept on the property, contracts, financial records, and photographs.

Arthur Lewis's 1963 book, *The Day They Shook the Plum Tree,* and John M. Bullard's *The Greens As I Knew Them* (1964) also provided interesting and quite different perspectives on the Colonel. Bullard was a New Bedford attorney who worked with Ned and was interviewed by Lewis. Bullard's privately published book counters the fairly cynical and dismissive portrait of Ned offered in *Plum Tree.* I also consulted Bullard's papers and notes for the book, which are on file at the Harvard Law School Library.

A note on the name "Round Hill": Over the centuries, the property has been referred to as both "Round Hill" and "Round Hills" to such an extent that either choice can be considered correct. Ned used the singular on virtually everything relating to the property, and for consistency I have done the same throughout the book.

## CHAPTER SEVENTEEN: SCATTERED TO THE WIND

The descriptions of Sylvia's friendship with Helen Guild both as children in Bellows Falls and as elderly women in Greenwich came from a lengthy interview Guild gave to *Boston Globe* reporter Frances Burns shortly after Sylvia's death ("She Loved Toys Because She Hadn't Had Them as Child," March 4, 1951). The description of her friendship with Mary Nims Bolles came from letters between the two from the Rockingham Free Public Library in Bellows Falls, and from Mary's memoirs. The distribution of Sylvia's estate was widely covered in newspapers nationwide.

# BIBLIOGRAPHY

## BOOKS

Allen, Everett S. *Children of the Light: The Rise and Fall of New Bedford Whaling and the Death of the Arctic Fleet.* Boston: Little, Brown, 1973.

Ambrose, Stephen E. *Nothing Like It in the World: The Men Who Built the Transcontinental Railroad, 1863–1869.* New York: Touchstone Books, 2001.

Anonymous, *History of the Chemical National Bank 1823–1913*, privately printed, New York, 1913.

Ashley, Clifford W. *The Yankee Whaler.* New York: Dover Publications, 1991. Reprint of 1942 edition.

Bedell, Barbara Fortin. *Colonel Edward Howland Robinson Green and the World He Created at Round Hill.* South Dartmouth: [self-published], 2003.

Black, Ladbroke. *Some Queer People.* London: Sampson Low, Marston & Co., n.d.

Browne, William Bradford. *The Babbitt Family History, 1643–1900.* Taunton, Mass., 1912.

Bullard, John M. *The Greens As I Knew Them.* New Bedford, Mass.: Reynolds–De Walt Printers, 1964.

Collier, Peter, and David Horowitz. *The Rockefellers: An American Dynasty.* New York: Holt, Rinehart & Winston, 1976.

Collins, Anne L., Virginia Lisai, and Louise Luring. *Around Bel-*

lows Falls, Rockingham, Westminster, and Saxtons River. Charleston, S.C.: Arcadia Publishing, 2002.

Congdon, James Bunker. *New Bedford, Massachusetts.* New York: Jared W. Bell, printer, c. 1841.

Crapo, Henry Howland. *Certain Comeoverers,* 2 vols. New Bedford, Mass.: E. Anthony & Sons, 1912.

———. *The New-Bedford Directory.* New Bedford, Mass.: Press of Benjamin Lindsey, 1841.

———. *The Story of William Wallace Crapo, 1830–1926.* Boston: Thomas Todd Co., Printers, 1942.

Crossen, Cynthia. *The Rich and How They Got That Way.* New York: Crown Business, 2000.

Dean, Sidney, ed. *History of Banking and Banks.* Boston: Pelham Studios, 1884.

*Directory of Directors in the City of New York.* Audit Company of New York, 1898.

Ellis, Leonard Bolles. *History of New Bedford and Its Vicinity, 1602–1892.* Syracuse, N.Y.: D. Mason & Co., 1892.

Emery, William M. *The Howland Heirs: Being the Story of a Family and a Fortune and the Inheritance of a Trust Established for Mrs. Hetty H. R. Green.* New Bedford, Mass.: E. Anthony & Sons, 1919.

———. *New Bedford Lawyers of the Past.* Old Dartmouth Historical Society. Reprinted from the *New Bedford Sunday Standard-Times,* 1943–44.

Evans, Cerinda W. *Collis Potter Huntington.* Newport News, Va.: The Mariner's Museum, 1954.

Evans, Thomas. *An Exposition of the Faith of the Religious Society of Friends.* Philadelphia: Kimber & Sharpless, 1828.

Flynn, John T. *Men of Wealth: The Story of Twelve Significant Fortunes from the Renaissance to the Present Day.* New York: Simon and Schuster, 1941.

Geisst, Charles R. *Wall Street: A History.* New York: Oxford University Press, 1997.

Gordon, John Steele. *The Great Game: The Emergence of Wall Street as a World Power, 1653–2000.* New York: Touchstone Books, 2000.

Hayes, Lyman Simpson. *History of the Town of Rockingham, Vermont 1753–1907.* Bellows Falls, Vt.: published by the town, 1907.

Hazard, Thomas R. *Recollections of Olden Times: Rowland Robinson of Narragansett and His Unfortunate Daughter.* Newport, R.I.: John P. Sanborn, 1879.

*History of the Chemical National Bank 1823–1913.* Privately printed, 1913.

Holbrook, Stewart H. *The Age of the Moguls.* New York: Doubleday & Co., 1954.

Howland, Franklyn. *A Brief Genealogical and Biographical History of Arthur, Henry, and John Howland and Their Descendants, of the United States and Canada.* New Bedford, Mass.: privately published, 1885.

Kindleberger, Charles P. *Manias, Panics, and Crashes: A History of Financial Crises.* 4th ed. New York: John Wiley & Sons, 2000.

King, Moses. *King's Notable New Yorkers, 1896–1899.* New York: Orr Press, 1899.

Klepper, Michael, and Robert Gunther. *The Wealthy 100: From Benjamin Franklin to Bill Gates—A Ranking of the Richest Americans, Past and Present.* Seacaucus, N.J.: Carol Publishing Group, 1996.

Lavender, David. *The Great Persuader.* Garden City, N.Y.: Doubleday & Co., 1970.

Leonard, John William, ed. *Who's Who in Finance and Banking.* New York: Joseph & Sefton, 1911.

Lewis, Arthur H. *The Day They Shook the Plum Tree.* New York: Harcourt, Brace & World, 1963.

Lovell, Francies Stockwell, and Leverett C. Lovell. *History of the Town of Rockingham, Vermont 1907–1957.* Bellows Falls, Vt.: published by the town, 1958.

Melville, Herman. *Moby Dick, or The Whale.* New York: Library of America, 1983. Reprint of 1851 edition.

Myers, Gustavus. *History of the Great American Fortunes.* New York: Modern Library, 1936. Reprint of 1909 edition.

Nash, Jay Robert. *Zanies: The World's Greatest Eccentrics.* Piscataway, N.J.: New Century Publishers, 1982.

Noyes, Alexander Dana. *Forty Years of American Finance: 1865–1907.* New York: G. P. Putnam's Sons, 1909.

Pease, Zephaniah W. *The Diary of Samuel Rodman: A New Bedford Chronicle of Thirty-seven Years, 1821–1859.* New Bedford, Mass.: Reynolds Printing Co., 1927.

Perrin, William F., Bernd Wursig, and J. G. M. Thewissen. *Encylopedia of Marine Mammals.* San Diego: Academic Press, 2002.

Philbrick, Nathaniel. *In the Heart of the Sea: The Tragedy of the Whaleship Essex.* New York: Penguin Books, 2000.

Reed, St. Clair Griffin. *A History of the Texas Railroads.* New York: Arno Press, 1981. Reprint of 1941 edition.

*The Robinsons and Their Kin Folk.* Third Series. New York: published by the Robinson Family Genealogical and Historical Association, 1906.

Ross, Ishbell. *Charmers and Cranks: Twelve Famous American Women Who Defied the Conventions.* New York: Harper & Row, 1965.

Smith, Arthur D. Howden. *Men Who Run America: A Study of the Capitalistic System and Its Trends Based on Thirty Case Histories.* New York: Bobbs-Merrill, 1936.

*Souvenir Edition of the Bellows Falls Times.* Bellows Falls, Vt.: W. C. Belknap & Co., 1899. Local history.

Sparkes, Boyden, and Samuel Taylor Moore. *Hetty Green: The Witch of Wall Street.* Garden City, N.Y.: Doubleday, Doran & Co., 1935.

Stern, Robert M. *New York 1900.* New York: Rizzoli International Publishing, 1983.

Wall, Joseph Frazier. *Andrew Carnegie.* Pittsburgh: University of Pittsburgh Press, 1989. Reprint of 1970 edition.

Wilson, Neill C., and Frank J. Taylor. *Southern Pacific: The Story of a Fighting Railroad.* New York: McGraw-Hill Book Co., 1952.

## NEWSPAPERS

Because Hetty Green was so widely covered during her own time, period newspapers and magazines were a vital resource, not just for the details they recount, but for the light they shed on how her contemporaries viewed her. I amassed hundreds of articles from dozens of newspapers, with the following newspapers providing the bulk of the material: *New York World; New-York Daily Tribune, New York Sun, New York Times, Brooklyn Daily Eagle, New Bedford (Mass.) Morning Mercury, New Bedford (Mass.) Evening Standard, New-Bedford Gazette and Courier*, the New Bedford (Mass.) *Standard-Times, Bellows Falls (Vt.) Times*. The *New York Times* proved to be a particularly valuable resource, thanks mainly to a marvelous computer search engine enabling researchers to search every issue from 1851 on, according to a word or phrase, and to print out a facsimile of the article. Professional researcher Roger D. Joslyn conducted the search on my behalf, sending me fat packets of articles every few days crammed not just with lengthy profiles, but obscure details on real estate deals, financial transactions, and even racehorses named for Hetty—few if any of which would have turned up in a traditional search of the *New York Times Index*.

## JOURNAL ARTICLES

Bradstreet, Elizabeth Anne. "Hetty H. R. Green Hall." *The Wellesley Magazine*, April 1931.

Briggs, Ruth Lawrence (as told to Meras, Phyllis). "And Then There Was Uncle Ned." *Wellesley*, spring 1988.

"The Burden of Money." *The Outlook*, February 28, 1917. Hetty memorial.

"Col. Edward Howland Robinson Green." *New England Historical and Genealogical Register*, vol. XC, July 1936. Obituary.

Cooper, Dan, and Brian Grinder. "Women on Wall Street: An Historical Perspective." *Financial History*, no. 73, fall 2003.

Daggett, Mabel Potter. "Hetty Green: Mistress of Finance." *Broadway Magazine*, January 1908.

Flynn, John T. "The Witch of Wall Street." *The Mentor*, December 1929.

Glasscock, Jean. "The College and the Colonel." *Wellesley*, spring 1988.

Gordon, John Steele. "The Fortunes of Hetty Green." *Audacity,* summer 1996.

Green, Hetty. "Why Women Are Not Money Makers." *Harper's Bazar,* March 10, 1900.

Griswold, J. B. "A Rich Man Who Gets His Money's Worth." *American Magazine,* September 1933. Ned Green profile.

Henry, Sarah M. "The Strikers and Their Sympathizers: Brooklyn in the Trolley Strike of 1895." *Labor History,* vol. 32, no. 3 (1991).

"Hetty Green's Philosophy." *Literary Digest,* August 5, 1916.

Hodges, Leigh Mitchell. "The Richest Woman in America." *Ladies' Home Journal,* June 1900.

Lefevre, Edwin. "Mr. Williams and the Chemical National Bank," publication unknown, 1902. From JP Morgan Chase Archives.

Menand, Louis. "She Had to Have It: The Heiress, the Fortune, and the Forgery." *New Yorker,* April 23, 2001.

Nicholls, C. W. deLyon. "Hetty Green: A Character Study." *Business America,* May 1913.

O'Quinn, Truemann. "Texas, Taxes, and Where Did Colonel Green Live?" *Texas Bar Journal,* September 1961.

Spencer, Miranda. "Money Mad." *Biography,* August 1997.

Tolf, Robert W. "The Incredible Story of Hetty H. R. Green." *Wellesley,* spring 1988.

Wyckoff, Peter. "Queen Midas: Hetty Robinson Green." *New England Quarterly,* June 1950.

## PAPERS

Anonymous, "An Open Letter: A Protest and a Petition, from a Citizen of California to the United States Congress," 1895. Library of Congress.

Bolles, Mary Nims. Untitled paper with memories of Hetty's daughter, Sylvia, by her lifelong friend. From the Arthur Lewis papers at Temple University.

Gelt, Joe, et al. "Water in the Tucson Area: Seeking Sustainability: A Status Report by the Water Resources Research Center, College of Agriculture, The University of Arizona," 2002. Found at Web site: http://ag.arizona.edu/AZWATER/publications.

Medeiros, Peggi. "Hetty Howland Robinson Green's Birthplace." Unpublished paper in the collection of the Kendall Institute, New Bedford Whaling Museum.

# INDEX